W9-BEU-385
USED

ENLIGHTENED
DEMOCRACY

ENLIGHTENED DEMOCRACY

THE CASE FOR THE ELECTORAL COLLEGE

TARA ROSS

Foreword by George Will

COLONIAL PRESS, L.P.
Dallas, Texas
www.colonialpressonline.com

COLONIAL PRESS, L.P.
8409 Pickwick Ln., No. 280
Dallas, Texas 75225

Copyright © 2004, 2012 by Tara Ross.
Foreword copyright © 2004, 2012 by George Will.

All rights reserved. First edition 2004.
Second edition 2012.

No part of this book may be reproduced in any form or by any means, electronic, mechanical, photocopying, scanning, or otherwise, without permission in writing from the publisher, except by a reviewer who may quote brief passages in a review.

The first edition of this book was published by World Ahead Publishing, Inc., Los Angeles, CA (hardcover: 2004) and Colonial Press, L.P. (paperback: 2005).

Second Edition

ISBN: 978-0977072224
LCCN: 2012911550

Printed in the United States of America

For my dear husband, Adam,
our sweet daughter, Emma,
and our newest little guy, Grant,
with much love.

CONTENTS

Foreword

Mr. George F. Will

America's constitutional system aims not merely for majority rule but for rule by certain kinds of majorities. It aims for majorities suited to moderate, consensual governance of a heterogeneous, continental nation with myriad regional and other diversities. All 537 persons elected to national offices—the president, vice president, 100 senators and 435 representatives—are chosen by majorities that reflect the nation's federal nature. They are elected by majorities within states or within states' congressional districts.

American majorities are not spontaneous; they are built. A two-party system builds moderate majorities by assembling them from coalitions of minorities. In multiparty systems, parties proliferate, each representing intense minorities. Then a group of parties strives to govern through (often unstable) coalitions improvised after the election.

A two-party system is buttressed by an electoral system that handicaps minor parties by electing a single person from each jurisdiction, chosen by majority or plurality. In presidential elections, states are the jurisdictions. Forty-eight of them have chosen a winner-take-all allocation of electoral votes: The presidential candidate winning the state is awarded its entire slate of electors. So in 1992 Ross Perot won 18.9 percent of the popular vote but carried no state and won no electoral votes. Bill Clinton's 43 percent of the popular vote won him 68.8 percent of the electoral votes. In 1912 Woodrow Wilson's 41.8 percent of the popular votes produced a strong presidency based on 81.9 percent of the electoral votes.

Political scientist Judith Best notes that the electoral-vote system, combined with winner-take-all allocation, creates a "distribution condition." Candidates cannot just pile up popular votes in the most populous states. They must win many states, because legitimacy, and the capacity to govern this extensive republic, involves more than crude arithmetic. The federal principle, Best argues, prevents the most dangerous kinds of factions—racial, religious, economic—"from uniting their votes across state lines. It confines them within little republics and forces them to compromise early and often with their fellow state citizens."

The 2000 election, the sixth in which the popular-vote margin between the winner and runner-up was less than 1 percent, was a reminder that the electoral-vote system quarantines electoral disputes. Imagine a close election—2000, or the 1960 election, in which Kennedy's margin over Nixon was just 118,574—under direct popular election. With all votes poured into a single national bucket, there would be powerful incentives to challenge the results in many thousands of the nation's 170,000 precincts. The outcome could remain murky for months, leaving whoever wins crippled by attenuated legitimacy.

America has direct popular election of presidents, but has it within the states. As Best says, the states are not mere administrative agencies for a unitary government; they are components of a compound—a federal-republic. And today's electoral-vote system is not an 18th-century anachronism. It has evolved, shaping and being shaped by a large development the Constitution's Framers did not foresee—the two-party system.

Tara Ross' book, *Enlightened Democracy: The Case for the Electoral College*, celebrates this important bulwark of America's federalist republic. The Constitution provides for the election of Presidents by states' electoral votes, rather than individual popular votes, for an important reason: It enables citizens of a heterogeneous, free society to live peacefully alongside each other.

Proposals have recently been made that would undermine the protections provided by America's unique presidential election system. In 2004, when the first edition of *Enlightened Democracy* was released, some Coloradans sought to do away with the winner-take-all allocation of their state's electoral votes, replacing it with a proportional division. In 2011, Pennsylvania considered legislation ending the state's practice—shared by 47 other states—of allocating all of its electoral votes to the candidate who wins the statewide popular vote. It would have joined Maine and Nebraska in allocating one vote to the winner in each congressional district, with the two remaining votes going to the statewide popular vote winner. Today, eight states and the District of Columbia, with 132 electoral votes, are pursuing an even worse idea than Colorado's or Pennsylvania's. They have agreed to a compact requiring their electoral votes to be cast for the national popular vote winner, even if he loses their popular vote contests. This compact would come into effect when the states agreeing to it have a decisive 270 votes.

Deep-blue California supports the compact. But if it had existed in 2004, the state's electoral votes would have gone to George Bush even though 1.2 million more Californians favored John Kerry.

Supporters of the compact say they favor direct popular election of presidents. But that exists—within each state. The Framers, not being simple, did not subordinate all values to simple majority rule. The electoral vote system shapes the character of presidential majorities, making it unlikely they will be geographically or ideologically narrow.

Today's electoral vote system provides incentives for parties to alter the attributes that make them uncompetitive in important states. It shapes the nation's regime and hence the national character. The Electoral College today functions differently than the Founders envisioned—they did not anticipate political parties—but it does buttress the values encouraged by the federalism the Framers favored, which Coloradans, Pennsylvanians, and all other Americans, should respect.

Acknowledgments

I am indebted to many people for their help with this book. It is the first manuscript that I've completed since having kids. Writing a book with no parental responsibilities can be hard, but writing a book as "Mommy" is its own special challenge! My daughter, Emma, has been fascinated with this process and was constantly popping into my office to ask: "How many pages do you have now, Mommy?" She seems to think that I am "winning" because I've written more than 270 pages. She made me promise that I would teach her more about the Electoral College soon. My son, Grant, is much too young to know what is going on, but he contributed to the process by sitting on my lap and pounding the keyboard when I let him. My husband, Adam, is always supportive and willing to read chapters when I need an objective set of eyes. He and Emma also played many games of tennis on the weekends so I could check footnotes during Grant's naps. In short, my family has shown wonderful patience, especially in the last few weeks before the book went to press.

I owe a special thanks to George Will, who took time to update his foreword for this edition of *Enlightened Democracy*. I was ready to reprint the old foreword, with his permission, and really felt that he went above and beyond the call of duty. "Thank you" does not seem adequate. I very much appreciate the confidence he placed in me.

I also appreciate several lawyers and academics who read all or part of the manuscript at some point during the drafting process: I am grateful to Dr. Judith Best, Prof. Robert Hardaway, Dr. John Samples, and Mr. Michael Wiggins for taking time to review the book and send comments. Several people read a white paper that I wrote for the Federalist Society in 2010, portions of which made their way into this book: Mr. Trent England, Dr. Michael Greve, and Mr. James C. Ho. My friend, Dr. Sung Ahn, also graciously spent time being an "objective set of eyes" for this manuscript. Thank you, everyone, for your help and advice.

I want to send a special thanks to my Democratic colleague, Mr. Curtis Gans. We share an appreciation for the Electoral College and both believe that it is a non-partisan institution, although we have other political differences. Curtis was kind enough to read my manuscript and offer comments as I worked to make it as non-partisan as possible. I know that he is still not in complete agreement with everything this conservative has to say, but I also believe this book benefited from his perspective. I am grateful for his suggestions—many of which found their way into this edition.

One of the graduating law students at the *Texas Review of Law & Politics*, Mr. Chris Jones, spent many hours helping me with final footnote checks in June 2012. To put this into perspective, the Texas Bar is administered in July of any given year, so Chris was giving up his valuable study time to help! As the "BlueBook Guru" on the *Review*'s 2011-12 staff, I found his input especially helpful. Legal citation forms have changed a bit since my law school days more than a decade ago, and he caught many outdated citation forms that I was using.

Finally, I am grateful to the numerous individuals who helped with the first edition of this book. They were a necessary prerequisite to this edition: Attorney General Edwin Meese III, Judge Robert Bork, Judge Kenneth W. Starr, Professor Lino Graglia, Mr. Leonard Leo, Mr. Todd Gaziano, Mr. John Fortier, Mr. Patrick O'Daniel, Mr. Doug Wilson, Ms. Elizabeth Kovacs, and Ms. Rachael Hendrickson.

Thanks to everyone who helped to make this book possible. I hope you enjoy the final result.

Introduction

*The mode of appointment of the Chief Magistrate of the United
States is almost the only part of the system . . . which has escaped
without severe censure. . . . I venture somewhat further, and hesitate
not to affirm that if the manner of it be not perfect, it is at least
excellent.*

—*Alexander Hamilton*[1]

Alexander Hamilton would doubtless be surprised to discover
that America's presidential election system has become a topic
of some controversy. Some voters stand staunchly in support of the
nation's uniquely successful election process, colloquially referred to
as the Electoral College. The system, these voters observe, was an
ingenious invention of the founding generation. It remains a good
solution for a nation as diverse as America. Urban and rural areas,
large and small states are all represented in the White House.

But other voters shudder at the mere mention of the Electoral
College. To these latter voters, one event stands as the perfect
example of the system gone awry: They find it unfair that George
W. Bush won the 2000 election, despite the fact that Al Gore won
more individual votes nationwide.

The story of that election is well known by now. Returns were
close throughout election night. As in other years, media coverage
focused on predicting state-by-state results. American presidential
elections are, after all, a battle to win the most state votes (called
electoral votes), rather than the most popular votes nationwide.

The networks called many of the so-called "swing states" for
Democratic candidate Al Gore early in the evening.[2] One of these

critical states, Florida, was first called for Gore at 7:49 p.m. Eastern Time by NBC. Other networks quickly jumped on board with the prediction, despite the fact that polls had not yet closed in the state's Republican-leaning western panhandle, which is in a different time zone. Within a matter of hours, the call for Gore was deemed premature, and it was rescinded. Shortly after 2 a.m., the networks declared Republican candidate George W. Bush the winner of Florida and, hence, the presidential election. By 4 a.m., they had withdrawn their prediction—again. The country went to bed without knowing the name of its next President.

The final results of the election remained in doubt days later. Neither candidate had yet obtained a majority of at least 270 electoral votes, which would be needed to win. To that point, Bush had earned a total of 246 electoral votes, while Gore had earned 262 electoral votes. Two state elections remained undecided: Florida (25 electoral votes) and New Mexico (5 electoral votes).[3] The outcome of the national election would turn on the results in Florida, with its large bloc of unclaimed votes. Florida's election, however, was unusually close. Bush was ahead in the state tally, but his lead was razor-thin. Lawsuits were filed, and recounts were requested. Weeks of doubt followed as state officials and judges attempted to determine whether Bush or Gore had won the state's electoral votes.

The legal wrangling and recounts endured in Florida for more than a month. The U.S. Supreme Court was asked to intervene, not once, but twice.[4] The Court's final ruling essentially stopped the Florida Supreme Court from ordering hand recounts in addition to the mechanized recounts that had already been completed. In doing so, it brought a halt to the legal contest in Florida.

Throughout this entire process, Gore remained ahead in the national popular vote tally. His popular vote lead has no legal significance under the American state-by-state presidential election system; nevertheless, it gave Gore supporters ammunition in the forthcoming public relations battle against Bush. Many argued that the system is unfair; Gore should not have to fight to win a majority of the states' electoral votes when he was virtually certain to win the popular vote tally among individual voters. America's system of electing Presidents took a pounding in the press.

Introduction

In the end, Florida's 25 electoral votes were awarded to Bush. Certified results held that he had won the state by 537 votes. Bush's win in Florida pushed him to a majority of 271 electoral votes and ultimately gave him the presidency, despite the fact that he finished more than 500,000 votes behind Gore in the nationwide popular vote tally.[5] Bush's Electoral College win made him the first President in more than 100 years to ascend to the presidency despite the fact that he had garnered fewer individual popular votes, overall, than his opponent.

The close and disputed nature of the Bush-Gore election perhaps pushed the American presidential election system to its limits, but it was not the only one of its kind. Elections in 1876 and 1888 also resulted in Presidents who lost the recorded popular vote, but won the electoral vote. The 1876 election resulted in many weeks of post-election uncertainty, as did the 2000 election.

The last "popular vote loser" President was Benjamin Harrison. In 1888, Harrison defeated Grover Cleveland in the Electoral College vote, but he lost the popular vote by nearly 100,000 votes. Yet the outcome of this election between Harrison and Cleveland was not surrounded by the controversy of post-election disputes and recounts, as was the Bush-Gore election. The most recent election to face post-election disputes on the scale of those faced in Florida was the election of 1876, in which Rutherford B. Hayes defeated Samuel J. Tilden.

The 1876 and 2000 elections were comparable, but the Hayes-Tilden election was arguably even more controversial than the Bush-Gore election. In 1876, the country waited for weeks to see which candidate would be declared the victor; it did not get an answer until two days before President Ulysses S. Grant's term expired.[6] Imagine if Bush and Gore had continued fighting over the 2000 election outcome through Christmas and New Year's. What if Gore had conceded the election in the middle of January 2001, rather than the middle of December 2000? This is a taste of what the 1876 election was like, although 19th-century Americans did not have CNN, Fox News, and MSNBC to add 24-hour drama to the process, as 21st-century Americans do.

The 1876 election was similar to, although perhaps more suspenseful than, the 2000 election in another way. In 2000, the outcome in Florida was disputed. In 1876, not only Florida, but also two other states remained undecided after Election Day.[7] When the Electoral College met, multiple sets of election returns were generated by these three states. It was left to Congress to sort out which of the conflicting sets of returns to accept. Congress dealt with the problem by creating an Electoral Commission to determine which slates of electors should be certified from each of the three contested states. This controversial Commission was composed of 15 Senators, Congressmen, and Supreme Court Justices. Although it was meant to be composed of equal numbers of representatives from each party, plus one independent, it ended up with one extra Republican. This Republican reliably voted with the Republicans (not surprisingly), causing the Commission's votes to fall along party lines. Congress eventually accepted its determinations, but not before a filibuster nearly sidetracked even this final decision.

One last resemblance exists between the 2000 and 1876 elections. In 2000, Bush's popular vote loss was challenged by some: They claimed the results were skewed when the networks prematurely called Florida for Gore. This early, erroneous prediction may have discouraged Republicans in western time zones from going to the polls. Former Speaker of the House, Newt Gingrich, observed in 2000: "I feel pretty strongly that had the networks not called Florida early that night, [Gore] wouldn't have won the popular vote. We wouldn't be in this mess. And I think Bush would be above 300 electoral votes."[8] Others hypothesize, specifically, that Bush lost anywhere from 8,000 to 37,000 votes in the Republican-leaning western panhandle of Florida due to the early call.[9] A similar situation existed in 1876, although voters then cared less about the outcome of the national popular vote. Hayes won the electoral vote and lost the popular vote by more than 250,000 votes, but these totals don't tell the whole story. The country was still in the midst of Reconstruction, and disputes surrounded the voting in many southern states, making it impossible to know what the outcome of a truly free election would have been.

Introduction

As with the 1876 election, Gore supporters continued to protest the results of the 2000 election, even after the election results were relegated to the history books. Many of these Americans focused on the controversy surrounding the recount in Florida; however, a smaller number of dissenters took the argument a step further. Gore's popular vote win, they stressed, should have guaranteed him the presidency, regardless of the electoral vote tally.

For those who were focused on the discrepancy between popular and electoral vote tallies, the 2000 election was a demonstration of the Electoral College's shortcomings. But for those who looked a little deeper, the election instead demonstrated the genius of the system. This book is written for those who are willing to look a little deeper.

A Misunderstood Institution

Pick up a newspaper and read about the Electoral College. The opinions of (often left-leaning) editorial boards are sure to undermine your respect for the system. *The Boston Globe*'s editorial board has blasted the Electoral College's "pernicious effect on American politics."[10] *The Miami Herald* has wondered: "Isn't it time to get rid of this horse-and-buggy-era political contraption?"[11] Editors at the *Los Angeles Times* bemoan the Electoral College

> in which the candidate who wins the most votes doesn't always win the presidency. Voters in some states matter much more than others, so candidates are encouraged to ignore the concerns of the less important ones and focus on those who really make a difference. That, in turn, tends to lower turnout because many voters believe their input doesn't matter. Is this any way to run a democracy?[12]

Editors at *The New York Times*, for their part, have a habit of tying the Electoral College to the long-vanquished institution of slavery. The editorial board describes the Electoral College as a "quadrennial ritual born in the economics and politics of slavery and the quill-pen era."[13] It was "established by the nation's founders in part to appease slave-owning states."[14] The *Sacramento Bee* describes the Electoral College as the "broken, obsolete way Americans elect the president"[15] and claims that the founding generation adopted the institution, hurriedly, at the end of the Constitutional Convention: "Nobody wanted it. It's not a venerable institution. It broke down immediately and has been amended many times."[16]

The education system piles on to this media-bashing. Schools do not always teach students about the origins of the Electoral College. Or, when they do teach the subject, some political science textbooks are too quick to oversimplify this aspect of constitutional history.[17] The Electoral College is quickly dismissed as the product of the Founders' fear that "ordinary citizens, most of whom could neither read [n]or write, were too poorly informed to choose wisely."[18] The media's approach, combined with spotty teaching in schools, has left the general electorate remarkably ill-informed about its presidential election system.

Given such a hostile environment, perhaps it is unsurprising that polls sometimes reflect a desire to move away from the Electoral College system. Polls consistently show support for a switch to direct popular election of the President. For instance, in 1988, an ABC and *Washington Post* poll showed that 77 percent of the public was in favor of direct election, rather than the Electoral College system.[19] Indeed, as early as 1944, 65 percent of the American public wanted to abolish the Electoral College.[20]

A close election in 1968 caused opposition to the Electoral College to hit one of its high points. At that time, 81 percent of the American public was in favor of abolishing the Electoral College, according to one estimate.[21] The furor over the Electoral College that year was caused by the campaign of third-party candidate Governor George Wallace.[22] He earned enough support to cause fears that the election would essentially be decided by the Governor himself. Many worried that Wallace would obtain enough electoral votes to prevent either the Republican or the Democratic candidates, Richard Nixon and Hubert Humphrey, from obtaining a majority in the Electoral College. In such circumstances, the presidential election would move to the Constitution's secondary election procedure in the House of Representatives. The situation could have put Wallace in a position to cut a deal because his endorsement could swing the votes of his electors and prevent the necessity of a contingent election. Such a situation never came about, however. On Election Day, Wallace won 46 electoral votes, but these votes were insufficient to prevent Nixon from winning the presidential election with a majority of 301 electoral votes.

Following Bush's defeat of Gore, a Gallup poll again showed that a majority of Americans, 59 percent, would support abolition of the Electoral College.[23] A *Time*/CNN poll showed a greater majority: 63 percent in support of abolition, compared to 29 percent in favor of retaining the Electoral College.[24] This number is lower than it has been in the past, despite the turmoil surrounding the 2000 election.

Few voters understand why American presidential elections are a battle to win the most state votes (called electoral votes), rather than the most individual popular votes nationwide. In 2000, Gore obtained more votes from individuals, but his national popular vote lead had no legal significance under the American state-by-state presidential election system. The constitutional election process instead looks to the total number of electoral votes. Some argue that such a system is unfair. Winning the popular vote tally among individual voters nationwide should be sufficient. The circumstances surrounding the 2000 election doubtless reinforced this feeling. Legal disputes surrounded the count in one state, Florida. Bush could not win without this state in his column, yet the results of the state's election remained in dispute for weeks on end. Many Americans felt that Gore should not have to fight for victory in one state when he'd already won a plurality of popular votes nationwide. In circumstances such as these, Electoral College opponents claim that the system "misfires."

Indeed, some argue that the Electoral College almost "misfired" again during the 2004 election. The popular vote totals were close: Bush obtained 62 million votes, while his opponent, John Kerry, obtained 59 million.[25] The electoral vote was also close, but Bush won the presidency because he obtained a majority of electoral votes: he won 286 votes to Kerry's 251.[26] The margin of victory happened to coincide with the number of electoral votes in one state. If Kerry had won Ohio, then he would have won the presidency with 271 electoral votes compared to 266 for Bush. The irony would certainly have been great if Bush had won the popular vote in 2004, but lost the presidency because Kerry obtained more electoral votes.

But such a situation would have been more than merely ironic. It also shows that the Electoral College does not serve one political party to the exclusion of the other. In 2000, it "benefited" Republicans, but it just as easily could have reversed course in favor of the Democrats in 2004. Support of the institution cannot be a partisan matter. Either the system serves America, as a whole, or it does not.

Today's negative views on the Electoral College are odd, given the universal admiration in which the system was held at the time of the Constitutional Convention. One influential delegate to the Constitutional Convention, Alexander Hamilton, publicly deemed the Electoral College "excellent."[27] The other Convention delegates agreed with him; they viewed the Electoral College as one of the great achievements of the Constitutional Convention.[28] Transcripts of the ratification debates do not record much opposition to the presidential election process, although other aspects of the proposed Constitution were debated intensely. Both at the Convention and during the ratification debates, the Electoral College was considered a clever solution to one problem facing the new nation: It would allow the will of the people to be expressed, but would still provide sufficient safeguards to protect minority interests. The unenthusiastic views of today's citizenry on this topic would almost certainly surprise the founding generation.

The Electoral College, Under Attack

Electoral College opponents have long tried to rid the country of its unique presidential election system. The Congressional Research Service reports that about 595 constitutional amendments regarding Electoral College reform were introduced in the Congress between 1889 and 2004.[29] Most of these amendments saw little legislative activity, although one proposal in the 91st Congress passed the House with the requisite supermajority. This resolution later died in the Senate.[30]

The Founders designed the constitutional amendment process to be a difficult, uphill battle: Two-thirds of Congress and three-quarters of the states must approve an amendment before it becomes part of the Constitution.[31] They knew that constitutional principles should be changed only after a great deal of thought and approval from the vast majority of the country. The Constitution is America's fundamental law; difficulty in changing it protects freedom. While there has been some discontent with the Electoral College, the discontent has never been widespread enough to enable an amendment to gain the necessary momentum needed to overcome the high hurdles erected by the Founders. But in recent years, Electoral College opponents think that they have found a way to gain their objective without the bother of a constitutional amendment.

The first edition of this book discussed a "De Facto Direct Election" plan that had been proposed by several academics.[32] At the time that book went to press, implementation of the plan seemed extremely unlikely. Instead, it was primarily a theoretical discussion in certain academic circles. Indeed, during peer reviews of *Enlightened Democracy*'s first edition, this author was asked why she had bothered to include a discussion of the proposal at all. The idea seemed so far-fetched and so unlikely to happen as to be almost unworthy of discussion. In the end, a brief description was included "in the event that the idea gains more steam in future years."[33] The idea was labeled a "silly academic proposal that sounds good to those who favored a direct popular election anyway."[34]

That label was appropriate then, and it is appropriate now. Unfortunately, not everyone has seen it that way, and the idea did gain more steam after the release of *Enlightened Democracy*. Indeed, the "silly academic proposal" has become a true threat to the republic in recent years.

In 2006, a California-based group, National Popular Vote Inc. (NPV) was created to promote legislation based on the De Facto Direct Election idea. A book, *Every Vote Equal*, was released to explain and defend the mechanics of NPV's legislation.[35] Where constitutional amendments have failed, NPV believes it can "reform" the Electoral College through a handful of simple state statutes.

NPV asks states to change the manner in which they allocate their presidential electors. Today, most states allocate their electors to the winner of the statewide popular vote. NPV proposes to instead allocate these electors to the winner of the national popular vote. If states with a majority of electors (currently 270) agree to the plan, the presidential election system will operate as a national popular referendum rather than a federalist, state-by-state process. To ensure that no state is left alone in its decision, NPV operates through an interstate compact. The compact goes into effect only when a critical mass of states agrees to join.[36]

The practical effect of this plan is to abolish the Electoral College, although NPV supporters deny it. With NPV in place, the Electoral College would exist on paper, but not in practice. As a practical matter, the election would be a direct national election, just as Electoral College opponents have long wanted.

As this book goes to press, eight states have agreed to the compact: California, Hawaii, Illinois, Maryland, Massachusetts, New Jersey, Vermont, and Washington (129 electoral votes total).[37] The District of Columbia, with three electoral votes, has also approved the plan, bringing the total number of participating electoral votes to 132. One other state legislature approved the plan, but the governor vetoed it: Rhode Island. If Rhode Island is included (a possibility discussed in Chapters Twelve and Fourteen), the total would be brought to 136 electoral votes—more than half the electors needed.

Remember that a constitutional amendment can succeed only with the support of three-quarters (currently 38) of the states. Yet NPV could be over halfway to its goal with only nine states, plus the District of Columbia, on board. Past efforts to eliminate or modify the Electoral College have failed miserably. Yet NPV is astonishingly close to success. This silly proposal has morphed into a force that must be taken seriously. Defenders of the Constitution need to rise up and defend the Electoral College or they may find that it is too late to save the institution.

On a Personal Note

This author is an accidental defender of the Electoral College. Since writing *Enlightened Democracy* in 2004, I've been asked many times what first prompted me to write a defense of America's presidential election system. The answer is a bit surprising.

I wrote a book about the Electoral College because I broke my arm in January 2001. Yes, really! I was a third-year law student, editor-in-chief of a law journal, and I somehow had to find time for a full load of classes so I could graduate. Easier when you can take notes in class than when you cannot! In the wake of the 2000 election, an independent study on the Electoral College seemed a practical solution for a busy law student with her writing arm in a cast. But something more was born that semester. My research into the system convinced me that the Electoral College is among the most important—if the least understood—aspects of our Constitution. Defending the system has become a natural position for me ever since, even as my student paper evolved into a more professional law review piece and, finally, a book.

When I first wrote *Enlightened Democracy*, I mentioned that the book is not a treatise on the Electoral College. It is a primer for any American who wants to better understand the history of and justifications for our presidential election system. This second edition is an updated version of the original and has the same purpose, but it also adds chapters specifically addressing the NPV effort, which did not exist when this book was first released in 2004. I firmly believe that more education about the system will result in more support. I also believe that more information regarding NPV will show what an unworkable solution it is, even for those who are otherwise in favor of eliminating the Electoral College.

The Founders were proud of the Constitution that they had created and deemed the Electoral College to be among its best features. They would likely consider it a great pity that most Americans now believe the Electoral College to be an anachronism, an institution that serves no real purpose in a global economy transformed by wireless Internet access, email, cell phones, iPads, Droids, and numerous other gadgets that give Americans constant access to news and information. Obviously, the world has changed since that summer in Philadelphia when the Founders drafted a new form of government. But these economic and technological changes have not undermined the importance of constitutional protections such as the Electoral College. To the contrary, these protections remain vitally important to our freedom.

The Founders did not create a system of checks and balances in the Constitution because they were worried about inadequate access to news or because the Internet hadn't been invented yet. They created constitutional protections because they knew that freedom would need to be protected from the flawed and imperfect nature of human beings. These concerns are as valid today as they were in 1787. The world may have changed, but the humans in it have not.

Ambition, power, and greed are still dangerous to self-government. Minorities still need to be protected. Rhode Island and Delaware are still smaller than their neighbors, and they still have unique interests that should be represented in the federal government. Moderation and compromise among federal officials and candidates are still beneficial. Americans still need a President who represents the variety of subcultures, regions, and industries that span the nation. The Electoral College ensures that presidential candidates develop a national base. They can't win if they are relying too heavily on specific regions or special interest groups.

The Electoral College is an institution worthy of respect, but it does need to be better understood by those that it serves. I wrote the original edition of *Enlightened Democracy* with the hope that it would help Americans to better understand the presidential election system that was deemed "excellent" if not "perfect" in 1787.[38] I hope the second edition serves the same purpose and encourages voters to defend the Electoral College against dangerous efforts such as NPV.

Part One

The Origins of the Electoral College

Chapter One

An American
Balancing Act

Dean Clarence Manion of the Notre Dame University College of Law once observed:

> The honest and serious students of American history will recall that our Founding Fathers managed to write both the Declaration of Independence and the Constitution of the United States without using the term "democracy" even once. No part of any one of the existing forty-eight State constitutions contains any reference to the word.[1]

Half a century later, his statement remains true, with the exception of two recent additions to the Constitutions of California and Oregon.[2]

This fact may come as a surprise to many Americans, who mistakenly believe that the United States was established as a democracy. The founding generation, however, intentionally omitted the word "democracy" from their governing documents. The Founders, by and large, were opposed to pure democracies, which allow bare majorities to tyrannize over minority groups. Instead, the founding generation intended to create a republic—or, arguably, a republican democracy—which would incorporate a spirit of compromise and deliberation into decision-making. Such a form of government, the Founders believed, would allow them to achieve two potentially conflicting objectives: Avoiding the "tyranny of the majority" inherent in pure democratic systems, while allowing the "sense of the people" to be reflected in the new American government.

Before traveling any further into the tangled thicket of the "intent of the Founders," it is important to recognize that an element of difficulty always exists in attempting to summarize the collective thoughts and deliberations of a group of individuals. Certainly, opinions among the delegates to the Constitutional Convention, the state ratifying conventions, and the general public differed widely on many issues. Indeed, some early Americans were opposed to adoption of the Constitution altogether. These early Patriots had differences of opinion, but their differences were, in many respects, transcended by shared concerns. One concern that was shared by many in the founding generation was how to resolve the tension between allowing self-government and providing protection for the political liberties of minority groups.

Members of the founding generation thought of themselves as having more reason than any other to know what it was like to have no voice in their own government. They themselves had been abused by a tyrannical monarch who took no account of their needs and opinions. As a result, self-governance was an important principle to these Founders. Yet their experiences in England had taught them another important lesson: They knew what it was like to be an ill-treated minority. After all, even if England had been a pure democracy rather than a monarchy, the American colonies, relegated to minority status, would have been quickly trampled by the majority of citizens at home in England.[3]

What form of government allows the people to govern themselves, but also prevents democratic majorities from endangering the freedom of minorities? How can the evils of democracy be avoided, while the benefits are allowed to flourish? The conflict was very real to many of the Founders. At one point during the Constitutional Convention in Philadelphia (one can almost imagine his exasperation), Colonel George Mason, delegate from Virginia, was led to observe: "It is curious to remark the different language held at different times. At one moment we are told that the [democratically elected] Legislature is entitled to thorough confidence, and to indifinite power. At another, that it will be governed by intrigue & corruption, and cannot be trusted at all."[4]

The Founders were students of history. They knew that democracy, in its purest from, could allow even "inflamed" majorities and "unreflective mob[s]" to rule.[5] Any majority, even a bare majority, always wins—even if they do so at the expense of rather large minority groups. The authors of the Constitution realized that freedom and self-government can only co-exist if devices are created to temper the momentary passions of the public. Only "reasonable" majorities should be allowed to rule. The Founders had another important incentive for establishing such a system: It would enable the country's most permanent minority constituency, the small states, to exist peacefully alongside their larger neighbors.

The importance of protecting both the majority and the minority, of allowing self-government but protecting political liberties, was summarized by Thomas Jefferson in his first inaugural address: "All, too, will bear in mind this sacred principle, that though the will of the majority is in all cases to prevail, that will, to be rightful, must be reasonable; that the minority possess their equal rights, which equal laws must protect, and to violate which would be oppression."[6]

The Founders would find encapsulating these conflicting values in the presidential election process to be especially difficult. When they finished crafting the Electoral College, however, it was nearly universally agreed that they had successfully created an election process that reflected the competing values of democratic self-government and the preservation of political liberty for minorities. The Electoral College made it nearly impossible for a presidential candidate to rely upon unreasonable or regional majorities at the expense of minorities or the small states. Instead, a candidate would need to generate national support before he could be elected.

The Evils of Democracy

The Constitution does not guarantee "every State in this Union" a democratic form of government, but rather "a Republican Form of

Government."[7] The difference is more than merely semantic. Republicanism expects that a country will thrive when the people are governed by representatives who are elected based on their wisdom, integrity and civic virtue. These representatives are intended to deliberate and reach wise compromises with other representatives.

A democratic, or populist, theory of government, by contrast, would assume that the "main repository of wisdom and virtue" is in the people themselves.[8] Representatives in a democracy merely carry out the majority will and are not expected to independently deliberate. Thus, 51 percent of the people can rule the other 49 percent without any need for compromise, even when the majority will tramples the rights of the minority.

The authors of the Constitution were opposed to the concept of a pure democracy. They had studied the history of many failed democratic systems, and they strove to create a form of government that would be quite different. Indeed, James Madison, delegate from Virginia, argued that unfettered majorities such as those found in pure democracies tend toward tyranny. Madison stated it this way:

> [In a pure democracy], [a] common passion or interest will, in almost every case, be felt by a majority of the whole; a communication and concert results from the form of government itself; and there is nothing to check the inducements to sacrifice the weaker party or an obnoxious individual. Hence it is that such democracies have ever been spectacles of turbulence and contention; have ever been found incompatible with personal security or the rights of property; and have in general been as short in their lives as they have been violent in their deaths.[9]

The rhetoric against democracies became quite strong during the Constitutional Convention. Early in the debates, Elbridge Gerry, delegate from Massachusetts, forcefully asserted that "[t]he evils we experience flow from the excess of democracy."[10] Edmund Randolph of Virginia concurred that "the general object was to provide a cure for the evils under which the [United States] laboured; that in tracing these evils to their origin every man had found it in the turbulence and follies of democracy."[11] Later in the Convention, Randolph reaffirmed his words, noting that the "democratic licentiousness of the State Legislatures proved the necessity of a firm Senate. . . . to controul the democratic branch of the [National] Legislature."[12]

Other delegates also sought to encourage creation of a system that would control the impulsiveness and emotion that they believed would sometimes characterize public opinion. Gouverneur Morris of Pennsylvania remarked that "Every man of observation had seen in the democratic branches of the State Legislatures, precipitation—in Congress changeableness, in every department excesses [against] personal liberty private property & personal safety."[13]

The arguments against pure democracy continued after the Constitutional Convention had concluded. Madison spoke to Jefferson of the dangers that could be created when the Government becomes "the mere instrument of the major number of the constituents."[14] Alexander Hamilton continued these arguments against democracies in a June 21, 1788 speech before the New York ratifying convention:

> It has been observed, by an honorable gentleman, that a pure democracy, if it were practicable, would be the most perfect government. Experience has proved that no position in politics is more false than this. The ancient democracies, in which the people themselves deliberated, never possessed one feature of good government. Their very character was tyranny; their figure, deformity.[15]

Other early Americans concurred in the judgment of these Convention delegates. John Adams, who signed the Declaration of Independence and later became President, declared, "[D]emocracy never lasts long. It soon wastes, exhausts, and murders itself. There never was a democracy yet that did not commit suicide."[16] Another signatory to the Declaration of Independence, Benjamin Rush, stated, "A simple democracy . . . is one of the greatest of evils."[17] A third signer, John Witherspoon, agreed: "Pure democracy cannot subsist long, nor be carried far into the department of state—it is very subject to caprice and the madness of popular rage."[18] Fisher Ames, a member of the Massachusetts convention that ratified the Constitution, agreed: "A democracy is a volcano, which conceals the fiery materials of its own destruction. These will produce an eruption, and carry desolation in their way."[19]

The concerns of these pro-Constitution Americans were shared, at least to some degree, by those who opposed ratification of the Constitution. Historian Paul Johnson once described the American form of government as one of "republican structure" and "democratic content."[20] True, those who opposed the Constitution (then referred to as "Anti-Federalists") were perhaps more likely to emphasize Johnson's "democratic content," as when Patrick Henry declared in a moving speech before the Virginia ratifying convention that the proposed government "is not a democracy, wherein the people retain all their rights securely."[21] Despite such statements in favor of the people's rights, however, these Anti-Federalists did not dismiss the importance of "republican structure."

The opposition of Anti-Federalists often centered on one of two perceived shortcomings in the federal Constitution. First, its (then-existing) lack of a Bill of Rights; or, second, the "consolidated" form of the new government. Anti-Federalists feared that the new government attempted to span too much territory; they argued that the new centralized government would have too much power over the state governments. The benefits of republicanism versus democracy were not dismissed; they were often assumed. Indeed, many Anti-Federalists promoted a "confederation of republics" instead of the Constitution that had been proposed.[22] The day before Patrick Henry's statement in which he condemned the new Constitution as "not a democracy," he took to the convention floor to declare, "[Y]ou ought to be extremely cautious, watchful, jealous of your liberty; for, instead of securing your rights, you may lose them forever. If a wrong step be now made, *the republic may be lost forever*."[23] His concern in both speeches was "[t]hat this is a consolidated government . . . ; and the danger of such a government is, to my mind, very striking."[24]

Another Anti-Federalist, who wrote under the pen name "Brutus," was more explicit in acknowledging the dangers of democracies. In his argument to do away with the consolidated federal government, he stated, "In every free government, the people must give their assent to the laws by which they are governed."[25]

Unfortunately, he concluded, "in a large extended country, it is impossible to have a representation, possessing the sentiments, and of integrity, to declare the minds of the people, without having it so numerous and unwieldy, as to be subject in great measure to the inconveniency of a democratic government."[26]

The pro-Constitution and anti-Constitution forces, then, generally agreed on the principles of republicanism versus democracy.[27] Their disagreement lay in how to express the principles of "republican structure" and "democratic content" in the new government that was to be created. They also disagreed about the wisdom of attempting to create a republic that would cover such a large territory. In the end, obviously, the arguments of the pro-Constitution forces carried the day, and the Constitution was ratified.

The Founders determined that democracy, in its purest form, is dangerous. The Constitution they crafted, therefore, explicitly rejected simple democratic rule by the majority in favor of a system that would require deliberation and compromise. Walter Berns of the American Enterprise Institute has summarized these conclusions reached by the founding generation as they drafted, debated, and ratified the Constitution. He stated:

> The American idea of democracy cannot be expressed in the simple but insidious formula of the greatest good for the greatest number. What the greatest number regards as its greatest good might very well prove to be a curse to those who are not part of that number. . . . [G]overnment is instituted to secure the rights of all.[28]

Reflecting the Sense of the People

These men who spoke so forcefully against the vices of a pure democracy were, however, the same men who supported the signing of the Declaration of Independence, a document that proclaimed: "[Governments] deriv[e] their just powers from the consent of the governed."[29] The Founders' statements against democracy were not indicative of opposition to self-government. To the contrary, the

Founders knew and often spoke of the need to allow the will of the people to operate in the new government that they were crafting.

At the Constitutional Convention in Philadelphia, Virginia delegate George Mason often emphasized the importance of retaining a democratic principle in the government. "Notwithstanding the oppressions & injustice experienced among us from democracy," he declared, "the genius of the people must be consulted."[30] One legislative branch, he argued, should be directly elected by the people. This branch would serve as the "grand depository of the democratic principle of the [Government]."[31] It would be able to "know & sympathise with every part of the community."[32] He admitted that the state governments "had been too democratic"[33] in the past, but cautioned the Convention delegates not to use these past failures as an excuse to "incautiously run into the opposite extreme."[34]

He need not have worried. Other delegates also realized that the government would not be legitimate or sustainable if it failed to reflect the voice of the people. James Wilson, delegate from Pennsylvania, argued that the "most numerous branch of the Legislature [should come] immediately from the people," because "[n]o government could long subsist without the confidence of the people."[35] James Madison "considered the popular election of one branch of the National Legislature as essential to every plan of free Government."[36] He reiterated these thoughts later, as the states considered whether to ratify the Constitution. In *The Federalist No. 39*, he described the "honorable determination which animates every votary of freedom to rest all our political experiments on the capacity of mankind for self-government."[37]

The delegates, then, faced a dilemma. Their fierce opposition to simple democracy ran headlong into their determination to allow the people to govern themselves. Fearful of tyrannical majorities, they distrusted straight democracies. However, they strongly advocated for the right to self-government—and they were faced with the challenging task of reconciling these two positions. How could they let the people rule themselves, while protecting the country from momentary passions or irrational majorities? The Convention delegates addressed the conflict by creating a republican government in which minorities would be given many opportunities to make themselves heard.

James Madison later described the solution that had been sought: "But it is the reason, alone, of the public, that ought to control and regulate the government. The passions ought to be controlled and regulated by the government."[38] James Wilson concurred, as he defended the proposed Constitution before his state's ratification convention: "The advantages of *democracy*," he noted, "are, liberty, equality, cautious and salutary laws, public spirit, frugality, peace, opportunities of exciting and producing abilities of the best citizens."[39] However, he added, democracy has disadvantages, such as "dissensions, the delay and disclosure of public counsels, the imbecility of public measures, retarded by the necessity of a numerous consent."[40] The Constitution, Wilson concluded, proposes a government that "[i]n its principle, it is purely democratical. But that principle is applied in different forms, in order to obtain the advantages, and exclude the inconveniences, of the simple modes of government."[41]

A Republic, If You Can Keep It

When asked by a Philadelphia matron what the Constitutional Convention had produced, Benjamin Franklin famously responded, "A Republic, if you can keep it."[42] The American republic that Franklin described is a blend of contrasts: It takes the will of the majority into account, but then ensures that the voice of the minority will also be heard and not stifled. The political well-being of the country would best be nurtured, the Founders believed, if they provided both the majority and the minority with a voice in their government.

More than one constitutional provision reflects the intent of the Founders to give minorities more influence than they would have in a simple democracy. For instance, the legislative power is divided between a House, in which representation is based on population, and a Senate, in which each state is equally represented.[43] The Constitution divides powers between the state and the federal governments, which allows states to govern themselves in some areas—most notably in the exercise of their police power—without seeking compromise or input from other states or the federal government. In addition, the Constitution sometimes requires a supermajority for action, rather than a simple majority, as when the legislature attempts to override a presidential veto or when states approve a constitutional amendment.

The Founders buttressed the new government with one last protective device: The Electoral College. The new presidential election system provided at least two reasonable concessions to the minority. First, a presidential candidate cannot be elected simply by gaining a majority in a handful of states. Instead, the presidential candidate must garner support across the nation to have a reasonable probability of being elected. Second, the minority is provided with several methods by which it may amplify its voice, allowing it to make a statement that would otherwise go unnoticed in a direct popular vote.

For instance, minority groups that congregate in one state or region of the country may increase their impact in the presidential election. The Hispanic vote has greater weight than it might otherwise have, as it can be influential in determining the outcome of the vote in Texas, California, or Florida.[44] The Jewish vote in New York carries similar influence.[45] Farmers in the Midwest have the ability to make a statement as well because they can affect the votes of several states. Vernon Jordan, former president of the Urban League, similarly noted how elections might change for black Americans without the Electoral College. "Instead of being crucial to victory in major states," he observed, "blacks would simply become 10% of the total electorate."[46]

The election of 1948 demonstrated the great weight that a minority can carry if its population is concentrated in one region of the country. Strom Thurmond received 2.4 percent of the vote in the 1948 election,[47] a relatively small percentage that could have gone unnoticed in a direct popular election. However, the Electoral College system enabled him to capture the votes of four states,[48] victories that allowed him and those he represented to capture national attention.[49] The election outcome is a remarkable demonstration of what a minority can achieve in our presidential election system, at least under certain circumstances.

(Simultaneously, it demonstrates the manner in which the Electoral College controls extremist or unhealthy third parties.[50] The benefits of moderation and compromise in politics, as encouraged by the Electoral College, are discussed more in Chapter Six.)

Some critics, however, continue to advance the notion that the Founders had dishonorable motives for creating the Electoral College. According to this view of the founding, the Founders were an "elitist" group of white men who deliberately sought to take the election of the President out of the hands of the people. In pursuing their politically correct theory, these critics frequently cite George Mason, who (in addition to his statements that "the genius of the people must be consulted") stated, "it would be as unnatural to refer the choice of a proper character for chief Magistrate to the people, as it would, to refer a trial of colours to a blind man."[51]

This negative view of the Founders as an elitist group has been reinforced at a level as high as the Supreme Court. In 1963, the Court, then led by liberal Chief Justice Earl Warren, stated that the "electoral college was designed by men who did not want the election of the President to be left to the people."[52] The Electoral College, under this view of the Founding, is an institution that should be eliminated—a fate befitting its undemocratic and anti-proletarian roots.

These critics have misinterpreted the role of the safeguards inserted into the presidential election process by the Founders. The Founders, as students of history, felt that its verdict was clear: A presidential election process would fail if based on the untempered expression of the people's will; however, the Founders also strongly felt that the voice of the people could not be removed from presidential election altogether. The system that they devised sought to reconcile these potentially contradictory goals. The Convention delegates knew precautions were necessary, but these protective measures could not filter out the will of the public and replace it with the will of the few. Instead, they should merely filter out public passions of the moment, while enabling the less volatile aspects of public opinion to emerge as the expressed will of the people. The system should allow the majority to win, but it should not exclude the minority altogether.

Discussions regarding the mode of presidential election emphasized the importance of providing the people a voice in the process. The delegates' praise for the final product reflected the importance that they placed upon electing Presidents chosen by the people. James Madison declared, "He [the President] is now to be elected by the people."[53] Alexander Hamilton promoted the Electoral College as an institution that would allow the "sense of the people" to "operate in the choice of the [President]."[54] James Wilson of Pennsylvania supported the proposed election system during the ratification debates, noting that the President "may be justly styled *the man of the people.*"[55]

In the American republic created by the Founders, majorities can—and should—rule, but only while they are reasonable. The minority views in a 1970 Senate report reflected this sentiment:

> Accordingly, the crucial question in considering electoral reform is whether one method of election is better than another at creating *reasonable* majorities. One method might be better at obtaining a strictly numerical majority, but only at the price of failing to protect minorities; another might protect minorities very well indeed, but only at the price of frustrating a truly *reasonable* majority.[56]

The Electoral College was considered by the Founders to have struck the perfect balance between minority protection and majority rule. It was a balance that they hit upon only after several months of deliberation and compromise in Philadelphia during the summer of 1787.

Chapter Two

The Great
Compromise

The Constitutional Convention of 1787 got off to a slow start.[1] At the urging of James Madison and Alexander Hamilton, a convention had been called by the Confederation Congress, which governed (in name, if not in practice) the American colonies immediately following the Revolutionary War. The Confederation Congress, however, did not want the nation's then-existing charter, the Articles of Confederation, replaced. It had instead restricted the purpose of the Convention to "the sole and express purpose *of revising the articles of Confederation* and reporting to Congress and the several legislatures such *alterations and provisions therein* as shall . . . render the federal Constitution *adequate to the exigencies of government and the preservation of the Union.*"[2]

It is doubtful that Madison and Hamilton ever intended to abide by these limited instructions. In their view, a stronger national government was needed to handle issues of interstate commerce and foreign relations, among other matters. The directive from the Confederation Congress, however, served as an excuse to convene delegates from all the states. Once they convened, it became clear to the delegates that the Articles of Confederation could not be successfully amended; instead, a new government would need to be created and proposed. Of course, this dawning revelation—plus the exigencies of travel—all took time, which caused an initial languid pace to the Convention's proceedings.

The meeting was scheduled to begin in Philadelphia on May 14, 1787, but on that morning, only a handful of delegates had arrived. By May 25, a quorum of seven states was present. The 29 delegates determined to proceed with the Convention, despite the fact that some states had no delegates in attendance.[3] Eventually, 55 delegates attended at least some portion of the Convention. Nineteen delegates never made an appearance, and Rhode Island refused to send delegates at all. The average age of these delegates never exceeded 43. Benjamin Franklin, at 81, was the oldest, while Jonathan Dayton from New Jersey was the youngest at 26. Despite their young average age, the delegates were unusually accomplished. Most of these delegates had served in Congress or the colonial or state legislatures, and they were well-versed in the works of such philosophers as John Locke and Baron de Montesquieu. Many were lawyers. When Thomas Jefferson, then in Paris, read the names of the delegates, he described them as "an assembly of demi-gods."[4]

George Washington was designated as the Convention's presiding officer, although he contributed very little to the discussions. The General found it inappropriate to express himself on pending matters because he was the Convention's president.[5] Moreover, he may have feared that his opinions would carry too much weight with the other men due to his celebrated status as a war hero—even at that early date he was already being regarded as "the Father of the Country."[6] Whatever his motivations may have been, Washington never rose to speak until the last day of the Convention, although he voted with the Virginians, and it was known that he was generally in favor of a stronger national government.

The delegates worked through the sweltering summer with the windows and blinds in Philadelphia's State Hall closed. They considered it imperative that the discussions be conducted secretly, so all delegates would feel free to speak their mind. Throughout the debates, the 36-year-old James Madison took comprehensive notes. He said later that his labor in that hot room throughout the summer nearly killed him. "I was not absent a single day, nor more than a casual fraction of an hour in any day, so that I could not have lost a single speech, unless a very short one," he later confirmed.[7] His notes remain the single best source on the debates in the Constitutional Convention.

The mode for electing the Executive was discussed early and often that summer in Philadelphia. The delegates considered it one of the hardest questions that they would be asked to address. They eventually discussed the election of the President on 21 separate days; the issue provoked more than 30 distinct votes.[8]

As with other issues at the Convention, much of the disagreement on the matter of presidential selection reflected the tension between the large and the small states.[9] The friction among the states was perhaps unavoidable. Each state had operated independently for decades— first as a colony, then as a state under the Articles of Confederation. Despite their drastic differences in size and population, these states were accustomed to acting essentially as sovereign nations. It would be no easy matter at this late date for the states, especially the small states, to sacrifice their sovereignty to a new union of states.

The matter came to a head as the delegates sought to finalize a structure for the legislature. The large and small states could not agree, and discussions nearly fell apart. The Convention was saved when a compromise—the "Great Compromise"—was proposed and accepted. One house of Congress would operate on the principle of equal state representation, while representatives in the second house would be elected based upon population. This compromise over the composition of the legislature shaped future discussions on presidential selection. The delegates eventually devised a manner whereby the principles of the Great Compromise could be reflected in the presidential election process. The result was the Electoral College system.

Discussions in the Convention

The presidential selection process was first discussed almost immediately after the Convention opened and established its standing rules. The delegates spent much of these early discussions debating the merits of legislative selection of the President versus those of other modes of appointment, such as a national, direct popular election. Early on, a few delegates suggested the use of electors, as when Luther Martin, delegate from Maryland, advised that they could be "appointed by the several Legislatures of the individual States."[10] These early elector proposals, however, were usually variations on the legislative versus popular election schemes already being discussed. The legislative and direct election proposals remained the primary methods under consideration for much of the Convention.

The small states were concerned about the prospect of direct popular elections. They felt that they would be outnumbered, which made them wary of agreeing to such a plan. Roger Sherman, delegate from Connecticut, stated that the "sense of the Nation would be better expressed by the Legislature, than by the people at large. . . . [The people] will generally vote for some man in their own State, and the largest State will have the best chance for the appointment."[11] Charles Pinckney of South Carolina concurred: "An Election by the people [is] liable to the most obvious & striking objections. They will be led by a few active & designing men. The most populous States by combining in favor of the same individual will be able to carry their points."[12] Moreover, these delegates noted, the size of the country would make it difficult for the populace to be informed about all candidates in a direct election.

The alternative, legislative selection, could not gain steam either, as it was also believed to have crippling disadvantages. Many delegates worried that such a method of appointment would rob the President of his independence from the legislature. Gouverneur Morris, of Pennsylvania, declared that such an executive would be the "mere creature of the [Legislature]: if appointed & impeachable by that body."[13] Instead, Morris continued, the President "ought to be elected by the people at large, by the freeholders of the Country. . . . If the Legislature elect, it will be the work of intrigue, of cabal, and of faction."[14] James Madison concurred:

> If it be a fundamental principle of free [Government] that the Legislative, Executive & Judiciary powers should be *separately* exercised, it is equally so that they be *independently* exercised. There is the same & perhaps greater reason why the Executive [should] be independent of the Legislature, than

why the Judiciary should: A coalition of the two former powers would be more immediately & certainly dangerous to public liberty. It is essential then that the appointment of the Executive should either be drawn from some source, or held by some tenure, that will give him a free agency with regard to the Legislature.[15]

The legislative selection proposal was bogged down by yet another problem: the concern over the composition of the legislature. After all, if the small states were not equally represented in the legislature, then they would not have equal representation in selecting the Executive.

Before the election issue could be resolved, these latter discussions regarding the composition of the legislature threatened to tear the Convention apart. The large and small states could not reach an agreement. Luther Martin later described the atmosphere at this juncture, stating that the Convention was "on the verge of dissolution, scarce held together by the strength of a hair."[16] The division among the delegates was resolved when an agreement was forged between the small states and the large states: it was decided that the small states would have equal representation in one of the two legislative houses. From that point on, the discussions surrounding the election of the President changed. The question was no longer *whether* to incorporate the principle of equal state representation into the election process. Instead, the question became *how* to implement it.

The Electoral College mechanism, when it was eventually proposed, made concessions both to the large and the small states. The large states would get more electoral votes in the college, reflecting their greater populations. The small states, however, were guaranteed at least three votes, regardless of population.[17] One further concession was made to the small states: In the event of a contingent election in the House, each state delegation would have one vote, regardless of size.[18] The compromise was quite an important gesture by the large states, as many delegates believed that most elections would be resolved in the House.

Each side, then, made sacrifices to the other at different stages in the election process.[19] James Madison expressed this sentiment when he described the presidential election process as the "result of a compromise between the larger & smaller States, giving to the latter the advantage in selecting a president from the Candidates, in consideration of the advantage possessed by the former in selecting the Candidates from the people."[20]

Evaluating the Final Results

Some have argued that the creation of the Electoral College was not so much a carefully thought out compromise as it was a hasty conclusion to the Constitutional Convention. The delegates, they contend, were tired and under pressure to complete the proposed Constitution. Because they could not come to an agreement on direct election versus legislative selection, they simply drew up a scheme that would be easily accepted by a public that was certain to elect George Washington as President anyway. Two vocal opponents of the Electoral College, Professor Lawrence Longley and journalist Neal Peirce have stated: "[T]he most basic reason that the electoral college was invented was that the Convention was deadlocked on simpler schemes like direct election and choice by Congress, and thus invented a system that could be 'sold' in the immediate context of 1787."[21]

The delegates were doubtless tired and ready to go home. James Madison admitted as much when he stated, "[T]he final arrangement took place in the latter stages of the session, [and] it was not exempt from a degree of the hurrying influence produced by fatigue and impatience in all such bodies."[22] However, he concluded, "the degree was much less than usually prevails in them."[23] The fatigue described by Madison was real, but it is unfair to dismiss the quality of the delegates' work based upon this one factor. To do so underestimates the importance of this task to the delegates.

The states were ceding sovereignty to a central, national government. Why would they cede this sovereignty without some assurance that they would be treated fairly in the new government? They had long been abused by a distant, powerful monarch, and they had won independence from that power at great cost. They would be unlikely to give up power to a new, centralized Executive without extensive deliberation into how that Executive would be selected and how his powers would be contained. To the contrary, James Wilson, delegate from Pennsylvania, deemed the presidential election process to be among the hardest issues faced by the Convention. He stated, "This subject has greatly divided the House, and will also divide people out of doors. It is in truth the most difficult of all on which we have had to decide."[24]

Hence, the Electoral College is more than a hasty conclusion to a long summer in Philadelphia. It is a carefully considered and thought-out solution to the problem facing the Convention: In a nation composed of both large and small states that have ceded some, but not all, of their sovereignty to a central government, how should an Executive be selected?

The Electoral College solved the problem by creating a federalist system that incorporated the principles of the "Great Compromise" struck earlier in the Convention. The presidential election process settled upon by the Founders is both a national and a local process. The states determine how to appoint their own electors, but these electors must vote for *both* national and local candidates (see Chapter Three).[25] The President is elected through a series of local election processes, yet he is a national President dependent upon a national people. The election requires the active involvement of each state, yet support from a regional constituency alone is insufficient to win the Electoral College. The President must win local support across the nation to be elected. "[T]he genius of the present [Electoral College] system," a Senate report concluded in 1970, "is the genius of a popular democracy organized on the federal principle."[26]

Early Supreme Court decisions recognized and upheld the federalist nature of American presidential elections. In 1892, the Court held that the Constitution "recognizes that the people act through their representatives in the legislature, and leaves it to the legislature exclusively to define the method of effecting the object. . . . In short, the appointment and mode of appointment of electors belong exclusively to the States under the Constitution of the United States."[27] Today, the Court still recognizes the critical role of the states, as states, in the presidential election process.[28] Most recently, in *Bush v. Gore*, the Supreme Court concluded that the "individual citizen has no federal constitutional right to vote for electors for the President of the United States unless and until the state legislature chooses a statewide election as the means to implement its power to appoint members of the Electoral College."[29] The election, Justice Thurgood Marshall once noted, is not one "by the Nation as such, but rather by the individual States."[30]

The solution devised by the Founders recognized that, in a federalist republic, the states would and should have a voice in determining the identity of the next President. This state participation was valued at least as highly as the voting rights of individuals in the presidential election process. After all, a federalist system would not easily be maintained in the absence of a federalist election method. And the Founders considered it imperative for the federalist republic to remain intact.

A Federalist Republic

The Constitutional Convention was called based upon the conviction of many early Americans that the United States needed an energetic, central, federal government. After the Revolution, the states struggled for several years under the system of government created by the Articles of Confederation. This government was rather weak and failed to bring the states together as a unified whole. Instead, states' treaties sometimes clashed with each other, commerce suffered, and the country was in debt because the national government could not force the states to contribute to the national treasury. Washington strongly felt that a more powerful national government was needed; he had spent many years struggling to lead the Continental Army under a Congress that did not have sufficient authority to fund and maintain a military. He observed of the Confederation, "Thirteen Sovereignties pulling against each other, and all tugging at the fœderal head, will soon bring ruin on the whole."[31] The Constitutional Convention was called in response to the recognition by many that only by creating a central, national government could the states effectively work together.

Yet this need for a strong central government clashed with other sentiments strongly felt by many in the founding generation. Many refused to support the creation of a central government. They had just won their freedom from England in the Revolutionary War.

After fighting so hard and sacrificing so many lives, why, then, would these early Patriots create a strong United States Congress to enslave them once again? They might as well have stayed under the thumb of the British Parliament and King.

The clashing sentiments of pro-nationalists and anti-nationalists were exacerbated by another issue: The Founders' review of history showed them that a republic could not successfully extend across a large nation. Large republics could not ensure that every district or segment of society had representation in its own government. Inevitably, someone would not be fairly represented. Republican principles could work well only when the representatives were close to the people.

The solution, the Founders proposed, was to create a federalist republic. Those matters requiring national attention would be left at the national level. Every other matter would be handled by state authorities. In this manner, every person would be adequately represented by his government, particularly on the issues that are closest to home and most impact daily life. Charles Pinckney praised this unique combination of national and state power during the South Carolina ratification debates. The records of the debates summarize his views:

> It had been an opinion long established, that a republican form of government suited only the affairs of a small state; which opinion is founded in the consideration, that unless the people in every district of the empire be admitted to a share in the national representation, the government is not to them as a republic; . . . [Much of the objection] would be done away by the continuance of a federal republic, which, distributing the country into districts, or states, of a commodious extent, and leaving to each state its internal legislation, reserves unto a superintending government the adjustment of their general claims, the complete direction of the common force and treasure of the empire.[32]

American federalism, in its simplest form, is the distribution of power between the federal and state governments. Each government is a sovereign in its own right. Each has a sphere in which its authority trumps the others. Such a system recognizes that larger and smaller governmental authorities may each be better at different tasks. National tasks are handled nationally, but other tasks are handled locally. The country is able to function together on issues requiring cooperation, such as defense, interstate commerce, and foreign affairs. On other issues, freedom is protected by leaving the decision-making process close to where the people live, thereby granting them the greatest influence on the outcome.

Federalism has benefits that were well-recognized by the Founders, who preferred local laws to national laws for several reasons. They knew that it is often easier to influence the content of local laws. Local officials represent fewer people and are therefore more directly accountable to the public. For example, as of the 2010 Census, Texas's 25,268,418 people are represented by 36 Congressmen.[33] Each Congressman, in other words, represents about 701,900 constituents. By contrast, Texas' 150 state representatives[34] represent an average of 168,456 constituents. If a voter or group of voters in Texas wished to influence policy, it would have a greater likelihood of success at the state level, rather than the federal level.

For example, assume that Joe Citizen, residing in Temple, Texas, has been told that his private property is being taken by the government, through its exercise of eminent domain. The government wants to build a highway where his house now stands. Joe wants to fight this process. He has found an alternate path for the highway—one that does not require the government to purchase and demolish his home, or the home of any other citizen. The question is: Would Joe prefer to take this argument to the federal government or to the state government? Most people would prefer arguing before a state legislature, rather than a federal bureaucracy. Joe is more likely to be heard and to have an impact on the process if it is closer to home.

Now take the example a step further. Rather than the state level, wouldn't he really prefer to argue before the county or city authorities? He can certainly have more influence on his local city council members than he can a member of his state legislature—let alone a member of Congress. City council members have small constituencies and would more likely be influenced by a crowd of, say, 50 protesters than would a Senate or House Committee, which is flooded with hundreds of requests even on a slow day. Local lawmaking protects freedom because it allows the people themselves to have the most direct and powerful influence possible on the laws and regulations that affect them on a daily basis.

Another benefit of local lawmaking is that it allows the diversity of subcultures across the country to be reflected in different states and their statutes. Californians, for instance, may be more concerned about environmental care than about creating inexpensive energy sources. America's federalist system allows California to pass legislation accordingly, and it may do so without negotiating with Texans who may care more about saving money on energy. Each state's laws will reflect the differing priorities of its voters. Voters are free to live in a state that reflects their priorities—or to argue for change in their state's laws, as applicable.[35]

Moreover, federalist principles encourage state legislatures to act responsibly. If one state's legislature goes too far in one direction, residents may leave the state for other states, thus encouraging the state legislature to adjust its laws. As an example, residents may leave if a state's tax rates get too high, encouraging lawmakers to restrain spending and bring taxes back to more reasonable levels. California's high taxes and spending rates have caused many companies to move to California's lower-tax neighbor, Nevada. Many people move to Nevada, Florida, or Texas, because these states do not have state income taxes.[36]

If a state is having difficulty addressing a particular issue, it can look to what has or has not worked in other states and adjust its laws accordingly. As one example, the National Governors Association Center for Best Practices builds specifically on this idea; it works to provide the nations' governors with policy ideas, based on what has worked in some parts of the country.[37] Moreover, states can experiment with new solutions without affecting the rest of the country, as when Ohio experimented with school vouchers in the Cleveland school system. Justice Brandeis once stated, "It is one of the happy incidents of the federal system that a single courageous State may, if its citizens choose, serve as a laboratory; and try novel social and economic experiments without risk to the rest of the country."[38]

The federalist system, in many ways, creates the same incentives and restraints as a free market system. Americans may live and vote and work in the state that best reflects their needs and principles. This freedom to pick up stakes and start afresh encourages lawmakers to create a climate that brings residents to their state.

Professor Judith Best of the State University of New York has explained one last benefit of federalism—a benefit that has particular importance in a presidential election process. A federalist presidential election system, she explains, allows the country to reap the benefits of "safe" factions (or special interest groups) without succumbing to the hazards of "dangerous" factions.[39] Special interest groups in America are based on such public policy issues as gun control, affirmative action, or other social and family issues. These groups, of course, should and do have a voice in America's republican democracy; however, they are best able to contribute to society when they check and control each other. Left to their own devices, these factions could tend toward the extremes of their public policy positions and endanger the freedoms of those who disagree with them.[40]

States are safe factions upon which to rely in the presidential election process. They may act as cohesive units because they share common interests such as environmental, transportation, and local economy concerns. In this capacity, the states are able to play against each other, providing the helpful check-and-balance function that may be provided by special-interest factions. However, because states are also heterogeneous entities composed of individuals with a wide variety of interests, the danger of extremism that often accompanies other special interest groups is muted. Dr. Best explains this dynamic:

> The federal principle keeps dangerous factions within bounds by penning them up in multiple small societies. If dangerous factions cannot directly combine their votes across state lines, their destructive potential is reduced. If they are confined within the boundaries of a state, the necessity to

compromise in order to achieve national representation can instill moderation.[41]

The country's federalist system prevents local needs from being ignored, controls dangerous factions, and requires a balancing of interests. The Founders recognized that the President should have the same motivation as the Congress, with its House and Senate, to consider local as well as national needs. He should represent the people as a whole, not a bare majority of individuals who may represent only certain regions or special interest groups. Removing states from the presidential election process would undermine the federalist nature of the American republic.

The degree to which the system is valued today will depend upon the degree to which the states, as states, are valued as participants in the process. Those that value the votes of individuals over the influence of states as the *sine qua non* of a modern democracy will downplay the importance of the Electoral College as an institution. Yet many reasons exist to emphasize state participation in the presidential election process, as the Framers of the Constitution understood from their reading of history.

※ ※ ※

The Framers deliberately created a federalist republic, rather than a pure democracy, because they believed that, ultimately, such a form of government would be the best protection for individual freedom. Moreover, many of the original 13 states would not have consented to being governed by the new American government were it not for the federalist protections in the new Constitution. Delaware's delegates to the Constitutional Convention, for instance, were not authorized to vote in favor of a Constitution that violated the principle of "one state, one vote."[42] Rhode Island refused to participate in the Convention, as it was worried about the powerful centralized government that might result from the process.[43]

Although some modern-day Americans may value individual voting rights more than the rights of the states, it is important to remember that consent of the governed is an equally important

39

component of freedom. This consent would not have been obtained without the protections that the Constitution provides for small states and other minorities. In all likelihood, such consent still could not be obtained today without such minority protections as the Electoral College and equal representation for all states in the Senate.[44]

Chapter Three

The Constitution's Election Process

O ver the course of that long, hot summer, the delegates to the Constitutional Convention reached compromises that would enable large and small states to peacefully co-exist in the same country. The compromises pertaining to the presidential election process were articulated in Article II of the United States Constitution; these provisions would provide the framework for the nation's first four presidential elections.[1] Soon thereafter, however, the emergence of political parties and the tumultuous election of 1800 were enough to push the fledgling nation into making a few minor adjustments. These changes were encapsulated in the 12th Amendment to the Constitution.[2] Today, American presidential elections are governed by this amendment and two still-effective clauses in Article II.[3]

The 12th Amendment and Article II procedures are fairly similar, except the original Article II provision did not provide for separate voting for the President and Vice President. Instead, the candidate with the most votes became President and the runner-up became Vice President. During the country's fourth presidential election in 1800, this combined voting procedure created problems. As a result, the 12th Amendment was adopted and governed the next presidential election in 1804.

Despite claims to the contrary, the constitutional process of selecting a President, while not as straight-forward as a direct popular vote, is not terribly complicated either. It is perhaps easiest to think of the election in two phases: First, the Electoral College vote, and second, the contingent election procedure, which is used only if no candidate wins a majority of electoral votes.

Unintended Consequences in 1800

The country's first two elections were relatively uneventful. Nearly everyone expected that the revered General, George Washington, would be the nation's first President. The bigger question was who would serve as his Vice President. John Adams was elected to the post. By the time Washington announced his retirement in 1796,[4] political parties were coalescing, and they were identifying specific nominees for President and Vice President. Today, voters expect each party to nominate one person for President and one for Vice President. In 1796, however, this practice was just taking shape. The emergence of separate nomination processes for President and Vice President caused an unanticipated conflict with the new Constitution's presidential election provision.

Two major party candidates competed for the presidency during the country's third presidential election in 1796. The Federalist Party nominated then-Vice President Adams for President and Thomas Pinckney for Vice President. The Democratic-Republican Party nominated Thomas Jefferson for President. (It could not agree on only one nominee for Vice President.) Unfortunately, the Article II constitutional provision did not allow electors to differentiate between their votes for President and Vice President. Instead, each elector was to cast two ballots for President. When these electoral votes were tallied, the first place winner became President and the second place winner became Vice President.

When the electors cast their votes, Adams placed first with 71 electoral votes, and he became the country's second President. The Federalist Party's vice presidential candidate, Pinckney, did not place second, however. Instead, that honor went to Jefferson, who won 68 electoral votes. His second place finish made him Vice President, even though he and Adams were from different political parties.

Pinckney placed third with 59 electoral votes. The remainder of the electoral vote was divided among ten men.

The Federalist Party avoided a mistake that the Democratic-Republican Party would later make in the election of 1800. Yet its actions, ironically, contributed to Pinckney's loss of the vice presidency. Recognizing the possibility of an unintended tie if all Federalist electors voted both for Adams and Pinckney, the Federalist Party instructed some of its electors to vote for Adams with one ballot, but to cast a blank second ballot in place of their vote for Pinckney. Unfortunately for the Federalists, too many Pinckney votes were held back, and Jefferson squeaked in between the two men to place second in the balloting.[5]

The fourth presidential election was more eventful,[6] and it brought the flaw in the Article II process more sharply into view. In 1800, the Democratic-Republican Party nominated Jefferson for President and Aaron Burr for Vice President. The Democratic-Republican slate defeated the Federalist Party candidates, Adams and Charles Pinckney, by eight and nine electoral votes, respectively. The presidential election should have ended there—but it didn't. Unfortunately, the Democratic-Republican Party failed to ensure that one elector would abstain from casting his vote for Burr. The result was an electoral tie: Jefferson and Burr each received the same number of electoral votes. Although the electors intended to elect Jefferson for President and Burr for Vice President, the constitutional provision did not allow them to distinguish between their votes for the two offices. The election was thrown into the Constitution's secondary election procedure, known as the House contingent election.

More trouble brewed in the House, which was still controlled by the outgoing Federalist Party. Many Federalists searched for a way to thwart Jefferson's election. Eventually, these Congressmen decided to throw their support behind Burr. Other Federalists, relegated to the minority for the first time, sought concessions from Jefferson in return for their vote.

A stalemate continued for the better part of a week.[7] Nine state votes were needed to win the election in the House, but neither candidate could obtain this majority. Over five days of voting, 34 ballots were taken, but the vote remained unchanged: Eight states for Jefferson, six for Burr, and two states divided. The sixth day of voting opened with yet another unchanged ballot, but after this 35th ballot, one Congressman yielded. James Bayard, the only Congressman from Delaware, indicated his decision to switch his vote to Jefferson. His action would place the critical ninth state in Jefferson's column. His decision broke the deadlock, which in turn made his vote for Jefferson unnecessary. In the end, he abstained from voting on the 36th ballot, as did Congressmen from Maryland, Vermont, and South Carolina. Jefferson ultimately won, ten states to Burr's four.

Results: Election of 1800

	Party	Nominee For	Electoral Votes	House Votes
Thomas Jefferson	Democratic-Republican	President	73	10
Aaron Burr	Democratic-Republican	Vice President	73	4
John Adams	Federalist	President	65	—
Charles C. Pinckney	Federalist	Vice President	64	—

Allegations later surfaced that the impasse had been broken because Jefferson cut a deal with Bayard via an intermediary, General Samuel Smith of Maryland. Jefferson, however, denied these claims. In a letter to Dr. Benjamin Rush, he later described his reaction to Adams at the time of the House deliberations, "I will not come into the government by capitulation. I will not enter on it, but in perfect freedom to follow the dictates of my own judgment."[8]

In all likelihood, Jefferson did not cut a deal, but Smith may have taken it upon himself to ascertain and pass on Jefferson's views regarding certain matters of concern to Bayard. Bayard, finding Jefferson's views satisfactory, eventually decided to change his vote.[9] Jefferson's election may also owe much to the intercession of Alexander Hamilton, who had no great fondness for Burr. Hamilton wrote many letters to Congressmen, urging them to obtain concessions from and vote for Jefferson instead. To Bayard he wrote a scathing letter alluding to Burr: "[G]reat Ambition unchecked by principle, or the love of Glory, is an unruly Tyrant."[10] The new Vice President had no great fondness for Hamilton, either. He would later kill Hamilton in a duel during July 1804.

Passing a constitutional amendment to separate the voting for President and Vice President might seem like an obvious solution to these electoral problems. Nevertheless, many congressional representatives in the early 1800s did not see the issue in such black and white terms. To the contrary, a fair amount of argument over the subject ensued.[11] The minority party, the Federalists, did not want to approve the proposed amendment. They argued that the election process, as it then stood, made it possible for the minority party to have a representative in the executive branch. In all likelihood, they feared that the Democratic-Republicans were taking advantage of the situation to deprive them of such an advantage in a future presidential administration. Some Democratic-Republicans, for their part, could see the possibility that they would be in the minority again someday. They hesitated to change the election procedure as well. After all, the Article II process had helped them to gain the vice presidency in 1796, when Jefferson defeated the Federalist vice presidential candidate, Thomas Pinckney.

An amendment to the election procedure failed to pass the Senate by a single vote when it was first proposed in 1801. In 1803, however, with the specter of a new presidential election on the horizon, the 12th Amendment gained enough support in the Congress to pass both the Senate and the House. North Carolina became the first state to ratify the amendment on December 21, 1803. The amendment became effective when New Hampshire ratified it on June 15, 1804. Tennessee ratified it later, on July 27, 1804. Three states rejected the amendment.[12]

The 12th Amendment still provides the framework for American presidential elections today.[13] Its procedures are virtually identical to those in the original Article II provision adopted at the 1787 Constitutional Convention, except the 12th Amendment procedures provide for separate voting for the President and Vice President in the Electoral College; they also made minor changes to the contingent election procedures, used when no candidate wins a majority of the electoral votes.[14]

The election process was tweaked and adjusted following the election of 1800, yet today it remains largely as the Founders created it. As a first step, the states cast electoral votes in the nationwide presidential election. If no candidate wins a majority of these state votes, then the House of Representatives must decide which of the top candidates will be the next President.

The Electoral College Vote

The Constitution does not provide for a national, direct popular vote to determine the winner of the presidency. Instead, it provides for an election in which each state is granted a certain number of representatives, called electors, to cast votes on its behalf.[15] This vote is national in nature, but it is a tally of states' votes, not individuals' votes. This national vote among the states is often referred to as the Electoral College vote.

States are allocated one elector for each of their representatives in Congress—both Senators and Congressmen.[16] Each state therefore automatically receives a minimum of three votes, because it is entitled to at least two Senators and one Congressman in the Congress, regardless of population.[17] Puerto Rico and the Island Areas are not given electors, as they are not states. The District of Columbia did not initially receive votes because it is not a state; however, adoption of the 23rd Amendment in 1961 provided it with at least three electoral votes, as if it were.[18] At this time, there are 538 total electors. Following the 2010 Census, California has the most electors (55), while seven states plus the District of Columbia have the minimum number (3).[19]

It is left to the state legislatures to decide how to appoint their electors for this national election,[20] and the general rule is that the legislatures may appoint their states' electors in any manner that they choose. (Potential exceptions to this general rule are discussed in Chapter Fourteen.) The Supreme Court reaffirmed this general principle in the litigation surrounding the 2000 election. In *Bush v. Gore*, the Court stated: "The individual citizen has no federal constitutional right to vote for electors for the President of the

United States unless and until the state legislature chooses a statewide election as the means to implement its power to appoint members of the electoral college."[21] Indeed, the Court noted, "[The state legislature] may, if it so chooses, select the electors itself."[22]

This is exactly what happened in the first presidential election when the legislatures of Connecticut, Delaware, Georgia, New Jersey, and South Carolina each appointed electors on behalf of their citizens.[23] On the other hand, Pennsylvania, Maryland, Virginia, and Massachusetts appointed their electors through popular vote; this vote took a different form in each of the four states.

In Pennsylvania, electors were elected on a general ticket by popular vote. Maryland provided for the election of electors on a general ticket, but directed that five were to be residents from the Western Shore and three were to be from the Eastern Shore. Virginia created 12 districts specifically for the election of electors. One elector was elected from each of these districts. These elector districts were separate from the ten districts created for the election of Congressmen. In Massachusetts, the state was divided into congressional districts. On Election Day, voters cast two ballots for elector in addition to the votes cast for Congressmen. The names of the two electors receiving the most votes in each congressional district were submitted for a second election, this one before Massachusetts' general court. From this list of names, the general court determined which elector would represent each congressional district; it also selected two at-large electors to represent the state.

A fifth state attempted, but failed, to implement a popular vote in this first presidential election. New Hampshire passed a statute providing for an election by a majority popular vote, but it also made provision for legislative selection in the event that the election resulted in no choice. Ultimately, the legislature appointed the electors in the 1789 election. Of the other three states, New York lost its vote altogether due to disagreement in the legislature regarding how to proceed, and North Carolina and Rhode Island did not vote, as they had not yet ratified the Constitution.

The second presidential election saw a similar variety of elector selection methods. Of the fifteen states that voted, nine relied upon their legislatures to choose their electors. Maryland, New

Hampshire, and Pennsylvania selected their electors by general ticket, while Virginia elected them by districts. Massachusetts held an election for the selection of electors, but divided its state into two five-elector districts and two three-elector districts for this purpose. North Carolina was divided into four districts. The members of the legislature in each district designated three electors to represent that district.

The states continued to rely upon a wide variety of methods for the appointment of their electors through the first several presidential elections; however, it did not take long for each state to move to statewide direct, popular elections instead. Most states had taken this step by the 1830s, although South Carolina did not utilize popular elections until after the Civil War.[24] Today, most states rely upon a "winner-take-all" system, whereby the presidential candidate winning the state's popular vote is awarded the state's slate of electors in its entirety. Maine and Nebraska are currently the only exceptions to this general rule, despite occasional rumblings from other states that they might also abandon winner-take-all.[25] Maine and Nebraska rely upon a congressional district allocation: Each gives two electoral votes to the winner of its own popular vote and select the remaining electors by congressional district.[26] Despite the technical possibility that their electoral votes could be divided among candidates, their votes usually are not split. Nebraska has split its vote once since it implemented the system in 1992.[27] Maine began using the system in 1972 and has never split its vote.[28]

While the state's authority to determine a method for appointing electors is not in doubt, one issue is unresolved. Some dispute remains regarding the extent of Congress's constitutional authority (or lack thereof) if there is controversy regarding which of two slates of electors rightfully represents a state.[29] The controversies surrounding the election of 1876, discussed in the introduction, were made worse in large part due to this unresolved issue. The Congress created an Electoral Commission to resolve the problems in 1876, but only after many other House and Senate proposals had been defeated. No one seemed to know how to handle the election dispute.[30] Following the chaotic election proceedings, Congress enacted the Electoral Count Act of 1887.[31] In this statute, Congress claimed authority to supervise the Electoral College process.[32] The law it passed limits state discretion as to issues of timing and grants Congress final authority in counting electoral votes. This federal law, as updated and expanded through the years, currently provides a timeline for the various procedures described in the Constitution.

Election Day is the Tuesday following the first Monday in November in any given presidential election year.[33] In 2012, the election date will be November 6, and in 2016, the election will be held on November 8. On Election Day, voters in the states are not voting for the presidential candidate himself. They are actually voting for a slate of electors (Republican, Democrat, or third-party), even though the names of the electors themselves are not on the ballot in most states.[34] Once the votes have been tallied, each state (except Maine and Nebraska) will certify the entire slate of electors for the party that won that state's popular vote. A "Certificate of Ascertainment" with the names of these electors is forwarded to Washington, D.C.[35]

The electors affiliated with each party were appointed prior to the election, usually at the state party convention during the election year. In some states, these electors are committed to vote for their party candidates by state law, although it is unclear whether these pledges can constitutionally be enforced. At other times, the elector is bound by a pledge to his party, but in still other cases, the elector is bound by nothing more than his conscience.[36]

These electors assemble in their state on the first Monday after the second Wednesday in December.[37] In 2012, these meetings are on December 17, and in 2016, they will be held on December 19. On this day, the electors cast the votes that officially determine who will be the next President of the United States. These votes are recorded on "Certificates of Vote," one of which goes to the President of the Senate.[38] These votes must be received by the Senate by the fourth Wednesday in December,[39] and they are counted on the January 6 following any meetings of the electors. The Congress meets in joint session to count the votes.[40] The President of the Senate presides at this meeting. Ironically, on January 6, 2001, then-Vice President Al Gore presided over the joint session that declared his opponent, George W. Bush, the winner of the 2000 election.

To be elected President, a candidate needs a majority of the states' electoral votes, which are cast in December. He does not need a majority of the direct popular vote on Election Day.[41] At this time, 270 electoral votes constitute a majority of the Electoral College and will win the presidency for a candidate.

The Contingent Election

If no candidate wins a majority of the Electoral College vote, the Constitution provides a back-up method for presidential selection. This procedure is often referred to as the Constitution's contingent election procedure. In this secondary election, the election of the President is sent to the House and the election of the Vice President is sent to the Senate.[42]

In the House vote for President, each state delegation is granted one vote. California, with its current delegation of 53 Congressmen, would cast one vote, as would South Dakota, with its single Congressman. In the event that a state's delegation is evenly divided, that state cannot vote until and unless the tie is broken. For instance, Maine's vote will result in a tie if one of Maine's two Congressmen votes Republican while the other votes Democrat. One of the Congressmen will have to agree to abstain or switch his vote before Maine's vote can be cast for a candidate. Otherwise, the state of Maine will abstain from the election.

A President is elected when one candidate wins a majority of the votes of state delegations (currently 26). State delegations may vote for any one of the top three presidential candidates in the Electoral College vote,[43] and re-votes are taken until a majority is achieved. A similar procedure is employed for election of the Vice President, except that each Senator is granted one vote and only the top two vice presidential candidates from the Electoral College vote are candidates in the Senate vote.[44]

The Constitution provides this outline for the contingency procedures that are to be employed in the House and Senate, but it does not delineate all the logistical aspects of this secondary election. If a contingent election were required in the House in a future election year, there would be numerous questions regarding what specific procedures should be followed.[45]

First, are state votes determined by majority or plurality within each state delegation? A closely related question is whether a quorum is required within each state delegation before the delegation may take its vote. The Constitution does not provide an answer,[46] so the House would likely turn to the rules that it passed during the contingent election of 1825. Under these rules, a state could not cast a vote except by "majority of the votes given."[47] For instance, in Massachusetts, which has nine Congressmen, five Congressmen constitute a majority and are therefore needed to cast the state's one vote (assuming that all Congressmen vote). If four Congressmen vote for Barack Obama, three for Mitt Romney, and two for Hillary Clinton, the state's vote is deemed "divided" and is not counted because Obama has only a plurality of the votes within the delegation. The state may vote if, for instance, one Congressman switches to Obama. Alternatively, if the two Clinton Congressmen abstain, then Massachusetts' vote will go to Obama because four votes constitute a "majority of the votes given."[48]

Second, is the election one that is taken by secret ballot? The Constitution requires that "the House of Representatives shall choose immediately, by ballot, the President,"[49] but it does not otherwise address whether balloting must be done publicly.[50] In 1801 and 1825, many Congressmen felt that votes should be cast by secret ballot, but the rules they passed do not necessarily require the ballots to be secret. In fact, many newspapers in 1801 and 1825 reported the votes of Congressmen.[51]

Last, is the contingent election conducted in the new or old House of Representatives? The Constitution provides that the new House is sworn in on January 3,[52] and federal law provides that the electoral votes are counted on January 6.[53] Accordingly, many scholars believe that the new House is responsible for conducting the contingent election. A few others, however, observe that the counting of the votes on January 6 is a mere formality. The outcome of the Electoral College vote is generally known much sooner. It is possible that, under the right set of circumstances, some might urge that the contingent election be held earlier, in the lame-duck House.

When Ross Perot entered the 1992 presidential race, the House did some investigation into the logistical aspects of a contingent election. Unfortunately, it dropped the issue when Perot dropped out of the race (temporarily, as it turns out).[54] The issue was never raised in any serious manner again. The lack of consideration regarding this issue is unfortunate. Obviously, fair and impartial contingent election procedures can most easily be identified before the outcome of any one election hangs in the balance. Once the procedures are actually needed, partisan considerations are certain to taint any discussion of logistical procedures that remain unresolved. The House of Representatives should consider these logistical issues and adopt procedures for a contingent election, even though no immediate need for them appears on the horizon.[55]

☙ ☙ ☙

America's method of presidential election remains largely as it was first conceived by the Founders in the summer of 1787. The procedure seems unnecessarily complicated to many modern-day Americans, yet the Founding Fathers believed the Electoral College to be an ingenious solution to the problems facing the new country. Max Farrand, in his *The Framing of the Constitution of the United States*, reports: "[F]or of all things done in the convention the members seemed to have been prouder of that than of any other, and they seemed to regard it as having solved the problem for any country of how to choose a chief magistrate."[56]

The Founders spent months of extensive deliberation on the topic of presidential election. They found it to be one of the hardest topics facing the Convention, because of the necessity of incorporating so many conflicting values into the election system. When the Electoral College proposal was completed, they viewed it as a unique and commendable solution—a solution that came as close to perfection as possible in an imperfect world. More importantly, creation of the Electoral College allowed the Founders to reflect the many, apparently contradictory, goals of the new republic in their presidential election process.

Part Two

An 18th-Century Solution For the 21st Century

Chapter Four

A Rapidly
Changing Society

Much has changed since 1787. The Founders could not have
foreseen the rapid technological advancements that have
facilitated national and global communications. They lived in a
world that included a healthy fear of tyranny, whereas many
Americans today have not been exposed to tyranny except as a
theoretical matter. States were then reluctant to give up their
sovereignty to a central national government, preferring to handle
most matters themselves. Today, states instead often run to the
federal government, hat in hand, asking for more funding for roads
or schools or medical care. Moreover, Americans increasingly believe
that they live in a democracy, rather than a republic; many schools
do not teach the republican principles upon which America was
founded.

Some academics have predicted for years that these changes
could lead to a constitutional crisis. Particularly before the 2000
election, critics often warned that election of a "runner-up" President
would throw the country into turmoil. Somewhat pessimistically,
they imagined a future election in which Americans would find
themselves unable to accept their new President: a popular vote
loser. Today's Americans, these critics predicted, are too closely wed
to the principle of "one person, one vote" to accept such a President.[1]

A book by well-known Electoral College critics Neal Peirce and Lawrence Longley told the story of a hypothetical 1996 presidential election that ended in electoral deadlock and disaster.[2] Professor Akhil Reed Amar of Yale University echoed their warnings, telling a House committee in 1997 that the Electoral College is a "brilliant 18th century device that cleverly solved a cluster of 18th century problems," but "this once brilliant device has become a constitutional accident waiting to happen."[3]

Are these critics right? Could it be that the Electoral College, although once an ingenious solution to many 18th century problems, has today become merely an anachronism—and a potentially dangerous one at that? Or does it still serve the protective purposes intended by the Framers, despite the fact that it sometimes functions a bit differently than originally expected? Are detractors right in saying that our country has changed so much that the benefits of the Electoral College, important in 1787, no longer outweigh any detriments?

These critics have a valid point, worth considering. If the Electoral College is to be kept, it must either serve new, useful purposes in our 21st century world, or it must serve the goals of the Framers in new ways.

Losing Appreciation for States' Rights

Modern Americans cherish their own rights more than the rights of the state in which they live. They may not understand why so many in the founding generation valued their federalist system, in which states have their own areas of total sovereignty. Today's Americans may not know why the founding generation considered adoption of the Tenth Amendment so important—if indeed they know what it says: "The powers not delegated to the United States by the Constitution, nor prohibited by it to the States, are reserved to the States respectively, or to the people."[4]

Yet the problem is still more serious. Many Americans do not always know (or question) upon what basis their federal government claims authority to act. As a result, they do not realize the extent to which one of the federal government's powers, found in the Constitution's Commerce Clause, has been grossly expanded to justify the federal government's intrusion into many matters that should remain the responsibility of individuals or the states. This constitutional provision simply authorizes Congress "[t]o regulate Commerce with foreign Nations, and among the several States, and with the Indian Tribes."[5] The Clause does not authorize governance in matters that are purely *intra*state (as opposed to *inter*state) in nature, yet Congress uses the Clause as a pretext to interfere in local matters. Unfortunately, modern American schools do not teach their students about these restrictions upon the federal government. As a result, many Americans remain unaware of the numerous ways in which the federal government illegitimately stretches its power beyond the parameters originally granted to it.

In 1787, the Founders deliberately avoided granting the federal government a general police power; instead, they severely limited federal power, giving the government only certain powers that were enumerated in the Constitution. The Founders considered the concept of limited, enumerated powers an important protection for their hard-won freedom. In modern-day America, by contrast, many Americans seem to have adopted the reverse attitude: They want a governmental solution for every woe. These Americans do not always stop to evaluate whether the federal government has the authority to provide the solution that they want, nor does it occur to them that their deferral of responsibility may have an unwanted side effect: They may inadvertently undermine their own freedom.

Instead, when the Supreme Court knocks down legislation such as the Gun-Free School Zones Act,[6] these Americans wonder why the Supreme Court would declare such a "good" or "useful" law unconstitutional. When the Court strikes down a portion of the Violence Against Women Act,[7] the decision is met with similar complaints. Teachers rarely instruct students on the constitutional principle of federalism, which prohibits the federal government from legislating on certain purely intrastate matters. Without this background, it does not occur to many Americans that a federal law may contain a good statement of policy, but still be unconstitutional. Perhaps the good statement of policy is more appropriately enacted by a state government, rather than the federal government.

The Civil War was among the first major events to undermine the value of state decision-making in the eyes of Americans. In the mid-1800s, many southern states opted to continue slavery, citing states' rights as a defense for their actions. Slavery was an appropriate casualty of the war, but the legitimate principle of states' rights unfortunately also took a beating during this time. Later, during the Great Depression, states and individuals lost even more of their independence. Franklin Delano Roosevelt's New Deal offered national, governmental solutions to those in economic hardship. Americans at the time did not dwell on the loss of these states' rights; instead, they were glad for any financial relief.

The Supreme Court initially struck down many of FDR's New Deal measures, arguing that these laws encroached upon purely *intra*state matters. These decisions followed both the Constitution and the Court's own precedents, and they correctly held that Congress may regulate only *inter*state matters when it is relying upon its Commerce Clause power. Congressional power is limited to those powers enumerated in the Constitution, and the Court found that many of FDR's New Deal measures exceeded this federal authority.

FDR, however, was determined not to have his programs thwarted so easily. He was fresh from a landslide victory in the 1936 presidential election, and he resolved to implement his New Deal programs in spite of the Court. He firmly believed that his programs were a necessary component of economic recovery. FDR used his post-election momentum to support a "court-packing" plan, in which the appointment of up to six new Justices was proposed.[8] At the time, he explained that his intent was not to threaten the Justices or influence the Court's rulings—but one would be excused for doubting his claims of innocence in this regard.

The court-packing plan became unnecessary. Justice Owen Roberts switched his vote on a 14th Amendment issue in *West Coast Hotel Co. v. Parrish*, a case that upheld the constitutionality of minimum wage legislation enacted by the state of Washington.[9] The Justice's decision became known as "the switch in time that saved nine" because FDR dropped his court-packing plan soon thereafter.[10]

Following the *West Coast Hotel* decision, the Justice continued his downward spiral, switching his vote on Commerce Clause issues as well. A few weeks later, he joined the majority in *NLRB v. Jones & Laughlin Steel Corp.*, a decision that upheld the National Labor Relations Act (NLRA).[11] This Act gave the National Labor Relations Board expansive power over the country's labor practices. Chief Justice Hughes wrote for the majority: "The authority of the federal government may not be pushed to such an extreme as to destroy the distinction . . . between commerce 'among the several States' and the internal concerns of a State. That distinction . . . is vital to the maintenance of our federal system."[12] In previous cases, similar logic had led the Court to strike down far-reaching federal programs such as the NLRA; however, in *Jones & Laughlin Steel Corp.*, the Court added a big "But." Chief Justice Hughes concluded:

> The cardinal principle of statutory construction is to save, and not to destroy. . . . [If there are] two possible interpretations of a statute, by one of which it would be unconstitutional and by the other valid, our plain duty is to adopt that which will save the act. . . . We think it clear that the National Labor Relations Act may be construed so as to operate within the sphere of constitutional authority.[13]

Following this decision, the Supreme Court embarked on a journey in which it allowed virtually any act of Congress to stand, even when it infringed on matters that were purely local in nature.

In 1942, this stance reached a somewhat ridiculous extreme. The Court upheld the Agricultural Adjustment Act, which set production quotas for farmers. A small wheat farmer in Ohio had been fined for growing more wheat than the Department of Agriculture wanted him to grow. This excess wheat was intended for use on his own farm, but the Court determined that his wheat use affected interstate commerce anyway. After all, the Court reasoned, had the farmer not grown and used his own wheat, he would have been forced to purchase wheat from others who *are* involved in interstate commerce.[14]

Had FDR's government programs been temporary, or had FDR been less stubborn in pushing his programs past the Supreme Court, perhaps the damage to states' rights could have been lessened. Unfortunately, FDR's actions upset the balance of power between the state and federal governments, perhaps permanently. His New Deal programs became predecessors for many national welfare programs that remain in effect today. Nor did the Supreme Court reverse course or temper its decisions in the years following the New Deal. Since FDR's administrations, it has rarely questioned the federal government's authority to legislate. Indeed, its 1995 decision invalidating the Gun-Free School Zones Act was the first decision in almost 60 years to strike down a law based upon federalism issues. Such a decision remains the exception, rather than the rule, when the Court reviews a case.

Today, modern Congresses often assume the authority to legislate in any area that (they think) will score political points in the next election. Perhaps most notoriously in recent memory, the 111th Congress took it upon itself to order all Americans to buy health insurance so that a national health plan might be implemented.[15]

The early generations of our country understood the need for national action, but they tended to default upon local action first. They understood, of course, that some issues can be addressed only at the national level. This need for national cooperation spurred early Americans to call for a Constitutional Convention. They knew that a centralized government would be necessary to handle certain interstate commerce and national defense matters. Yet they tempered this recognition that national action would be beneficial in certain circumstances with a second belief: They assumed that states and towns could handle a matter until a sufficient argument was made to the contrary.

In recent decades, Americans have not relied primarily upon their state or local governments to provide a framework for public policy issues. They have instead presumed the need for a national solution and considered the possibility of local action only as a last resort. As they have devalued the importance of federalism, so have they changed their views on institutions such as the Electoral College. A re-emergence of federalism would likely reinvigorate support for the institution.

Developing a Populist Mentality

Compounding Americans' decreased understanding of federalist principles, their perceptions regarding their form of government have changed as well. The Founders distrusted unchecked democracies, with their historic propensity to degenerate into mob rule, and they instead sought to establish a republic in which the people's voice would be expressed in a tempered fashion. Today's Americans, by contrast, overwhelmingly believe that they live in a pure democracy. They cherish individual expression and populist ideals and seem to view other forms of government as "thwarting" the will of the people.

The founding generation established republican safeguards as a protection against tyranny, but modern Americans have never been exposed to such tyranny (or mob anarchy for that matter) and such a threat seems more hypothetical than real.[16] Instead, they are more likely to view republican safeguards as a hindrance to the principle of "one person, one vote." Why should this sacred democratic principle be less important in presidential elections, they might ask? To the contrary, shouldn't it be even more important than in other elections? George C. Edwards, III, then-director of the Center for Presidential Studies at Texas A&M University, expressed this frustration that many seem to feel:

> There's no justification for the Electoral College—none. We have invested so much in this nation in the principle of "one person, one vote." We've expanded the franchise to make sure that everyone votes. And for someone—no matter who wins the popular vote—to quite legally take the presidency, entirely contrary to democratic principles, is very hard to justify.[17]

Some have argued that the forces nudging the American republic towards such undiluted democratic ideals were present early in the nation's history—as early as 1824. That election year, Andrew Jackson lost to John Quincy Adams in the House of Representatives, despite winning a plurality both of the popular vote and the Electoral College vote. Jackson won 99 electoral votes and 41.3 percent of the recorded popular vote. John Quincy Adams, by contrast, won 84 Electoral College votes and 30.9 percent of the recorded popular vote.[18] The remainder of the vote was split between William H. Crawford and Henry Clay.[19] The value of this popular vote tally is questionable because many states at that time still selected electors through their state legislatures. Nevertheless, Jackson spent the next four years claiming that the will of the people had been thwarted and that the election had been stolen from him in the House.

Adams won in the House contingent election with the help of Henry Clay, who threw his support behind Adams and was instrumental in obtaining state delegations' votes on Adams' behalf. Adams subsequently made Clay Secretary of State, and Jackson supporters wasted little time in arguing that a "corrupt bargain" had been struck between the two men. Allegedly, Clay initially sought to strike a deal with Jackson, but Jackson refused to "go to that chair" except "with clean hands."[20] Of these events, historian Paul Johnson states, "We shall probably never know whether there *was* a 'corrupt bargain.' Most likely not. But most Americans thought so. And the phrase made a superb slogan."[21] Jackson used the issue, in combination with his plurality win in the popular vote totals, to generate public dissatisfaction with the results. Eventually, he was able to win the 1828 campaign, based in part on this issue.

In reality, up until that time, there had been no perception among the electorate that the winner of a direct popular vote should win the presidency; presidential candidates had no reason, therefore, to run their campaigns with such a goal in mind. Nevertheless, the election of 1824 was one of the first events leading to a belief among Americans that popular vote winners should be elected to the White House.

The constitutional amendments after 1824 mirrored the increasingly populist mentality in America. The Civil War resulted in passage of the 15th Amendment, which prevents states from denying minorities the right to vote "on account of race, color, or previous condition of servitude."[22] The 17th Amendment soon followed, removing the election of Senators from the state legislatures and placing that responsibility in the hands of the people.[23] In 1920, the 19th Amendment was ratified, ensuring that women could not be denied the right to vote based on their gender.[24] Other changes to government were less formal, but reflected the growing populist forces nonetheless. For instance, although many state legislatures initially selected electors on behalf of their citizens, today all states hold a direct popular election for the state's electoral votes.

Many critics of the Electoral College maintain that the country's presidential election process has become outdated in a society that increasingly believes itself to be democratic. They discount the ability of the American people to accept Presidents who were not elected with a majority of the popular vote. During the 2000 election, in which George W. Bush was elected despite his popular vote loss, one journalist claimed that the results of that election were "a mess" because "democratic principles count for more" than they did in the early years of our country.[25]

His words ring hollow, at least with the benefit of hindsight. President Bush may have been elected without a popular vote majority in 2000, but he also closed out his first term without any great constitutional crisis. Indeed, he was re-elected with both a popular and electoral vote majority in 2004. The American public, although increasingly democratic, by and large seems to have accepted the outcome of the 2000 election, governed by republican principles.

Evolving into a Global Society

It doesn't take a genius to realize that the ability to communicate, even over distances, has improved dramatically since 1787. Access to news and information was once slow and sporadic. Today, it is instantaneous and practically unavoidable. Presidential candidates can make themselves known to the entire nation through debates, media outlets, and the Internet. Americans can easily educate themselves as to the names, background and policy positions of each candidate, whereas such a task was difficult to impossible in 1787. Traditional journalists no longer have a monopoly on the news. Instead, they compete with blogs and social networking sites that pour out information (and, sometimes, misinformation), commentary, and humor—all from bloggers' home laptops. An

American doesn't have to take the word of the network news anchors regarding the War in Iraq or protests in Iran. Instead, he can read the thoughts of Iraqis and Iranians, directly, on Twitter or elsewhere.

Americans' ability to communicate with each other has changed dramatically as well. New technology has made users available to each other virtually anywhere in the world. High school students may use these new devices to message each other—gone are the days of passing physical notes in class. The Internet is available at the touch of a button, even in the middle of the grocery store check-out line or during a flight on a commercial airliner. A person can sit in the middle of his favorite park, surfing the Internet on one screen, instant messaging a friend in Australia on a second screen, and playing games with another friend on a third.

Global communication has become so easy and fast that some people even claim that massive self-rule is now possible. Perhaps voters can jump on the Internet and vote for or against legislation. What's the point of voting for representatives in Congress with such technology at the nation's disposal? (One can only imagine the horror of the Framers at such a system, totally bereft of safeguards against majority tyranny and faction.)

Along with the improvement in communications has come a similar change in the nature of commerce. The economy has increasingly become, not just more national, but also more global. Furniture purchased from the store down the street may be made in China. Dialing a technical support center often connects customers to service representatives in India. Opening an email inbox could deliver spam email from all around the world. Wireless technology allows stores to perform instant inventories: Taking a widget off a shelf at the local store can automatically notify a distribution center several states away that more widgets are needed in stock.

At first glance, these changes would seem to undermine the purposes of the Electoral College. The Framers implemented the system based partly on the assumption that the electorate could not be fully informed about each candidate. They could not foresee a world in which truly national candidates would not only be possible, but common. They certainly never predicted that technology would exist allowing their great-great-great grandchildren to vote, simultaneously, via the Internet, if they so desire. Further, some academics contend that federalist principles count for less in today's increasingly global society. State boundaries no longer define the most relevant or meaningful political communities, they argue. The economy is more global than local these days.

❧❧❧

The Electoral College undoubtedly operates in a different society from the one that existed in 1787. Global communications and the rise of national political parties have facilitated the rise of national candidates. They have enabled the average voter to be as informed as he would like to be regarding public policy issues and candidates. He can easily debate these issues with those in other states and countries.

Moreover, the Electoral College, in practice, operates differently than it did in 1787. Electors no longer operate as independently as they once did, but they usually merely rubber-stamp the decision of the states' electorates. State legislatures no longer select the electors; instead, electors are selected based on a popular election within each state. Over time, these elections have changed so that all states' electors (except Maine and Nebraska) are now awarded on a "winner-take-all" basis. Confounding the Founders' expectations, the contingent election is a rarity in this day and age.

Despite these changes, the Electoral College has not become an out-of-date electoral tool obstructing the American electorate. It has instead shown an amazing ability to adapt to modern-day America. It operates differently than expected, but still serves the political goals it was intended to serve.

Chapter Five

The Benefits
of Federalism

Prior to his presidency, Ronald Reagan discussed the principle of federalism as it relates to the Electoral College. In a 1977 radio broadcast, he described the security the system affords to all states, but especially to small states:

> The very basis for our freedom is that we are a Federation of Sovereign States. Our Constitution recognizes that certain rights belong to the state and cannot be infringed upon by the National government. This is the guaranty that small states or rural, sparsely populated areas will have a proportionate voice in national affairs.
>
> Those who want to do away with the electoral college really mean they want the President elected in a national referendum with no reference as to how each state votes. Thus a half dozen rural states could show a majority for one candidate and be outvoted by one big industrial state opting for his opponent.[1]

His words ring true in any century. Federalism remains important, even in the midst of the Information Age. Americans may operate in a global economy, but, as one columnist recently opined, this globalism has not caused the country to become "one undifferentiated national mass."[2] To the contrary, modern-day

American states retain unique interests that should be protected in a free society, and the federalist nature of America's constitutional system provides this indispensable protection.

Separating power between the state and federal governments still protects freedom. Local governance is still preferable on issues that do not require national cooperation. Governance close to home keeps elected officials more directly accountable to enact good policies, as discussed in Chapter Two. Joe Citizen will still have an easier time affecting policy if he brings his concerns to local government officials, rather than to national ones. His vote is more likely to change the outcome of one of these local elections than a national election—and those campaigning for office are always keenly aware of this fact.

The presidential election process devised by the Founders is a cornerstone of America's constitutional system. The Electoral College provides a vehicle whereby this nation of states can elect a President who is truly representative of the diverse interests of the various states. The federalist nature of the presidential election requires candidates to hear and address the unique interests of the various states. The alternative, a direct national election, would most likely produce a President who represents narrower special-interest groups, such as those based on region, state, or ideology.

Critics of the Electoral College allege that the country's presidential election process does less to protect federalism than it does to trample the rights of individuals. Implementation of a direct popular election system, they argue, would not undermine the federalist system. Instead, they contend that the primary consequence of a direct election system is to protect democratic principles. These principles, they argue, should be applied to the nation's most important election: the election of the President of the United States.

The "Wasted Vote" Theory

Critics of the Electoral College often claim that the state-by-state presidential election is unfair and causes some votes to be "wasted."[3] The culprit, they say, is the "winner-take-all" method employed by most states. In perhaps a bit of hyperbole, critics

Lawrence Longley and Neal Peirce have alleged that "[t]he operation of the winner-take-all system results in effective massive disenfranchisement of voters supporting losing candidates."[4] The National Popular Vote organization uses similarly dramatic language claiming that "voters are effectively disenfranchised in presidential elections in about two thirds of the states."[5] These critics argue for reform: A citizen's vote should not be "wasted" simply because he is voting Democratic in a red state or Republican in a blue one.

As this argument goes, a Texan who voted for Barack Obama in the 2008 election wasted his vote, because John McCain was awarded the state's entire slate of electors under the winner-take-all method. McCain won the state with a popular vote total of 4,479,328, but Obama won a fair number of votes, too: 3,528,633.[6] Despite the 3.5 million popular votes cast for Obama, he did not win so much as one electoral vote from Texas. McCain was awarded the entire slate of 34 electors.[7]

Critics condemn this situation as intolerable. After all, in a direct popular election, Obama votes could have instead been included in the final national tally for Obama, and they would not have been wasted simply because they were cast in Texas. Alternatively, critics continue, if Texas were to apportion its electoral votes by district, then this effect of wasted votes would at least be greatly reduced, because some of Texas' electoral votes could have been awarded to Obama in the 2008 election.

These criticisms are unconvincing for two reasons. First, the critics forget that the winner-take-all system is not mandated by the Constitution. Indeed, the NPV alternative now under consideration in many state legislatures relies heavily on the fact that any state may change its method of allocating electoral votes at any time.[8] The Constitution mandates that each state, through its state legislature, decide for itself how to allocate its votes.[9] States may cast their electoral votes as a bloc, divide them among multiple candidates, or even cast them according to a lottery system (if they really want to do so). Each state legislature has "plenary" power when choosing a manner of allocating its state's electoral votes[10]—and it does not have to agree with neighboring state legislatures on the best method. Each state legislature determines how its state and citizens can best be served in the electoral vote and adopts a method accordingly. If a state's citizens disagree with the chosen method, then they simply need to appeal to their state legislators to change the rules. Texans are free to elect state representatives who are willing to make this change—if, in fact, they feel that such a change would serve the state's best interests.

Some might dismiss this point, arguing instead that the small states are essentially bullied into adopting a "winner-take-all" system once large states, such as California and Texas, have already done so. Arguably, small states have great incentive to cast their votes in a bloc, regardless of what the larger states do. Nevertheless, two small states have apparently determined otherwise. Maine and Nebraska, with four and five votes, respectively, have each adopted a different system.[11] Their elections do not follow the winner-take-all rule; instead, votes are allocated based upon congressional district. The freedom of states to do exactly as they wish is one of the great benefits of federalism.

The wasted vote theory is a bit disingenuous for a second reason. These votes aren't wasted. They were simply cast on the losing side of a popular vote within the state. If the 2008 election had been conducted based on nationwide popular vote totals, would people claim that any vote for McCain was "wasted" because Obama won the popular vote? Of course not. The votes for McCain were cast in an effort to win. In the event of a loss, they would simply have been votes for the losing candidate—just like any other election.

The nation does conduct democratic, popular elections—but they are conducted at the state level, rather than the national level. Professor Charles R. Kesler of Claremont McKenna College puts it this way: "In truth, the issue is democracy with federalism (the Electoral College) versus democracy without federalism (a national popular vote). Either is democratic. Only the Electoral College preserves federalism, moderates ideological differences, and promotes national consensus in our choice of a chief executive."[12]

Comparing Election Systems

Perhaps the best method of demonstrating the benefits of a federalist presidential election process is to expose the evils suffered without it. As it stands today, presidential candidates have no incentive to poll large margins in any one state. Winning 50.1 percent of the votes in a state is as effective as winning 100 percent of the votes. Either way, the winner is awarded the entire slate of electors for that state—except, of course, in Maine and Nebraska. Presidential candidates therefore tour the nation, campaigning in all states and seeking to build a national coalition of voters that will enable them to win in most states.[13] They cannot focus on one or a handful of states to the exclusion of others. Doing so causes them to risk losing the election. Polling large margins in isolated regions of the country will not help their cause. Instead, their support must have a national component if they are to win a majority of the states' electoral votes in the election.

Presidential biographer James MacGregor Burns has described this phenomenon as "the immense widening of the electorate."[14] Presidential candidates are motivated "to widen and 'flatten out' their vote, [and] to win states by dependable but not wasteful popular majorities."[15] The campaigns of presidential candidates stand in sharp contrast to the campaigns of congressional candidates, who are often campaigning in a district that has been specifically drawn to be "safe" for one of the parties.[16] The different campaign strategies required causes many Congressmen (particularly those in safe districts) to be more ideological than the typical Senator or President, who instead tend to be (or must at least appear to be) more moderate. The former are often able to aim their campaigns at individuals who are similar to themselves; the latter must build coalitions, either at the state or national level. Without coalitions, Presidents and Senators are unable to win. The Electoral College serves the nation well to the extent that it encourages presidential candidates to build coalitions, rather than to aim their campaign solely at one group of voters.

Now imagine an America in which Presidents are elected by direct popular election. Some scholars have claimed that elections would not be significantly different in this new world. Campaign strategies, they claim, would remain essentially the same, even if the Electoral College system were eliminated.[17] It is difficult to see how this could be true. Rule changes impact strategy all the time.

Consider a hypothetical rule change for baseball.[18] If the two teams that scored the most runs during the year were able to go to the World Series, would not the strategies of all the teams change accordingly? In this new baseball world, amassing high run totals against weak opponents would be extraordinarily beneficial. Playing good hitters against an especially talented pitcher is probably a waste of time; perhaps it is better to leave hitters on the bench, where they can rest for the next game against a vulnerable opponent. The coaches' decisions on these and other issues would be greatly impacted by the changed incentives inherent in the new rules of the game.

Presidential campaign strategies, too, would be significantly adjusted if the incentives for various behaviors were changed. The Electoral College, together with the winner-take-all system, treats candidates who win 50.1 percent of a state's votes identically to candidates who win 100 percent of a state's votes. A direct popular vote procedure would reverse this situation. Winning 100 percent of the votes in a state would be infinitely preferable to winning 50.1 percent of the votes. In fact, it may be easier to rack up votes in a friendly state than to gain 50.1 percent of votes in each of two states of similar size, although the pay-off would be essentially the same.

The result? Ronald Reagan concluded his radio broadcast in 1977 by describing the likely consequences of such a change: "Presidential candidates would be tempted to aim their campaigns and their promises at a *cluster of metropolitan areas in a few states* and the smaller states would be without a voice."[19]

Democrats would almost certainly spend most of their time in the large population centers in California and New York. Republicans would campaign in the South and Midwest. Each candidate would promise anything and everything to the regions in which he is strong, ignoring the needs of the rest of the country. Large cities would be focused on almost exclusively as the candidates seek to turn-out as many votes as possible in "their" region of the country. Small states, rural areas and sparsely populated regions would find themselves with little to no voice in presidential selection. The parties would not be able to risk selecting candidates from small states.

By the time a President got himself elected under such a system, he would be indebted to—and would essentially represent—isolated regions, not the country as a whole. In this scenario, a handful of states (or heavily populated cities) win, while the remaining states suffer significantly.

Many critics argue that this description of the two types of elections is not entirely accurate. They contend that the current system does not encourage presidential candidates to tour the nation so much as it encourages them to focus their time and energy on the mid-sized "swing" states. "Safe" states and small states do not receive nearly as much attention on this national tour.

There is, obviously, an element of truth in this. Presidential candidates do not focus as much of their efforts on the safe states that they already feel certain of winning. This is, after all, one of the major goals of the Electoral College. Presidential candidates should not camp out in "friendly" states, ignoring and failing to learn about the needs of the remaining states.

To the degree that safe states don't receive a proportionate amount of attention during campaigns, the logical conclusion is that those states, by and large, must already feel that one of the two presidential candidates represents their interests pretty well. When a candidate ceases to adequately understand and represent one of "his" state's interests, the discontent in that state is usually expressed pretty quickly, forcing both candidates to again focus energy on understanding and gaining the support of constituents in that state.

Consider, for example, a state such as West Virginia. Democrats considered West Virginia a safe state for years; thus, the state probably saw less campaign time than it would have had it been more evenly divided. But in 2000, the George W. Bush campaign recognized an opportunity to gain a foothold in the state. Voters in West Virginia perceived that Al Gore's environmental policies would be harmful to the coal-mining industry in their state.[20] Bush took advantage of this discontent, and he spent more than $2 million communicating his message to voters in that state (compared to $830,000 spent by Gore).[21] When election results were tallied, Bush became the first Republican to win an open race for the presidency in West Virginia since 1928.[22]

In 2004, West Virginia was no longer considered a safe state for Democrats. Because party loyalties were in question, both parties spent increased time and energy on winning the state's electoral votes.[23] In the end, West Virginia voted Republican in both the 2004 and 2008 presidential elections. If party loyalties were to shift fully, then West Virginia would follow in the steps of states such as Texas, which used to be a safe state for Democrats, but now consistently votes Republican.

An honest assessment of American history shows that no state is permanently "safe" or "swing."[24] Instead, the identity of these states changes all the time. Texas used to be as undeniably Democratic as it is Republican today. States such as Georgia, Kentucky, and Louisiana all voted for Bill Clinton in the 1990s, but they were considered safe Republican states in 2008. States such as North Carolina and Virginia have voted Republican for decades, but went "blue" in 2008 and are considered swing states in 2012. California is often viewed as irreversibly Democratic, but Republican candidates such as George H. W. Bush, Ronald Reagan, Richard Nixon, and Gerald Ford might disagree. Each won the state. Indeed, even the George W. Bush campaign spent time in California in 2000, thinking that it might be able to win.[25] Ultimately, the Electoral College ensures that the political parties must reach out to all the states.[26] As a matter of history, no political party has ever been able to ignore any state for too long without feeling the ramifications at the polls.

A second argument made by critics is similarly flawed. True, the winner-take-all system can cause large states (especially large swing states) to elicit more attention than small states.[27] However, these critics erroneously compare the amount of campaigning in small states under the current system against the amount of campaigning in large states, also under the current system. Instead, they should compare the amount of campaigning in small states under the current system with the amount of campaigning that would occur in small states under a new one. Moreover, they should remember that "attention" encompasses far more than the tangibles that political scientists can measure: factors such as candidate visits, advertising dollars spent, and television time purchased. "Attention" includes intangibles that are used to appeal to voters.

How did California voters react when President Barack Obama decided not to allow construction of the Keystone Pipeline? How did Texas voters react when President George W. Bush issued his executive order prohibiting the use of federal funds for certain types of embryonic stem cell research? How many voters will not vote for Obama under any circumstance because of Obamacare? How many voters will love him forever for the same decision? Such decisions and their ramifications are part of governing, but they are also at least a part of "campaigning." They do as much as a TV commercial (if not more) to influence voting decisions—as candidates and incumbents certainly know.

As the system stands today, states with small numbers of electoral votes undoubtedly receive less attention than those states with large electoral vote allocations. However, a direct vote system would magnify, not improve, this problem. Small states will likely never receive as much attention as large states, but the Electoral College allows them to receive as much attention as possible—enough to keep them from being the victims of tyranny by the majority.

At the time of the 2010 census, California had a population of 37,253,956 people,[28] and it was allocated 55 electoral votes.[29] Wyoming, by contrast, had a population of 563,626 people,[30] and it was allocated three electoral votes.[31] California has more than 66 times as many people as Wyoming, but only 18 times as many electoral votes. If, as critics contend, Wyoming receives a disproportionately small amount of attention now, when the difference is three to 55 electoral votes, how much greater would the problem be if the relevant difference were half a million people to more than 37 million people?

Wyoming will never receive as much attention as California during a presidential campaign, but such will be the case under any election system. The relevant issue is not to eliminate this disparity, but to minimize its severity. Under the Electoral College, the states are as evenly represented as possible, given that they are not all the same size. The majority, often localized in the big states, may still clearly wield its influence as the majority. The protections of America's federalist republic allow this majority influence to stand, as they should in any self-governing society, but they also give the minority enough leverage to keep itself from being tyrannized by the majority in the other, larger states.

Last, opponents of the Electoral College dispute that a presidential candidate in a direct election system would have the luxury of relying upon one or two regions of the country to get elected. After all, there are simply not enough votes in one or two regions to deliver an election to a candidate. This observation may be true, but only if it is assumed that the general election is held between two, or perhaps three, main candidates, as it usually is today. Neither California nor Texas has a large enough population to deliver an election under this scenario. Similarly, relying upon one special interest group will not be sufficient to obtain election—none of these groups can guarantee that enough of their supporters will cast ballots on one issue alone. Under a direct election system, however, the situation could easily change.

The likely consequence of a change to a direct popular vote is the breakdown of the two-party system (discussed more in the next chapter) and a general election among many candidates. Dr. Judith Best has hypothesized that a straightforward change to direct popular elections at the national level would result in multi-candidate races and the constant necessity for runoff elections.[32] Without a strong two-party system in place, candidates would crop up for every special interest conceivable: the "feminist candidate, the Hispanic candidate, the moral majority candidate, the environmental candidate, the gay rights candidate, the military candidate."[33] These candidates won't garner many votes, but they will each obtain some. The more divided the vote, the fewer votes are needed to get into a runoff election. (Note that runoffs are not possible through the more circuitous route to change proposed by groups such as NPV. Instead, the presidency is awarded to the candidate obtaining any plurality, even a very small one. The ramifications of direct elections without runoffs will be discussed in the next chapter.)

California may not have the ability to deliver 40 percent of the nationwide vote (the minimum plurality sometimes suggested for a straightforward change to a direct popular election), but it does have the ability to help a candidate win the 15 to 20 percent of the vote potentially needed to qualify for a nationwide runoff—or, in the case of NPV, the 15 or 20 percent that could be the final winning plurality. Absent the two-party system, a special interest group such as a union or the National Rifle Association may also find itself able to help deliver this critical mass of votes. As multi-candidate races become the norm, presidential candidates would find themselves with more and more incentive to promise "their" voters anything and everything to get this much smaller percent of the vote needed to win.

Individuals v. States

An interesting twist to the prior arguments raised by Electoral College critics focuses on the reality that even if *small states* benefit from the Electoral College, they do so at the expense of the *individuals* who reside in small states. The Electoral College, its detractors argue, violates the principle of "one person, one vote" and creates a disparity in individual voting power. Worse, from their point of view, the disparity in individual voting power sways in favor of voters who happen to reside in large states.

This complaint can be confusing at first because it sounds like the opposite of another complaint—that the two vote add-on for small states (giving all a "guaranteed minimum" of three electoral votes) creates a bias in their favor. The two extra electoral votes given to all states, regardless of population, do create an advantage for those states. As a statistical matter, however, the advantage plays in favor of the *state as a whole*, rather than the *individual voter*. By contrast, the mathematical advantage granted by the winner-take-all system plays in favor of individual voters in the larger states.[34] These voters have a statistically higher probability of materially affecting the outcome of the election. An example may help to explain this phenomenon.

If a citizen resides in California, with its electoral bloc of 55 votes, then the mathematical probability that his vote will affect the outcome of the election is greater than if he lived in Montana, which has more citizens than some of the smallest states, but only three electoral votes.[35] Electoral College critics Lawrence Longley and Neal Peirce conclude that citizens in California during the 2000 election had "2.663 times the potential for determining the outcome of the presidential election of a citizen voting in the most disadvantaged state—Montana."[36]

Most of the time, one vote by one citizen will not determine which way the state's popular vote comes out. However, in the event that it does so, this mathematical model says that voters in large states have more power than those in small states. If a California citizen votes for Obama in the 2012 election and that one vote determines that Obama, not Mitt Romney, wins the state's slate of electors, then that one voter's ballot has determined the outcome of 55 electoral votes. A voter faced with the same situation in Montana does not have this much power. If his one vote determines that Romney, not Obama, gets Montana's vote, he has determined the outcome of only three electoral votes.

As a mathematical matter, perhaps voters in larger states have a disproportionately larger chance of changing the outcome of the election.[37] Yet the odds of any one voter providing the "tipping point" in an election are still exceedingly small, as is sometimes acknowledged even by Electoral College opponents.[38] Further, any individual disadvantage for those who reside in small states is outweighed by the larger advantage given to the state as a whole. The advantage given to small states is more than a theoretical mathematical advantage. Indeed, it has very real practical effects and should not be dismissed easily. Moreover, individual voters within small states benefit when their states benefit—and they will do so in *every* election, as opposed to the infinitesimal odds of "hitting the jackpot" and being the one voter who changes the outcome of one election in one year.

Residents living in the same state often share similar concerns. For instance, in Midwest states, voters may share opinions about agricultural policy. Voters in Alaska may share the same attitude about drilling for oil on their land. Nevada voters may band together against those who wish to dump nuclear material on their soil. Without the Electoral College, presidential candidates would likely never take the time to visit these smaller states and learn about the concerns of these residents. Without the Electoral College, candidates would not need votes from at least some of these small states to win the presidency.

The Electoral College, then, accomplishes an important goal: It ensures that the voices of small states are not drowned out altogether, as they otherwise could be. It ensures that the large states will not rule as majority tyrants over their smaller neighbors. As the small states are protected, so are the voters who reside within them.

Preserving Federalism

A direct popular election would probably cause some people to *feel* like they are better protected. After all, the principle of "one person, one vote" ensures that everyone is treated equally—right?[39] In the presidential election process, this sentiment may feel true, but it is not. Individuals are best protected in the presidential election system when they can combine with others in their state and make their voices heard as a bloc. Obviously, voters will lose in their states sometimes (just as they would sometimes lose in a national direct popular election); however, they are protected even in their loss. No presidential candidate can afford to ignore any segment of the country.

To be logically consistent, Electoral College opponents should criticize other federalist features of our government as they have the Electoral College. After all, disparaging the Electoral College as "unfair" requires that similar criticisms be directed at the Senate or at other, similar features of our government that were created as protections for the small states. No one, however, is seriously questioning the right of the Senate to exist. The Electoral College is simply one of several constitutional devices created by the Framers to protect the diverse interests of the states.

The Electoral College continues to protect the interests of the states, and thus their voters, just as it did in 1787.[40] It forces presidential candidates to build a support base that is national in character. A focus on any one area or special interest—urban or rural, east or west, coastal or interior—will cause the candidacy to fail. Solutions must be proposed that appeal to as many states' interests as possible, as at least some of the small states will be needed to win the presidency.

The truth of the matter is that many of the people who complain about the Electoral College are more concerned about their own individual votes than about how their states can best be served. They are entitled to this opinion, of course, and they may fight in their own state legislatures to have the rules for their states changed. However, they might be better served to remember the important safeguards provided in a federalist system and then apply themselves towards thinking how their states can best represent themselves within this structure. These protections still serve the states today.

Chapter Six

Moderation and Compromise

Currently, presidential candidates must build a national base among the states before they can be elected. They cannot target any one interest group or regional minority. Instead, they must achieve a consensus among enough groups, spread out over many states, to create a broad-based following among the voters. Any other course of action will prevent a candidate from gaining the strong base he needs to win the election.

The necessity of building such a national base has led to moderation and a strong two-party system in American politics.[1] Third parties are not usually able to achieve more than a minimal base of power, particularly because they tend to target narrower or special-interest groups. Third parties or special interest groups can wield influence only by working toward consensus with one of the major parties. On their own, they cannot usually win more than a fraction of the electoral vote—if they even manage to win that much.

Some see this trend toward moderation and a two-party system as a liability. They argue that certain points of view on the far left or right do not have representation. Perhaps voters identify with a third party more than they identify with one of the two major parties. The two-party system, however, has a definite benefit: Hand in hand with the Electoral College, it tends to prevent the rise to power of extremist groups and radical minorities.

Maintaining a Two-Party System

A major third-party candidate has entered several recent elections. In 1992, Ross Perot of the Reform Party ran against Republican George H.W. Bush and Democrat Bill Clinton. Clinton won the electoral vote, but he won a plurality rather than a majority of the popular vote. Perot ran again in 1996 against Clinton and Republican Bob Dole, with the same result. In 2000, Perot was replaced on the Reform Party ticket by Patrick Buchanan; Ralph Nader of the Green Party had also joined the field.[2] Neither of the major party candidates, George W. Bush and Al Gore, was able to achieve more than a plurality of the vote.

Political operatives and pundits chastised these third-party candidates, arguing that they would upset the election results. The candidates were encouraged to drop from the race, and voters were told that a vote for a third-party candidate is a wasted vote. Prior to the 1992 election, conventional wisdom held that a vote for Perot was a vote for Clinton, because it wasn't a vote for George H.W. Bush.[3] In the same way, many believe that Gore would have won in 2000 if Nader had not taken so many votes from him.

In American politics, third-party candidates are not usually successful in their bid for the presidency. Any success that they do have comes from grabbing the attention of a major party and influencing that party's platform, at least at the edges. The Reform Party was unsuccessful in its bid for the presidency in 1992, but its voters arguably did capture the attention of the major parties that year. One of the major campaign platforms for the Reform Party in 1992 was fiscal responsibility. Reform Party supporters, by and large, argued for a balanced budget and restraints on spending.[4]

Is it any coincidence that both parties made a push for fiscal responsibility before and during the 1994 mid-term elections? Democrats supported a 1993 budget reconciliation bill that raised taxes,[5] arguing that increased taxes were necessary to bring the budget back into balance. As the election neared, Republicans countered with their "Contract with America," which promised an "audit of Congress for waste, fraud or abuse," cuts in "the number of House committees . . . [and] committee staff," and an "honest accounting of our Federal Budget by implementing zero base-line budgeting."[6]

Third parties usually form when one of the two major parties is either unable or unwilling to work with a bloc of minority voters. This third party, if it is big enough, may be able to impact an election in one of two ways: It can focus on a state or states and win a handful of electoral votes there, or it may be able to win enough votes in a swing state to shift the outcome. In either event, if it demonstrates its ability to affect an election, it usually encourages one of the two major parties to work with it. The result is compromise and moderation because it is unproductive for either the third party or the major party to refuse to do so. Refusing to work together basically guarantees that both will go down in defeat.

Bucking the two-party system is an exercise in futility in American presidential politics.[7] The election of 1912 is perhaps the prototypical example of why this is so.[8] That election featured a three-way race among the incumbent, Republican William Howard Taft, Democrat Woodrow Wilson, and third-party candidate (and former President) Theodore Roosevelt. During the 1908 election, Roosevelt had chosen Taft to succeed him as President; however, he became disappointed with the decisions that Taft made, and he was determined to re-enter the political arena and win the Republican Party nomination.

Results: Election of 1912[9]

	Party	Electoral Vote	Popular Vote
Woodrow Wilson	Democrat	435	6,294,326
Theodore Roosevelt	Bull Moose (Progressive) Party	88	4,120,207
William Howard Taft	Republican Party	8	3,486,343

Roosevelt's campaigning won him the support of many Republican voters nationwide; however, the leaders of the Party chose to ignore the voters' preferences. When the party convention was held, they announced that the incumbent Taft would be the Republican Party nominee. Upon hearing this announcement, many backers of Roosevelt marched out of the convention. The Bull Moose Party, led by Roosevelt, was born.

Roosevelt campaigned hard in his attempts to re-win the presidency. He worked so hard that his campaign took a near-tragic turn. As Roosevelt prepared to attend an October rally in Milwaukee, he was shot in the chest by a gunman. Roosevelt resolved to give his speech anyway. He spoke to the crowd at a level barely above a whisper, explaining that he would need absolute silence, as he had just been shot. The crowd was able to see a bullet hole in the notes for his speech, which Roosevelt had carried in his breast pocket. Roosevelt claimed, at the time, that the thick speech may have saved his life. He spoke for more than an hour before he was taken to the hospital and treated.

Despite Roosevelt's gallant campaign efforts, he could not win the presidency. When the election totals came in, the Republican vote was badly split between Taft and Roosevelt. Although Roosevelt and Taft earned a combined 7.6 million popular votes to Wilson's nearly 6.3 million popular votes, they were able to win only a combined 96 electoral votes. Wilson was elected with 435 electoral votes, although he would likely have been defeated by a unified Republican Party.

The Republican Party would have done well to learn the lessons of earlier presidential elections, such as the election of 1836.[10] In that election, the Whigs could not agree on a nominee. In its defense, the party was still relatively new and was not well-organized. Instead, the party deliberately decided to fracture its vote among several regional candidates. Its hope was not to win, but to keep the Democratic candidate, Martin Van Buren, from obtaining a majority of electoral votes. They hoped to send the decision to the House of Representatives. Van Buren, however, benefited from the Whig strategy and defeated his nearest opponent in the Electoral College by 97 votes.

Results: Election of 1836

	Party	Electoral Vote	Popular Vote
Martin Van Buren	Democrat	170	764,176
William H. Harrison	Whig	73	550,816
Hugh L. White	Whig	26	146,107
Daniel Webster	Whig	14	41,201
W.P. Mangum	Indep. Democrat	11	-0-

The Whigs quickly learned their lesson. In 1840, they united behind William Henry Harrison of Ohio.[11] They ran a fierce national campaign and took the presidency back from Van Buren, 234 electoral votes to 60, although Harrison won the popular vote by a much smaller margin: 1,275,390 to 1,128,854.

The lesson of these and other, similar presidential elections? Cooperate and compromise.[12] The electoral vote cannot be won if voters split into various, marginal groups. Neither third parties nor major parties succeed when they insist on going it alone, ignoring others who may have differing viewpoints. The result is that American public policy tends to remain in the middle: not too far left, not too far right. This moderation can be admittedly frustrating when one's personal views might tend a little to the left or the right on a particular issue or issues, but as a general rule, the requirement for moderation protects Americans' freedom. Extremists cannot obtain power when moderation rules.

The Solar System of Governmental Power

Some proponents of a direct election system argue that the Electoral College is a divisive, not a moderating, factor in American politics. They further dispute the critical role that the Electoral College plays in upholding America's strong two-party system.[13] Of course, these proponents may acknowledge, America's system of checks and balances is the foundation upon which moderation and compromise has been built. However, they argue that changing the presidential election system, alone, would not undermine these protections or enable "rigid ideologies and inflammatory class appeals" to gain too much power.[14]

Electoral College opponents Neal Peirce and Lawrence Longley argue that a direct popular vote is "hardly a risky, untried governmental principle . . . . It is the tried and true way of electing every nonappointive government official in the United States today."[15] Moreover, they argue, other defenses against immoderation and factionalism still exist. Legislation, for instance, must pass both houses of Congress. The Bill of Rights and the judiciary serve as a check on unrestrained power. A variety of checks and balances still remain on the President, even without the Electoral College.[16] Changing the presidential election process, they contend, will not suddenly undermine the entire political system.

These arguments are not completely without merit. The American form of government contains multiple safeguards, and it does not rely exclusively upon one particular mechanism to protect citizens. If an "extremist" President were elected, he would not have absolute power, and the harm to the nation could potentially be somewhat mitigated by Congress or the judiciary. However, it is also important to remember the degree to which presidential power has grown in recent years.

Presidents act through executive orders more often than they did in the past,[17] and they have significant power in the area of judicial and other government appointments.[18] Moreover, they act as Commander-in-Chief of the armed forces and serve the country as its foremost ambassador in foreign countries.[19] During national emergencies, the scope of presidential power expands even more.[20] While the other two branches of government act as checks on the executive branch, the President may take many significant actions before these checks come into play. The check placed on the President by the Electoral College, along with the two-party system, should not be written off too quickly.

Speaking in support of the Electoral College, John F. Kennedy once referred to the checks and balances in the Constitution as a "solar system" of power:

> [I]t is not only the unit vote for the Presidency we are talking about, but a whole solar system of governmental power. If it is proposed to change the balance of power of one of the elements of the solar system, it is necessary to consider all the others.[21]

The system of checks and balances works as a whole, taken together. Eliminating the Electoral College would get rid of only one of several protective devices. Perhaps the impact would be minimal, as anticipated by many direct election proponents. On the other hand, it could throw the physics of the entire solar system (as JFK would say) out of balance.

Proponents of a direct election system often make the mistake of assuming that they can change one factor but leave all other dynamics unchanged. For instance, critics Neal Peirce and Lawrence Longley suggest that runoffs in a presidential election would not happen often.[22] To support their contention, they cite the fact that all but one President was elected with at least 40 percent of the popular vote. Gubernatorial races, they note, usually show similar results.[23] None of the races they cite, however, has ever been held in the absence of a two-party system; therefore, these campaigns cannot provide evidence for what would happen without it.

Judith Best makes a similar point, contending: "Many of the proponents of the direct nonfederal election with a 40 percent plurality rule assume that they can make such a major change in the rules without changing the way the game is played and without changing the nature of the winning team. That is nonsense."[24] Her opinion is shared by Professor Michael Glennon of Tufts University, who compares the American political system to a Rubik's Cube:

> One may not like the appearance of one side, and may wish to change that side, but one must remember that the other sides will then change as well. . . . [No one] is far-sighted enough to know how the political cube will look after we finish twisting it to eliminate the Electoral College.[25]

It is a known quantity that JFK's solar system, with the Electoral College in it, moderates political campaigns, contributes to the stability of the two-party system, and controls the rise of extremism, as the Founders expected. What is the point of spoiling a system that has proven itself in such a way?

An Alternative Universe, With Runoffs

Predictions of what would happen in a direct election system should assume that it is at least possible that changing the rules of the presidential election game will cause more than one aspect of the political process to change. Indeed, a relatively quick deterioration of the two-party system is quite likely under such a set of changed incentives. In order to evaluate the likelihood of this outcome, the consequences of change should be assessed from two perspectives: First, what if the presidential election system is changed, but a runoff provision is included (as has been the case with most historical proposals)? Second, what if the system is changed, but no runoff provision is included (as is the case with the recently proposed NPV)?

For years before NPV was introduced, most proposals to replace the Electoral College with a direct election system included a requirement that a certain plurality be obtained before a candidate could win the White House. If this threshold (usually about 40 percent) was not obtained, then a runoff would be held. These plans relied upon a plurality threshold—as opposed to a majority requirement—because direct election proponents hoped that the plurality would usually be obtained, thus avoiding the necessity of constant runoffs.[26]

The proposal for a plurality threshold may sound like a plausible solution at first glance, until one realizes that there is a lack of historical or anecdotal evidence supporting it. Instead, the most likely result is that this system, too, would eventually undermine the two-party system. Even with the 40-percent rule, voters no longer have the same disincentives to vote for a third party.[27] One has only to look to history to see how easily such a system could disintegrate into multi-candidate races, which would, in turn, devolve into a system of regular runoffs.

Consider the election of 1992. One of the primary factors that prevented some people from voting for Perot was that they felt their vote would be "wasted." A vote for Perot is a vote for Clinton, voters were told. Now imagine the 1992 election without an Electoral College. Suddenly, the incentives change. Clinton no longer has to be beaten; he just needs to be held under the 40-percent mark. To get in the runoff, Perot voters do not need to win, they simply need to overtake George H.W. Bush. If they can accomplish these two goals, a runoff between Clinton and Perot will follow. A vote for Perot is no longer wasted. The Reform Party has a specific, achievable goal with which to motivate its supporters.

In the actual 1992 election—even with all the disincentives inherent in the Electoral College system—Perot received 18.9 percent of the popular vote. Bush received 37.4 percent of the vote, and Clinton received 43.0 percent. Had this election been a direct popular election, it would have been only 3 percent away from triggering a runoff. With such incentives, would not Perot supporters have had a much easier time getting voters to switch their vote? Dissatisfied Bush and Clinton supporters risk very little if they vote for Perot. After all, they would always have a second chance to vote for one of the major parties during the runoff. Is a strong third-party showing, triggering a runoff, really so unbelievable? Once one runoff has been triggered, why would multiple third parties not jump into the race in 1996?

The country already hosts about 50 political parties with differing levels of activity.[28] Some of these political parties represent precisely the kind of extremist factions that most Americans do not want to find as one of their two choices in a runoff: the American Nazi Party, the Prohibition Party, the National Socialist Movement (a white nationalist group), and the Pansexual Peace Party, which is based on Wiccan principles.[29] Most of these alternative political parties obviously do not achieve a significant amount of public support, at least in part because the Electoral College makes it more beneficial for voters to work toward compromise with one of the two major parties. However, the fact that so many alternative political parties exist, even in the face of every conceivable disincentive, indicates that some could grow larger and magnify if those disincentives were removed.

At least five political parties have ample reason to believe that they could get a significant percentage of the popular vote in the absence of an Electoral College system: the Republican Party, the Democratic Party, the Constitution Party, the Green Party, and the Libertarian Party. If the Electoral College were removed today, each of these parties could make credible runs for the presidency. Indeed, each of these parties ran a candidate for President in 2008, even with the presence of the Electoral College. In a world in which five parties could make legitimate runs for the presidency, a runoff is almost certain. Moreover, the runoff would be between two candidates who had attained some small percent of the vote—no more than 39 percent, but perhaps as little as 20 or 25 percent each. A runoff would then be held between these two minority candidates so that one of them could be deemed the winner.

As such a situation became the norm, more and more candidates would be motivated to enter presidential contests over the years. Support from a smaller and smaller percentage of the population would be needed to qualify for the runoff. Over time, candidates would become more and more extreme and uncompromising. Dr. Best explains this dynamic:

> [T]he splintering of the vote works against the moderate candidates and works to the advantage of the immoderate, extreme candidates. It does this because the middle is where the inclusive coalitions can be built. By undermining coalition building prior to the general election, a runoff fragments the middle, not the extremes; the extremes are rarely fragmented—fanatics have solidarity. Coalition building seeks to spotlight most people's second choice, which is a satisfactory and inclusive choice.[30]

Other electoral systems utilizing a direct popular vote have seen increased influence by extremist, radical groups due to the fractured nature of the popular vote. Professor Robert Hardaway of the University of Denver has noted the results of a December 1993 Russian election in this context. In that election, the top three political parties were the Liberal-Democratic Party of Russia (22.9

percent), the Russia's Choice Party (15.5 percent) and the Communist Party (12.4 percent).[31] The election was a legislative one, not a presidential one. But if it had been the latter, Hardaway notes, then Russia would have avoided a runoff between the fascist LDPR and the communists by only a few percentage points, even with a democratic election and roughly two-thirds of the population voting for other candidates.[32]

A perhaps more concrete example can be found in French presidential politics. Consider the election of 2002, in which 16 candidates competed for the presidency.[33] The incumbent, Jacques Chirac, finished in first place, with 19.88 percent of the vote. Radical right-wing candidate Jean-Marie Le Pen came in second with 16.86 percent of the vote. Socialist candidate Lionel Jospin came in third with 16.18 percent. More recently, in 2012, ten candidates fractured the electorate in a similar manner.[34] The top vote-getter, Socialist candidate François Hollande, obtained only 28.6 percent of the vote, compared to 27.2 percent for the more moderate incumbent Nicolas Sarkozy.[35] The third-place candidate, far right National Front candidate Marine Le Pen, came in not far behind at 17.9 percent.[36] Close behind her was the Communist-backed Left Front candidate, Jean-Luc Mélenchon.[37]

As demonstrated in these examples, the French direct election system has worked against coalition-building and moderate candidates in that country.

An Alternative Universe, Without Runoffs

A direct election system that includes runoffs cannot prevent the rise of factions. It is more likely to encourage them. But some direct election proponents claim that omitting runoffs from the equation will solve the problem. Thus, proposals such as NPV, which give the presidency to the winner of any nationwide plurality, should have the same effect as the Electoral College and its winner-take-all system.

As this book has argued, the practical effect of the current system is that it discourages third parties from entering presidential races. Voters and candidates feel that their vote is "wasted" if they vote for a third-party candidate. They'd rather make their preference between the top two candidates known. NPV relies on the same dynamic, removing "winner-take-all" from the state level and implementing it at the national level. In this way, third parties will still be discouraged, but these direct election advocates will be able to achieve the more purely democratic process that they desire.

Both Electoral College and direct election advocates would be relying upon the same principle—winner-take-all—to control the rise of extremist third parties.[38] The difference is that Electoral College supporters temper winner-take-all with a dose of federalism. Direct election advocates would not. Does the added federalism component make a difference in discouraging American third parties? There is evidence to suggest that it does.

If a national direct election system such as NPV were implemented, its winner-take-all feature would doubtless discourage third parties to some degree, echoing the similar dynamic at the state level today. One can easily find a score of political science treatises that agree that winner-take-all elections tend to produce strong two-party systems.[39] Indeed, this book has relied upon some of these theories in arguing that the Electoral College, combined with the state level winner-take-all allocation of electoral votes, should work to uphold the two-party system. (And, historically, that theory has worked out in practice, as discussed above.) But these same political science textbooks will note a history of exceptions to the general rule: Well-known examples include India and Canada, which are multi-party systems.[40] Some political scientists will even include the United Kingdom as an additional example: Conservatives and Labour are two major parties, but the third-party Liberal Democrats remain a viable force.[41]

Exceptions to the general rule can be found even within America's own history of elections. Some examples at the presidential level, such as Perot's 1992 race, were discussed above. Examples also exist at the state level. During the 2010 mid-term elections, for instance, several Senate and gubernatorial races included a third-party candidate. On the Senate side, Alaska and Florida witnessed strong showings by third-party candidates—the candidate in Alaska, Lisa Murkowski, was a write-in candidate, no less! At least one candidate in each race was under pressure to drop out.[42] None of them did so. In Florida, for example, Marco Rubio

(R), Kendrick Meek (D), and Charlie Crist (I) faced off for the open seat left by retiring Senator George LeMieux. With mere weeks to go before Election Day, polls showed Rubio leading the field with 40 percent or more.[43] The other two candidates trailed, but if their supporters were to combine forces, they could have potentially overtaken Rubio. Pressure was put on Meek to drop out of the race or, failing that, his voters were urged to put their support behind Crist in an effort to overtake Rubio. Neither of those came to be. Final election results showed a three-way split among voters: Rubio (48.9 percent); Crist (29.7 percent); and Meek (20.2 percent).[44] Of course, none of these Senate races represent a major intrusion into the strength of the two-party system in America. But they do show that third parties are not always as easily discouraged as political science theory says they should be.

Political scientists admit that winner-take-all, standing alone, has not universally proven enough in supporting a strong two-party system. Indeed, some political scientists have gone so far as to say that the United States is the only example of a "truly two-party" system.[45] "The other major democracies," they conclude, "all have persistent third or fourth parties that call into question the predicted equilibrium of two parties."[46] Could it be that the federalism component in America's presidential elections is a critical factor that has kept America from joining the list of exceptions?

As a general matter, a third-party candidate must overcome two major parties before he can succeed in a winner-take-all election. This can be a very steep hill to climb. But in America's federalist presidential election process, this same third party has an even more daunting task: He must overcome both of the major parties, not just one time in one pool of voters, but many times in many pools. And he must accomplish these against-the-odds victories simultaneously. The third-party candidate who came closest to accomplishing this feat was George Wallace, in 1968. Despite winning five states, he was far from successful. He won only 46 electoral votes compared to Richard Nixon's 301 electoral votes.

At the end of the day, the reliance of direct election advocates upon a winner-take-all system, as opposed to a runoff system, is not completely without merit. They are, after all, exhibiting reliance on a principle that has already proven itself successful in this country. But they would do well to remember that winner-take-all may very well be stronger if it is combined with federalist principles. The Electoral College, combined with the winner-take-all system, has a proven history of sustaining America's strong two-party system. If federalism is ripped from the structure of American presidential elections, it would be a blow at the two-party system and the moderation and compromise that have historically accompanied it. Even NPV proponent Robert Bennett seems to admit as much when he acknowledges "a measure of uncertainty about the long-term effects on the two-party system of a move that would replace the electoral college with a nationwide popular vote."[47] His words echo JFK's admonition that it is impossible to know what the fallout will be if the political solar system is changed.

Americans are an independent people who enjoy their right and ability to go their own way and do their own thing. Ask a room of voters for their top presidential pick (as this author sometimes does) and you would probably get a dozen or more answers. If such an independent people were given the opportunity to divide their votes among many candidates, they would be quite likely to do so.

A proposal such as NPV cannot provide Americans with a President who has garnered nationwide support. NPV gives the presidency to the winner of any nationwide plurality, *even if this number is very low*, perhaps as low as it was in the 2012 French election. If an American President were elected with a mere 28.6 percent of the vote, he would take office knowing that a large majority of Americans voted against him. He would enter office without a mandate of any kind.

Freedom in the voting booth sounds instinctively appealing, but it is important to remember the fractious nature of multiple party systems and the generally unhealthy results for a country so badly divided. Americans are better off leaving in place every possible safeguard against such division: in this case, not only winner-take-all, but also federalism.

ΧΟΧ ΧΟΧ ΧΟΧ

Direct popular election proponents sound plausible when they argue for election of the President by a "majority" of the people. In reality, however, a President elected by the majority of citizens will rarely be achievable, unless the election system itself incentivizes compromise.[48] Given the choice of *any* candidate, a majority will never agree on their ideal candidate. Individuals' opinions vary too widely.

Given the general inability to obtain majority consensus, the Electoral College provides the country with the next best alternative. Electing Presidents by states' votes, rather than individuals' votes, creates a method of electing a President who is a good compromise candidate for the majority of Americans. The Electoral College requires moderation, compromise, and coalition-building from any candidate before he can be successful. Direct elections, with or without a system of runoffs, discourage such behavior.

Granted, America is a long way away from a multi-party, fractured political system. Psychologically, if nothing else, the electorate is used to thinking in terms of a two-party system. It could take a while before the system deteriorated. However, if the Electoral College facilitated the growth of the two-party system that has brought so much stability to American elections, would it not be natural to assume that eliminating the Electoral College would eventually lead to the end of the nation's stable two-party system? Even if the danger of an American election featuring Fascists and Communists is somewhat remote, why remove one of the safeguards that have kept such a scenario exactly that—remote?

Chapter Seven

Stability and Certainty in Elections

Many Electoral College proponents argue that fraud will increase under a direct election system. Any vote stolen in any part of the country would have some impact on the final outcome. Stolen votes can have an impact under the Electoral College system—but the only realistic way to impact the election is to somehow predict in advance where stolen votes will matter. No such predictive power is needed with respect to direct elections. Moreover, the Electoral College tends to magnify the margin of victory and promote finality in elections.

Opponents of the Electoral College disagree, arguing that fears of fraud under a direct election are "probably exaggerated," and "fraud in a closely contested state with a large bloc of electoral votes may already be enough to swing the entire national election."[1] These opponents emphasize the unequal weight given to votes from state to state, thus placing a premium on stealing votes in certain parts of the country. Fewer stolen votes are needed to change the outcome of a state election than are needed to change the outcome of a national election. As the reasoning goes, in a nationwide election, one stolen vote does not have much of an impact; therefore, the incentive to steal votes is reduced.

Opponents further dispute that the Electoral College makes election outcomes more certain. They see potential for chaos if an ambitious elector in a close election tries to swing the election. Or they worry about a future election in which no presidential candidate is able to obtain a majority of electors. Deal-making in the contingent election could leave the election results uncertain for weeks.

In a few, limited circumstances, the arguments of Electoral College opponents could ring true. These circumstances are the exception, rather than the rule, however. As a historical matter, the Electoral College has generally served to promote certainty in election outcomes and to reduce the incentive for fraud.

Magnifying the Margin of Victory

The 2000 election was an unusual election in many ways: The popular vote was remarkably close, but, amazingly, the electoral vote margin was razor thin, too. Historically, most elections have not been close in the Electoral College, even when popular vote margins are thin. The Electoral College system, when combined with the winner-take-all rule, tends to magnify the margin of victory, giving the victor a certain and demonstrable election outcome.[2]

The election of 1960 was one such close election. John Kennedy won only 49.7 percent of the popular vote, compared to Richard Nixon's 49.5 percent; however, Kennedy won 56.4 percent of the electoral vote, compared to Nixon's 40.8 percent. Eight years later, this magnification effect worked in favor of Nixon. Although he won the popular vote by less than one percent, he won 55.9 percent of the electoral vote to Hubert Humphrey's 35.5 percent. Jimmy Carter was the beneficiary of the magnification effect in the close election of 1976. Carter won 40,830,763 popular votes compared to Gerald Ford's 39,147,793 popular votes. The margin between the two numbers was only two percent of the total number of votes cast for both men. Yet, the Electoral College magnified the victory. With 297 votes, Carter won a solid 55.2 percent of electoral votes.

This magnification effect is not a recent phenomenon. The Electoral College produced a similar lop-sided effect in the 1888 election. That election resulted in a popular vote winner who lost in the Electoral College. Grover Cleveland won the popular vote by 0.8 percent; however, Benjamin Harrison won the electoral vote by a much larger margin: 58.1 percent to 41.9 percent.

Results: Close Elections

		Electoral Vote		Popular Vote	
		Actual	Percent	Actual	Percent
1888	Benjamin Harrison	233	58.1%	5,449,825[3]	47.8%
	Grover Cleveland	168	41.9%	5,539,118	48.6%
1960	John Kennedy	303	56.4%	34,226,731	49.7%
	Richard Nixon	219	40.8%	34,108,157	49.5%
1968	Richard Nixon	301	55.9%	31,785,480	43.4%
	Hubert Humphrey	191	35.5%	31,275,166	42.7%
1976	Jimmy Carter	297	55.2%	40,830,763	50.1%
	Gerald Ford	240	44.6%	39,147,793	48.0%

Indeed, as popular vote totals start to spread apart, the magnification effect increases dramatically. For instance, in 1952, the winning candidate won 54.9 percent[4] of the popular vote, but a much larger 83.2 percent of the Electoral College vote. In 1956, the difference was 57.4 percent (popular vote) to 86.1 percent (electoral vote); and 1964 was 61.1 percent (popular vote) to 90.3 percent (electoral vote). The magnification of the electoral vote can work to solidify the country behind the new President by bestowing an aura of legitimacy.

The presidential elections since 1804 (the year that the 12th Amendment was passed) have generally seen wide margins of victory in the Electoral College. These margins have gotten wider, on average, through the years as the winner-take-all rule has been adopted by more states and the two-party system has solidified. Since 1804, only two elections—those in 1876 and 2000—were won by fewer than 20 electoral votes. Only seven elections were won by fewer than 50 electoral votes. Four of these seven elections were held in the 1800s. Of the 28 elections held between 1900 and 2008, 17 Presidents have been elected after winning the electoral vote by a margin of 200 votes or more. Barack Obama's 2008 victory came close to this margin: He won by 192 electoral votes.

Margin of Victory in the Electoral College: 1804 to present

	1804 – 1896 elections	1900 – 1996 elections	2000 – 2008 elections	Total
N/A—Decided in contingent election	1	0	0	1
1-50 electoral votes	4	1	2	7
51-100 electoral votes	8	2	0	10
101-200 electoral votes	8	5	1	14
200 or more electoral votes	3	17	0	20
TOTAL	24	25	3	52

These consistently wide margins of victory in the Electoral College have come about despite the fact that the margin between the top two candidates in the popular vote was less than 10 percent in 16 of the 28 elections held since 1900—in 3 of these elections, the margin was less than 1 percent! This margin exceeded 20 percent only five times since 1900.

A direct popular election, by contrast, would not grant certainty nearly as often. Close popular votes such as those discussed above could easily result in demands for recounts on a national scale. America rarely has close Electoral College votes; it does, however, have close popular votes fairly consistently. Do Americans really want a presidential election system that could result in hotly contested recounts once every several elections?

A direct popular election would compound matters in a second manner. As discussed in Chapter Six, the likely outcome of such an election system is that presidential elections will devolve into multi-candidate races. As more candidates enter presidential races, individual votes will be divided among an ever-increasing number of candidates. The result will be lower vote totals per candidate and an increased likelihood that two or more candidates will have close popular vote totals. Recounts could be held simply to determine who is entering the runoff (assuming there is one); then they could be held again to determine who won the runoff. Certain, immediate election outcomes under this scenario will be a thing of the past.[5]

Arguably, the picture that has just been painted is a worst-case scenario; however, it should not be dismissed lightly. Many pundits have noted that the American President is the most powerful man in the world in many respects. Americans should assume that ambitious men will come along who will use every means at their disposal to obtain the position. The Electoral College provides a buffer against the uncertainty and turmoil of constant recounts and election disputes. This buffer is even more important when ambitious candidates lack the will or the inclination to concede for the good of the country.[6]

Bush's 2000 win by a mere five electoral votes is unusual and should not be used as a reason to condemn the Electoral College.[7] When reviewing the historical record as a whole, the general impact of the Electoral College, when combined with the winner-take-all system, is to magnify the margin of victory for the winning candidate. The magnified electoral vote count generally makes outcomes certain and close elections a rarity. A direct election system would not produce this certainty nearly as often.

Reducing Fraud and Error

The Electoral College provides yet another benefit: It reduces the incidence of fraud and error. Obviously, no system can completely eliminate the element of human error. Neither can any system eradicate the tendency of some dishonest individuals to cheat. An election system can, however, minimize the extent to which these human errors or fraudulent behavior impact elections. The Electoral College minimizes the impact of fraud and error by isolating problems to one state or a handful of states.[8]

Electoral College opponents disagree with this analysis, pointing to elections such as the 2000 presidential election in which the election could have been changed by just a handful of stolen votes. In 2000, Bush won the election without a state to spare. He won one state, Florida, by only 537 votes.[9] Six hundred stolen votes in Florida in the 2000 election would have changed the outcome and crowned Gore the winner. Another election similarly referenced in this regard is the 1960 election. Nixon lost the election by only two states: Texas and Illinois.[10] A shift of 4,430 votes in Illinois and 23,129 votes in Texas would have swung the election in Nixon's favor.[11] Moreover, many believe that fraud was rampant in these two critical states during the election. The fraudulent voting may or may not have been enough to swing the election. The extent of the fraud may always remain a matter of disagreement.

While these two examples of close elections do suggest that fraud and error could impact the Electoral College outcome, they do not indicate, in and of themselves, that American presidential elections are highly susceptible to fraud or that an alternative system would ameliorate this impact. Electoral College opponents have once again made the mistake of assuming that infrequent problems in the current system damn the entire system. Instead, they should compare the current system with the likely outcome in a changed system. No system is perfect, but one will prove better than the alternatives in the long run.

The Electoral College defends against fraudulent behavior and human error in two ways: First, the system makes it difficult to predict where stolen votes will make a difference. Not impossible, obviously, but more difficult. In a direct election system, any stolen vote matters, but under the Electoral College system, stolen votes impact the election only if they are stolen in the right location. Second, to the degree that fraud and errors do occur, the Electoral

College makes it possible to isolate the problem to one state or a handful of states.[12]

The 1960 election provides an illustration of the ability of the Electoral College to control a situation that could otherwise degenerate into chaos and uncertainty. Nixon had ample reason to demand a recount in Illinois and Texas, particularly given the expressions of concern regarding voter fraud in these states. A few examples of this alleged fraud have been cited by Richard Reeves, author of *President Kennedy: Profile of Power*. For example, Reeves reports that 6,138 votes appear to have been cast by 4,895 voters in Fannin County, Texas. In Chicago's sixth ward, 43 voters apparently cast 121 votes in one hour.[13] Nixon could not have been blamed had he challenged the votes in these two states, although he chose not to do so.

In his memoirs, Nixon explains the reason that he conceded the election, rather than demand a recount in Texas and Illinois. He explained, "A presidential recount would require up to half a year, during which time the legitimacy of Kennedy's election would be in question. The effect could be devastating to America's foreign relations."[14] He was right, and his actions saved the country from a difficult situation. A recount, with or without the Electoral College, would have created a fair amount of disorder and confusion. Nevertheless, the chaos created under a direct election system would be far greater than the lesser disarray that Nixon sought to avoid under the Electoral College system.

The overall official results of the 1960 election revealed a difference of only 118,574 votes between the two men.[15] Under a direct election system, such an extraordinarily close vote could easily have been used to justify a demand for nationwide recounts by Nixon. The Electoral College system, however, made the close popular vote irrelevant. Instead, had Nixon demanded recounts, these disputes would have been isolated to the two states that really mattered: Illinois and Texas. Moreover, the allegations of fraud have focused on these two states for a reason. Even if votes were stolen somewhere else in the country on that Election Day in 1960, the other stolen votes were not remarked upon because they would not have affected the election one way or another. The Electoral College successfully isolates problems of fraud and error to one or a handful of states. The remaining electoral votes, in other states, can remain above the fray, as they are undisputed. The country is given a clear set of problems to resolve one way or another before moving on to a definitive election outcome.

The Electoral College served a similar purpose during the 2000 election. Yes, of course, 600 stolen votes in Florida would have changed the election. But stealing these votes would have required knowing in advance that such a small number of votes in Florida could swing the outcome of the election. Even if someone had successfully made such a guess, surely this prediction would have been the exception, rather than the rule. Moreover, the Electoral College made it possible for the nation to isolate the problem to Florida. The nation was in suspense for weeks at the end of 2000, waiting to see how the election would come out. But the situation could have been much worse. Recounts could have ensued in virtually every state of the Union; instead, the focus was on a handful of counties in Florida.[16]

Under a direct election scheme, a national recount (complete with lawsuits in many states, not just Florida) could easily have occurred and left the country in suspense for months. Today, some might question whether Bush "really" won Florida's vote; however, the votes in other states are not questioned. The broad national coalition that Bush pieced together outside Florida is undeniable. Without the Electoral College, even this certainty would be absent. Instead, given the close popular vote in 2000, many today would likely be questioning whether Bush or Gore "really" won the national popular vote. There would have been no certain point at which the country could have stopped the legal wrangling over recounts.

The 2000 and 1960 elections exhibited the amazing ability of the Electoral College to control situations that could very easily degenerate into chaos. In each instance, the country was given a certain and definite election outcome, even in the midst of dispute.

Imperfect World, Optimal Solution

Today, both the electoral and the popular votes must be extremely close before voting disputes and recounts are threatened.

By contrast, a direct popular election would require only a close popular vote before these scenarios became possible. National recounts and legal challenges would be a constant possibility, particularly because the likelihood of multiple candidacies, lower individual vote totals, and smaller margins among candidates would increase. Confusion would reign while cities, counties and states across the nation attempt to tabulate and re-tabulate votes. Imagine Florida in 2000, but on a national scale.

The current system makes it possible to be certain as to the precise number of electoral votes for each candidate. Human fraud or error is less likely to impact the outcome, and, if all else fails, state legislatures are constitutionally empowered to take action and resolve uncertainty.[17] It is not possible, however, to be certain as to the precise number of popular votes for a candidate. Human error cannot be driven out of the equation—and errors across the country could easily combine to influence the outcome of a close election.

Moreover, a direct popular vote system would increase, rather than decrease, the incentive for fraud. After all, any stolen vote would have at least some effect, regardless of its location. Today, if fraud is suspected in one state, it may not trigger a recount if the vote in the state was not close. The Electoral College minimizes the impact of fraud, isolating it to the one or two states where the vote was close or disputed. In a direct election, any stolen vote in any location could matter. When taken together with the increased possibility of close popular vote margins, the potential for national challenges and recounts would be greatly increased.

The Electoral College system cannot completely eliminate the incentive for fraud. Where people are vying for power, there will always be motivation to cheat. That is human nature. A successful electoral system can hope only to isolate the incidents of dishonesty and provide controls on situations that would otherwise get completely out of hand. The Electoral College system isolates fraud to the state in which it occurred. In most elections, the national election cannot be changed without a concerted plan of action, spanning several states. Recounts, when necessary to ferret out illegal votes, can be isolated in a state or two. The country is given a definite election outcome, even in the face of electoral challenges.

Part Three

Refuting
Remaining Criticisms

Chapter Eight

The Faithless
Elector Problem

The tumultuous 2000 election highlighted a feature of the Electoral College system that had doubtless gone unnoticed for decades. Following certification by Florida's Secretary of State of her state's slate of electors, Bush had 271 electors pledged to vote for him, while Gore had 267 pledged electors—but these pledges, alone, did not seal the outcome of the election. Bush was the presumed winner because he had a majority of the pledged electors; however, these electors had not yet officially voted and their votes had not been counted by Congress. When push comes to shove, the electors are individuals with the ability to cast votes contrary to the expectations of voters, although some electors take pledges (of dubious enforceability) not to do so.

Given the unusually close election, faithless votes by only three electors could have thrown the election to Gore. A switch by two electors could have prevented either candidate from obtaining a majority of electoral votes, thus triggering a contingent election and leaving Congressmen to decide which of the two men would be the nation's next President. At least one group, calling itself "Citizens for True Democracy," devoted a website to this effort.[1] Despite the intense political pressure, most electors remained faithful to their party during the December 18, 2000, meetings of the Electoral

College. Only one elector—a Gore elector—chose to abstain, rather than cast her vote. (Even her decision, however, was one of symbolic protest. Presumably, she would not have abstained if her vote would have swung the election for Gore.) The final vote tally was thus 271 to 266. Bush won, but his victory was not guaranteed until these votes were officially cast and counted by Congress.

At the time the Electoral College was created, some early Americans may have believed that electors would serve as representatives for a citizenry that would be unable to keep abreast of all the presidential candidates' platforms and activities, particularly those of non-local candidates. The electors would act as representatives for the people, learn about candidates, and decide which candidates might deserve a vote for the presidency. Today, the situation is reversed: Voters are more familiar with the positions of presidential candidates than the qualifications of electors. As a result, many argue, the role of elector as an independent decision-maker has become outdated in modern-day America. In this day and age, why should an individual elector have the ability to cast a vote that does not follow the outcome of the popular vote within his state? The possibility of an elector exercising autonomy in decision-making is enough to make most voters cringe.

America has changed much in the past 200 years. As this book has argued, these changes have not undermined the usefulness of the Electoral College in many respects, but it is hard to see what positive purpose the role of elector plays in today's society. As discussed below, the fear of a "faithless elector" swinging an election outcome has proven groundless in practice; however, the possibility of such faithlessness coming into play in the future is real. If any change is to be made to the presidential election system, it should be to eliminate the role of elector and automate the process of casting the states' electoral votes.

Independent Deliberators or Mere Formality

Communications in early America were slow, erratic, and unreliable. Most American voters would have found it difficult to be informed regarding each and every presidential candidate. It is more likely that voters would have known local candidates and maybe a handful of the more widely known national candidates. The Founders included at least one provision in the Constitution that would balance out this possibility of local bias. Article II of the Constitution provides that electors "[shall] vote by Ballot for two Persons, of whom one at least shall not be an Inhabitant of the same State with themselves."[2] The 12th Amendment contains a similar provision, requiring that either the vote for President or the vote for Vice President be for an out-of-state candidate.[3]

Some academics argue that the Founders created the role of elector, at least in part, because they knew that voters would be handicapped by slow communications and unable to know all the candidates. The Founders probably anticipated that electors would be "distinguished citizens" who would act as representatives for the people in the presidential election process.[4] At the time the system was created, such a solution would certainly have been understandable as a logistical matter. Some academics, however, dispute this reading of history. They argue that the Founders never intended the electors to be completely independent.[5] Perhaps the role of elector instead evolved primarily because the drafters of the Constitution did not want to decide for the states how they should go about casting their electoral votes. Either way, any expectation that electors would act independently did not last long.

In the early 1800s, many electors were already being chosen for their party loyalty and other similar factors.[6] By the 1830s, voters in all states except one had been given the power to choose their electors directly.[7] Afterwards, the instances in which state legislatures selected the electors were few and scattered. South Carolina was one exception: Its legislature continued to select electors until 1860. Florida's legislature selected electors in 1868, and Colorado selected its electors in 1876.[8] Today, however, electors are most commonly nominated at state party conventions.[9] The outcome of the state's popular election determines which slate—Republican or Democrat—will be appointed the official slate for the state.

The electors themselves are typically party loyalists who are committed, either by state law or party rules, to vote for the candidate nominated by their party.[10] Some of these state statutes are arguably not enforceable under the Constitution. The Supreme

Court has heard only one case on the subject, and the opinion it issued in this 1952 case was somewhat limited in scope.[11] In that case, the Alabama chapter of the Democratic Party refused to certify an individual as a candidate for presidential elector.[12] This individual was qualified for the office of elector, except that he refused to take the Democratic Party pledge to support the Democratic nominee for President.[13] Even if individual electors may vote as they please once they get to an Electoral College meeting, the Court observed, a political party may require a pledge of loyalty before supporting an individual as candidate for elector.[14] The Court did not take a position on other types of pledges, such as those required by *states*, rather than *political parties*. It therefore remains unclear whether a state can force an elector to vote in a particular way.[15] Also unclear is what would happen if the elector violated a pledge. Could a law punishing such a violation be enforced? Even if punishment could be handed down for the elector's action, the vote probably could not be retracted. Further questions exist regarding whether Congress must accept the vote of a faithless elector.

Despite these unanswered legal questions, the problem of unfaithful electors has proven more of a theoretical problem than a real one. Between 1796 and 1996, Neal Peirce and Lawrence Longley report that no more than 17 of 21,291 electoral votes were "indisputably cast 'against instructions.'"[16] Moreover, eight of these votes, cast during the 1824 election, may or may not have been "faithless," depending upon one's reading of the facts. That year, the North Carolina slate of 15 electors voted en bloc for Andrew Jackson, despite the fact that as many as five of them may have been pledged to vote for John Quincy Adams. In New York, three electors pledged to Henry Clay defected, but they did not do so until it was already clear that Clay would not qualify for the tie-breaking contingent election in the House.[17]

The next electors to defect were in 1948 through 1972. Several of these electors broke their pledges in an effort to make a statement regarding civil rights issues. Three defectors were, oddly, all Nixon electors. One elector defected in each of his three presidential races. Four more electors have broken their pledges since the Nixon races, one each in 1976, 1988, 2000, and 2004. (The 2004 incident, in which a Democratic elector voted for the vice presidential candidate on a presidential ballot, appears to have been accidental.)[18] None of these faithless votes changed the outcome of an election. Two faithless electors in 2000, however, easily could have. The 2000 election, more than any election in recent memory, tested the durability of the elector system.

Faithless Electors Since 1796[19]

Year	Name of Elector	Pledged to:	Cast Ballot For:
2004	Unidentified MN elector[20]	John Kerry (D)	John Edwards (D)
2000	Barbara Lett-Simmons (D.C.)	Al Gore (D)	Abstained
1988	Margaret Leach (WV)	Michael Dukakis (D)	Lloyd Bentsen (D)
1976	Mike Padden (WA)	Gerald Ford (R)	Ronald Reagan (R)
1972	Roger MacBride (VA)	Richard Nixon (R)	John Hospers (L)
1968	Lloyd W. Bailey (NC)	Richard Nixon (R)	George Wallace (AI)
1960	Henry D. Irwin (OK)	Richard Nixon (R)	Harry F. Byrd (D)
1956	W.F. Turner (AL)	Adlai Stevenson (D)	Walter B. Jones (D)
1948	Preston Parks (TN)[21]	Harry Truman (D)	Strom Thurmond (SR)
1824	5 of 15 electors (NC)	John Q. Adams (DR)	Andrew Jackson (DR)
1824	3 of 36 electors (NY)	Henry Clay (DR)	J.Q. Adams (DR) W.H. Crawford (DR) A. Jackson (DR)
1820	William Plumer (NH)	James Monroe (DR)	John Q. Adams (IDR)
1796	Samuel Miles (PA)	John Adams (F)	Thomas Jefferson (DR)

After Gore's concession to Bush on December 13, 2000, much discussion centered on the possibility that "only three" faithless electors could throw the election to Gore. Some Gore supporters publicized the names and telephone numbers of Republican electors and instigated campaigns to encourage some Bush electors to change their vote to Gore.[22] Despite the week of speculation and pressure, most electors remained faithful to their party during the Electoral College vote on December 18, 2000. As previously noted, only one elector—a Gore elector—chose to abstain, rather than cast her vote. She reportedly abstained to make a statement about the lack of congressional representation for the District of Columbia.

The 2000 election was one of the most emotionally and politically charged in recent memory, yet only one elector changed her vote during this election—and she did so for symbolic purposes, rather than to affect the election's outcome. This result provides good anecdotal evidence that the danger of a faithless elector changing the outcome of an election is not great.[23] Most electors are extremely reluctant to break the trust placed in them, even when placed under great pressure. Moreover, most of these electors are chosen precisely because of their loyalty to the party. The combination of loyalty and trust makes the electors unlikely to exercise independence.[24]

As a result, the role of elector has become a formality. By and large, neither the populace nor state legislatures—nor the electors themselves—expect electors to act independently. Instead, electors are universally expected to cast votes in accordance with the popular vote outcome in their states. If an elector were to suddenly decide to exercise independence, after all, the state's citizens would likely revolt.

This state of affairs is confirmed by the fact that the names of the electors do not appear on the ballots in most states. In 1940, 15 states used the presidential short ballot, on which the names of the electors do not appear.[25] By 2004, this situation had reversed itself: Only eight states included the names of electors on their ballots.[26] Some ballots include a disclaimer announcing that "[a] vote for the candidates will actually be a vote for their electors,"[27] but the identity of the electors does not seem to be taken seriously, as a general matter. Indeed, their identities are treated so flippantly that the U.S. National Archives and Records Administrations advises those curious about their names to wait until *after* the election, when the "Certificates of Ascertainment will be posted online as quickly as possible."[28] As a result of this system, most voters have no reason to know the name of the elector for whom they have voted, unless they take time to investigate. In other words, we now have the exact opposite situation as contemplated at the Founding: the candidates themselves are well-known, but the electors are completely unknown to the average voter.

It is hard to see how independent deliberation by electors in this day and age will do anything to advance the goals of the Electoral College, as described above. To the contrary, the public is more informed about the character and policies of presidential candidates than they are about those of the electors. In many cases, they may not even know the names of the electors. The advent of mass communication and other changes to American society have not changed the usefulness of the Electoral College in most respects; however, it is fair to say that they have lessened the importance of the role of elector.[29]

The Automatic Plan

Many political commentators and academics have come to the conclusion that the role of elector serves no significant purpose in modern-day America. Therefore, a potential reform proposal, usually referred to as the "Automatic Plan," is sometimes discussed as a potential modification to the current Electoral College system.

In all likelihood, the present system can continue to function successfully without thwarting the will of the people as it is expressed in the state-level democratic elections held during American presidential elections. The role of elector will remain simply a formality and a tradition, as it has been for decades. However, the probability that a faithless elector could change the course of an election, while remote, is not zero. If any change is to be made to the presidential election process, it should be to abolish the role of the elector. Electoral votes should be cast automatically based upon the popular vote in the state.

Of the reforms that have been proposed to the Electoral College, the Automatic Plan is one that would remove the possibility of faithless electors from the system, while leaving the framework of the system largely untouched. Implementation of the Automatic

Plan would require a constitutional amendment to eliminate the provision that allows states, through their legislatures, to decide for themselves how to select their electors. Instead, the new constitutional provision would provide for the automatic allocation of electoral votes based on the popular vote outcome in each state. These votes would be awarded on a winner-take-all basis within each state, precisely as they are awarded today in all states except Maine and Nebraska.

Most critics of the Electoral College feel that the Automatic Plan does not go far enough, as it leaves the bulk of the system unchanged. Worse, they shudder at the thought of the winner-take-all system and other perceived inequities being officially incorporated into the Constitution. As they see it, the Automatic Plan does nothing more than to ensure that the principle of "one person, one vote" will never be honored at the national level.[30]

These critics are right in saying that inequality in individual voting will be further solidified in the presidential election process as a result of such an amendment, but they downplay the benefits that will also be solidified, including federalism and protection for minority groups. As this book has observed, the Electoral College will likely never be appreciated fully by those who do not value principles of federalism and who continue to value individual votes over the good of the states and their voters as a whole.

If any reform is to be adopted to the Electoral College, it should be to award the electoral votes automatically, based upon certified election returns within each state. Such a solution would preserve the benefits of the current system. It would continue to keep the large states from trampling on the smaller states, and it would support continued stability and moderation in American politics. Moreover, it may aid in the unraveling of several logistical tangles that exist in the current system.

Unraveling Logistical Tangles

The death of a presidential candidate either immediately before or after Election Day would create a series of complications, and each state would handle these complications differently due to their differing statutory schemes. For instance, the method by which presidential candidates can or cannot get on the ballot varies by state; thus, the death of a candidate before Election Day would be addressed in a variety of ways nationwide. Additionally, the political parties each have their own rules regarding replacement of the party nominee in the event of death, thus, they would individually work with the states once they have settled upon a replacement nominee.

Death of a candidate prior to Election Day could be extraordinarily complicated, regardless of whether the country is relying upon direct election or the Electoral College; however, most of these matters are issues of state or federal law that are beyond the scope of this book.[31] This book will address only one aspect of these matters: How the Automatic Plan might help to solve some potential logistical problems if a candidate passes away during the latter part of an election year.

The Constitution does not provide a contingency plan if a winning presidential candidate passes away either between the general election and the meetings of the Electoral College or between the meetings of the Electoral College and the counting of the electoral votes by Congress in January. It does, however, provide for presidential succession if the winning candidate passes away after congressional counting of the electoral votes, but before Inauguration Day.[32] The 20th Amendment applies to this latter period, providing that the Vice President-elect succeeds the President-elect if the President-elect passes away before he is inaugurated.[33]

Unfortunately, the 20th Amendment is not helpful before this point. If a candidate passes away between the general election and the meetings of the Electoral College, then the burden falls on the electors. Should they vote for the deceased candidate? Should they instead vote for the vice presidential candidate? Does state law always allow them to do so? Whom should they choose as a replacement Vice President? Presumably, the candidate's political party would take action to designate a replacement (if there is time), but the party and its electors must act in a coordinated fashion in all these matters or they risk losing the election.

What if the candidate passes away after the meetings of the Electoral College but before the congressional counting of votes?

Difficulties still arise because the winning candidate is not officially the President-elect until he has been formally declared the winner by Congress.[34] Congress would need to decide whether to count ballots cast for a deceased candidate. If it does, then the dead candidate will become President-elect and the provisions of the 20th Amendment could kick in, enabling the Vice President-elect to become President. If it does not count these ballots, then no candidate will have a majority of electors, and the House will choose a new President from the remaining living presidential candidates. Note that, in this scenario, the House does not have the option of choosing the Vice President-elect because he was not one of the remaining *presidential* candidates.

The country has not yet been faced with the death of a winning presidential candidate at the end of an election year, but it came close twice: once in 1872 and once in 1912.

In 1872, Republican Ulysses S. Grant ran for re-election against Democratic-Liberal Republican candidate Horace Greeley. The November 5, 1872, election revealed that Grant would soundly defeat Greeley in the electoral vote. Greeley had gained only 66 pledged electors to Grant's 286 during the general election. Greeley, however, passed away on November 29, 1872,[35] a mere five days before the Electoral College vote on December 4. The situation threw his electors into a bit of a quandary.[36] Who were they to vote for? Three electors decided to vote for Greeley, even though he had passed away. (Congress later refused to count these votes, determining that votes could not be cast for a deceased candidate.) Sixty-three other Greeley electors split their votes among several alternative Democratic candidates. No crisis ensued in 1872, mostly because Grant clearly would win the vote regardless of what the Greeley electors decided.

Several elections later, in 1912, confusion among electors became possible yet again. President Taft's running mate, James S. Sherman, passed away on October 30, mere days before the election. Individuals who voted for the Republican slate on Election Day did so without knowing who the replacement candidate would be. The Republican Party eventually selected a replacement, but did not do so until after the general election. The potential for confusion among electors was mitigated that year by two factors: First, Taft placed third in the election, so the actions of his electors were not as important as if a winning candidate had died. Second, the Republican Party had plenty of time between Election Day and the Electoral College vote during which to settle upon a replacement, in sharp contrast to Greeley's last-minute death in 1872.

These elections were uneventful, but difficulties could arise in the event that a *winning* presidential candidate passed away with mere days to go before the electoral vote could be officially cast. If the presidential and vice presidential candidates both died during the same event (perhaps a terrorist attack), then the potential for confusion escalates. In that event, for whom should the electors vote? What if Grant, not Greeley, had passed away on November 29, 1872? What would his electors have done? In 1912, the Republican electors had plenty of time to come up with a concerted plan of action, but what if they had no time to do so? Would their confused and fractured vote help a losing presidential candidate to default into office, despite a low number of electoral votes? In the 1872 election, with no time for planning, the Greeley electors exhibited precisely this kind of confusion, as their votes were scattered among several men.

Professor Akhil Reed Amar and others have discussed this problem in conjunction with issues of terrorism.[37] Such concerns continue to resonate today. Terrorists could not only try to change the direction of a presidential vote through their attacks, but they could take advantage of logistical loopholes in the presidential election system to throw the country into turmoil as it sorts out who should be its next President.

These logistical tangles should be unraveled immediately. Many timing issues can and should be addressed by state and federal statutes; however, a constitutional amendment would be needed for passage of the Automatic Plan. The plan can solve at least a portion of these logistical issues through several rather simple provisions: First, the amendment should provide that electoral votes be automatically cast for the winning presidential candidate, eliminating the interim period between the general election and the Electoral College vote. The potential for confused and fractured voting by electors if a candidate passes away too close to the meetings of the Electoral College would be eliminated.[38]

Second, the amendment should provide that electoral votes won by a presidential candidate should be deemed automatically cast for the vice presidential candidate if the presidential candidate passes away between Election Day and the counting of the electoral votes by Congress.[39] (It should also make provision for the death of a vice presidential candidate, perhaps by deeming the votes automatically cast for the next in line for the presidency under already-existing constitutional and statutory presidential succession provisions.) The Congress might even consider moving up the day on which it counts these votes to ensure that the winning presidential candidate is formally designated President-elect as quickly as possible.

A provision such as the Automatic Plan would make it possible to know for sure who the President-elect will be based upon the votes that are cast on Election Day.[40] Once a President-elect is designated, the presidential succession mechanisms in federal law and the 20th Amendment can take effect.

Chapter Nine

The Contingent
Election

The contingent election is a little-understood and much-disparaged component of America's presidential election system. Critics observe that the contingent election procedure could result in one person casting the deciding vote in an election, a situation that is "distasteful in a democracy."[1] It has been called "the most egregious violation of democratic principles in the American political system."[2] Even Electoral College proponents are likely to hesitate at the prospect of a contingent election. One Electoral College proponent, for instance, labeled the prospect of a contingent election a "horror."[3]

These critics note that many prospective problems could arise if a contingent election were ever needed. A President and Vice President of different parties could be elected. The election procedure could degenerate into self-interested deal-making among representatives. In a worst case scenario, the President-elect could find himself feeling indebted to the Congressmen who secured his election. Such sentiments could damage our system, which values separation of powers among the branches.

The potential for these problems is real, but also more remote than it appears on the surface. Further, most solutions that have been proposed do not remedy the problem. They make matters worse. But one idea that could be considered is automating the secondary election process. This automated process would operate in a manner similar to the automated processes that have been proposed for elimination of the role of elector. Yet even this new potential solution is probably unnecessary.

Without reform, the contingent election would most likely continue to function as it has over the course of the past 200 years, without causing any serious upheaval to America's political system. America rarely uses its secondary election process. The Electoral College, combined with the winner-take-all system, usually magnifies the margin of victory for one candidate and grants certain election outcomes. Nearly 200 years have passed since the country last witnessed a contingent election for the presidency. In all likelihood, the election process will not provoke more than one secondary election in the next 200 years—if it provokes that many.

Allowing the contingent election to stand "as is" would grant one additional—and important—side benefit: It would prevent unnecessary tinkering with the governmental solar system of power. As JFK observed, unanticipated consequences easily may result if one portion of the solar system is altered. Because the dangers of a contingent election are more theoretical than real, it may be better simply to leave the system unchanged.

Understanding the Process

The original Article II election procedure did not provide for separate voting for the President and Vice President. Its contingent election procedure, therefore, could be triggered in either of two situations: First, if no candidate won a majority of the electors.[4] In this situation, the House chose a President from the top five candidates; the Vice President would be the top electoral vote-getter of the four remaining candidates. Second, if two candidates obtained votes from a majority of electors (remember that each elector could cast two ballots), but each candidate had an equal number of votes.[5] In this case, the House chose from the two candidates who had tied. The person who placed second in this House election would be Vice President, since he would also have the most electoral votes of the remaining presidential candidates.[6]

Following the confused election of 1800, Congress enacted the 12th Amendment to separate the voting for President and Vice President, both in the Electoral College voting and in the secondary contingent election procedure. The 12th Amendment provides for a contingent election in the event that no presidential candidate receives a majority of the electoral vote.[7] In such a situation, the House chooses the President from the top three presidential candidates. A similar procedure exists in the Senate, but the Senate may choose a Vice President from only the top two vice presidential contenders. In the House election for President, each state delegation has one vote. In the Senate election for Vice President, each Senator has one vote. If the House of Representatives fails to make a choice before Inauguration Day, then the Vice President-elect acts as President until such time as a choice is made.[8] If the Vice President has not yet been chosen, then the Presidential Succession Act should apply,[9] making the Speaker of the House of Representatives acting President until a choice can be made.

Critics raise three main complaints about this system.[10] First, the Senate and House may elect candidates from different parties. The House considers three presidential candidates, while the Senate considers only two vice presidential candidates. By definition, one presidential candidate will not have the option of working with his preferred Vice President if he is elected. Second, many predict that a future contingent election would degenerate into political, partisan, or self-interested deal-making. For example, a representative from an evenly-divided state delegation would be tempted to cut deals in exchange for switching his vote (and thus his state's vote) to a different presidential candidate. Third, many complain that all states, large or small, each get one vote in this special election—regardless of the size of the state or the number of voters who cast votes in each state's general election.

The first two concerns are reasonable. Arguably, the contingent election process should guarantee that a President and Vice President from the same party are elected. Imagine what could have happened in a hypothetical contingent election in 1992. This secondary election procedure would have resulted in House consideration of Ross Perot, George H.W. Bush, and Bill Clinton as presidential candidates. Dan Quayle and Al Gore would have been considered as candidates for Vice President in the Senate, but the Senate would not have the option of selecting Ross Perot's preferred vice presidential candidate, Reform Party candidate Admiral James Stockdale. Moreover, the Senate can choose a Vice President from a different political party than that of the President chosen in the House. Perhaps the contingent election process would better serve the country if it endorsed either the Clinton-Gore, Bush-Quayle, or Perot-Stockdale ticket. It may be unproductive for the country to end up with, say, President Clinton and Vice President Quayle.[11]

Moreover, critics have genuine worries about deal-making in the House. These issues, in fact, plagued the contingent election in 1825 when Andrew Jackson lost the election to John Quincy Adams in the House of Representatives. Adams won in the House with the help of Henry Clay, who was subsequently made Secretary of State in the Adams administration. Jackson claimed that a "corrupt bargain" in the House stole the election from him, and he eventually went on to win the 1828 election.[12]

Despite the country's experiences following the election of 1824, a reasonable argument can be made that the danger from deal-making is not quite as great today as it was during the country's early years. Improved communications have increased the ability of voters to quickly discover which way their Congressmen voted. Presumably, voter attention to the actions of Congressmen would act as a disincentive to deal-making because congressional members must seek reelection if they are to continue in office. Those who wish to act for political or selfish advantage cannot do all their deal-making behind closed doors. They must be able to explain their actions to the public, particularly on an issue that is as high profile as a vote for President. In all likelihood, Congressmen will probably vote fairly predictably: for their party candidate, the popular vote winner, or the state's popular vote winner. Voters can act in reliance upon this expectation when they vote for their congressional candidate—an election that will always occur at the same time as presidential elections because Congressmen run for re-election every two years.

Finally, the objection regarding the contingent election, that states vote in delegations rather than as individuals, is simply a variation on the argument that Electoral College opponents have made to the current presidential election system. Votes are cast by state delegation in the Electoral College for the same reason that states are given two extra electoral votes, regardless of population. These devices ensure that small states are not forgotten in the process of selecting a chief executive. They buttress federalist principles and reinforce the need of presidential candidates to build a national coalition as they campaign for the presidency.

One Electoral College opponent nevertheless complains that the process is even more "'democratically' problematic than is choice by the electoral college itself."[13] He notes that the 26 least populous states contain less than 20 percent of the population.[14] Why should these states get to choose the next President, without the support of more heavily populated states? The list of small states that he cites, however, includes states as different from each other as Rhode Island and Wyoming. It is hard to imagine a candidate that could achieve the support of Rhode Island (currently very "blue"!) and Wyoming (currently very "red"!) without also achieving the support of at least some of the safely blue or red large states. The contingent election itself is rare. Rarer still would be a contingent election with an outcome dictated solely by the 26 smallest states.

The procedure of casting votes by state delegations is in accordance with the federalist goals of the Electoral College system. Arguably, the divided voting between the House and Senate, together with the possibility of deal-making in the House, makes the contingent election an imperfect procedure. Finding an alternative, however, is more difficult than it may appear at first glance. Critics' proposed solutions typically lead to more problems than they solve.

Runoff Election

Some have proposed holding a runoff between the two leading candidates (along with their running mates) if neither presidential candidate wins a majority of the electoral vote.[15] Other proposals dispense with the majority requirement, arguing that a candidate can win the presidency with a plurality of electoral votes, as long as he passes the 40 percent mark. (The proposals do not bother to explain what is magical about the 40 percent mark. Why not 39, 30, or 25 percent?) The runoff, once triggered, could be conducted either by electoral or popular vote. One advantage of this proposal is that the President and Vice President who are eventually elected would both be from the same party. However, many problems accompany this proposal.

Creation of a runoff system would undermine the certainty, stability, and moderation that have generally characterized American presidential elections.[16] Certainly, a runoff system, combined with the Electoral College vote, would not deteriorate into multi-candidate races as quickly as a pure direct election system would. Obviously, it remains harder to siphon off electoral votes from candidates than to shave a few percentage points from their national popular vote total. However, the harmful effect of introducing a "second chance" to vote into the presidential election system should not be underestimated.[17] Critics who wish to replace the contingent election procedure with a national runoff have yet to address the fact that their system has the potential to create many of the problems already discussed in connection with a direct election system, including deterioration of the two-party system, multi-candidate races, and difficulty in controlling factions.

The American electorate generally has confidence that the votes cast on Election Day are the votes that will determine, with finality, the winner of the presidency. They don't get a second chance to express a different opinion. In what might be dubbed the "Perot" or "Nader" effect, they can't vote for their favorite (but unelectable) candidate the first time, knowing that they can vote for the candidate that they actually expect to win on the second try. Runoffs contain the potential to change this situation. Voters are given a second chance to vote. Psychologically, they may feel more comfortable voting for third-party candidates during the general election. As multiple candidacies accrue, each candidate, again, needs a smaller and smaller percent of the electoral vote to make a runoff.

Local races commonly result in runoffs, but local races differ from the presidential contest in a few important respects. First, certainty and finality in a presidential election are more important than certainty in an election for mayor or governor. If a mayoral contest is undecided for a few weeks, any harm is likely to be minimal. The presidency, by contrast, is the top executive office in the nation. Certainty, finality, and quick transitions between administrations are essential, particularly for national security reasons. Second, runoffs can be conducted more quickly and efficiently in local races than they can across 50 states. Last, runoffs or third-party candidates in local races do not undermine the national two-party system as multi-candidate presidential races could. When third-party candidate and professional wrestler Jesse "The Body" Ventura is elected Governor of Minnesota, it is viewed as a novelty. Absent further incentives at the national level, no one seriously expects to suddenly start running serious independent or third-party candidates for national office based solely upon Ventura's success.

Selection by a Joint Session of Congress

A second proposal would send the presidential election to a joint session of Congress in the event that no candidate wins a majority of the electoral vote. Each member of Congress would have one vote. Voting for the President and Vice President would be combined, rather than separated as they are today. The small states would still retain a slight advantage because they have two Senators and one Congressman, regardless of population.

Some object to this plan because it would allow the winner of the popular vote plurality to lose the election if his party is in the congressional minority.[18] Some congressional members might vote for the popular vote winner (or the popular vote winner in their state), but they would doubtless be under great pressure to vote along party lines. In all likelihood, most congressional members would vote with their party, making it difficult for a President of the minority party to be elected, regardless of the amount of support that he carries among the populace.

Although this proposal cures the problem of separate voting for President and Vice President, it otherwise seems subject to many of the same defects already inherent in the contingent plan.

Congressional members would still be under great political pressure to vote along lines not dictated by the popular vote. Deal-making could still result if congressional membership is evenly divided between the two parties. No great advantage results from a switch to this plan, except to the degree that some might prefer to allow individual members of Congress to vote, rather than state delegations. In both plans, the small states retain a slight edge, although this advantage is undoubtedly greater in the current contingent system.

Neither the current contingency plan nor the joint session plan is perfect. Both carry the potential for deal-making among politicians, although the incentive to cut deals on high-profile issues may be reduced in an era of mass communication. Deal-making is a potential danger in either of these systems, but it is not the greatest downfall. The greater weakness is the permanent advantage given to the presidential candidate from the majority party.

Given that voting by a joint session of Congress does not have overwhelming advantages in comparison to the contingency plan, it seems best to maintain the status quo. Constitutional amendments should be rare, enacted only as a last resort. The solar system of governmental power certainly should not be altered without a strong argument in favor of changing it.

Potential Solutions

The Electoral College, by design, prevents the need for secondary election procedures most of the time.[19] It instead tends to magnify the margin of victory, giving the country a certain winner even when popular vote totals are close. As a result, the contingent election has not been used to select a President since the election of 1824. Secondary election procedures are rare in the United States. In all likelihood, America could continue with its current system without any great harm—which is, in and of itself, a good argument for leaving the current system largely as it stands. A few remedies, however, may be considered as further precautionary measures.

First, the procedures for the contingent election should be clarified. If a contingent election were suddenly needed today, the only available precedent for the logistical details surrounding the

House election would be the rules adopted by the House in 1801 and 1825. These rules, however, leave some unresolved questions, many of which were discussed in Chapter Three.[20] Are votes within each state determined by a plurality or a majority? Are votes by open or secret ballot? Which House conducts the election—the House existing at the time of the presidential election or the new House, which will be sworn in the following January?

These procedural issues should be established before the contingent election is actually needed.[21] Of course, any discussion on these matters will be fraught with partisanship, but at least where the event is a mere hypothetical, there can likely be a relatively unbiased committee discussion. Before the time of need, it is unclear which procedure will give which party in the future an advantage. In the midst of an undecided election, any debate over logistics could (and most likely would) quickly devolve into partisan bickering.

Second, recombining the separated voting for President and Vice President could be beneficial, as it would prevent the election of two candidates from different parties. It is hard to see any benefit if Presidents and Vice Presidents from different parties are elected. As early as 1796, when President John Adams (Federalist Party) was required to work with Thomas Jefferson (Democratic-Republican Party) as his Vice President, the two had difficulty working together productively. To the contrary, the relationship between Jefferson and Adams broke down soon after the two men had been inaugurated. Afterwards, Jefferson recalled, Adams never again "consulted me as to any measures of the government."[22]

Last, a system could be considered that would eliminate the possibility of partisan or self-interested deal-making. This system, however, should retain the federalist principle and leave the small and large states on a relatively even playing field. Finding a solution that serves both purposes is more challenging than it may appear.

One solution could be considered as a resolution for both of these problems. Just as the role of elector can be automated to resolve the problem of deal-making or faithlessness by electors, so could the voting in the House be automated. In this new procedure, each state would still get one vote in the secondary election. However, rather than leaving it to legislators to determine how to cast this vote, the outcome of the state's popular election would determine which candidate will receive the state's one vote. Essentially, Congressmen would be deemed to have voted for the winner of the popular vote in their states. Both the presidential and vice presidential elections could be resolved through this single procedure. The District of Columbia could also be given one vote, as if it were a state. The total current number of state votes awarded in this secondary election procedure would thus be 51.

For example, had the 2000 election resulted in a contingent election, these new procedures would give the Bush/Cheney ticket 30 state votes and the Gore/Lieberman ticket 21 state votes (20 states, plus the District of Columbia). Bush and Cheney would be deemed the winners of the presidency and vice presidency, respectively, because they won a majority of these secondary state votes. Another potentially controversial race, caused by the third-party candidacy of George Wallace in 1968, would be resolved in a similarly easy manner: Richard Nixon (32 state votes); Hubert Humphrey (14 state votes—13, plus the District of Columbia), and George Wallace (5 state votes). Nixon would be deemed the winner.

This alternate procedure would accomplish several important goals: First, it would allow Presidents and Vice Presidents to be elected together, with their running mates. Second, it would automate the process and eliminate the possibility of deal-making among congressional members in the event that a secondary election procedure is needed. Third, it provides a certain and immediate answer to the question of who won the election. Last, it avoids the dangers of a runoff election, which encourages multiple candidacies and the "second-chance psychology" of the electorate.

The primary drawback of this new contingent procedure is that there is no way to automate the process in the event that no candidate receives 26 state votes. If, for instance, two candidates each received 25 state votes and a third-party candidate won one state vote, a back-up plan would be needed. In that case, there is no real alternative except to go to voting by the House or a joint session of Congress. As a mathematical and practical matter, however, the likelihood that no candidate would win either the electoral vote or the automated state vote is slim to none. After all, the Electoral

College discourages third parties, inflates margins of victory, and encourages candidates to build national coalitions. In the event that a contingent election was needed, one of the candidates would almost certainly have obtained a majority of state votes through this automated procedure.

On the other hand, a strong argument exists that JFK's principle applies even to the generally unpopular contingent election. Perhaps Americans should not tinker too much with the solar system of governmental power, particularly when they do so merely to avoid remote or rare problems such as those that could occur in a contingent election.[23] The nation's presidential election process, with the contingent election in it, has served the nation well for more than 200 years. Perhaps it is best to leave the election process untouched. As the saying goes, "If it ain't broke, don't fix it."

Perhaps the specter of a contingent election, in and of itself, has done its part to uphold and maintain our stable, two-party system in America. If one election a century ends in political deal-making in the House, that may be a small price to pay for an otherwise stable and certain system.

Chapter Ten

Concerns
About Legitimacy

Within days of the 2000 election, a Knight Ridder/Tribune columnist wrote that George Bush's Electoral College win, combined with a popular vote loss, "could trigger a crisis of legitimacy."[1] The circumstances under which Bush won, the columnist concluded, constitute the "kind of electrifying election finish that would surprise—and even enrage—many Americans, particularly those who voted for Gore only to find that the majority doesn't necessarily rule."[2] A *New York Daily News* editorial echoed his words. In an age of "one person, one vote," this journalist opined, an electoral vote win combined with a popular vote loss "would rob Bush of the legitimacy he needs to govern effectively."[3]

Electoral College critics have warned the country for years that such sentiments would arise in the event that a popular vote winner failed to win the presidency. In any given year the potential for such a legitimacy crisis exists, these critics lament, because in any given year America's presidential election system could allow a "wrong winner" or a "runner-up President" to win the election. The perpetual possibility of runner-up Presidents, one detractor grumbled, is "the great anomaly in the American democratic order."[4]

These legitimacy arguments are perhaps the silliest raised by Electoral College opponents. If a President is elected by a majority of electoral votes but a minority of popular votes, why should he be considered less legitimate than a President who won a runoff election, but squeaked his way into that runoff by earning, say, 30 percent of the vote in a general election? Or why is he less legitimate than a President elected under NPV's plan, which awards the White House to candidates who obtain any minimal plurality? None of these Presidents would govern with a majority of the individual popular vote. But at least the President elected through the Electoral College must win one type of endorsement that the others do not: He must win concurrent victories across many states in order to obtain a *federal* majority. The President elected in a direct election system could easily be a default winner who was opposed by the majority of Americans in the general election.

The rules that govern the presidential election process exist for a strong and valid reason: to ensure that Presidents represent national coalitions, rather than isolated segments of the country. A President is legitimately elected if he campaigned and won under these rules. To the small degree that voters do not perceive the election outcome as legitimate, this minor problem can and should be cured by educating voters on the important rationales underlying our Electoral College system.

Playing by the Rules of the Game

In any game, rules are established for a certain purpose. As discussed earlier, one example is America's traditional pastime, baseball.[5] Any baseball fan knows that teams do not get to the World Series by scoring the most runs throughout the course of the season. Instead, teams earn their spot in the playoffs by winning the most games in their league. Naturally, rules *could* be established that would allow the two teams that score the most runs to play in the World Series, but such rules would not accomplish the stated objective of a championship game: Allowing the two best overall teams to face off at the end of the year.

A revised set of rules might allow a team, for instance, to earn a spot in the World Series by having one great month and several poor months. Or perhaps a team that is great at taking advantage of weak opponents (but rather poor at facing off against good opponents) would win a berth in the World Series. Excellent performances throughout the baseball season would not be required to earn the championship. Occasional, stellar performances could be sufficient.

The rules for the presidential election contest are established with a similar purpose. They seek to identify the best national candidate, overall. The system leans in favor of candidates whose strengths play out evenly, rather than those who perform brilliantly in one part of the country but terribly in other regions.

Once these presidential election rules have been proposed and established as the best method of achieving the country's stated objectives, is not a winning candidate legitimate any time that he plays by and wins under the rules in effect?[6] Indeed, a President is unfairly labeled "illegitimate" when he simply followed the rules of the game.

Some academics cannot accept this reasoning simply because they cannot accept the legitimacy of any election procedure that allows a presidential candidate to win, despite losing the nationwide popular vote. Other commentators accept the reasoning to some extent, but they are afraid to accept it fully. They may agree that the Electoral College is beneficial to the degree that it produces winners of "federal pluralit[ies]"; however, if a candidate were to ever win a "large majority of the popular vote" while losing the electoral vote, they claim it would be evidence that reform is necessary.[7] After all, a President should have the "support of the people."[8]

Either stance demonstrates a lack of understanding of the Electoral College. Assume, for argument's sake, that a presidential candidate wins the election, but the final vote totals reflect a rather large discrepancy between the outcome of the popular vote and the electoral vote. Perhaps the losing candidate won the popular vote by a landslide, while the winning candidate handily won the electoral vote. Such a situation has never come about, but if it were to occur, the benefits and legitimacy of the Electoral College remain unchanged. The discrepancy between vote totals is not evidence that the electoral system has failed the American people.

The Electoral College was devised to ensure that a President will have the "support of the people"; however, this support must be broad-based. It would be mathematically difficult for two candidates to create a large gap between the popular and electoral votes; however, if they did, the most likely explanation is that the losing candidate spent too much time camped out in one region of the country—precisely the type of behavior that the Electoral College is designed to prevent. Such a candidate would deserve to lose. He might technically have the support of the majority of individuals, but this majority would be in danger of being a tyrannical or regional majority. The Constitution dictates that the other candidate, who successfully obtained the *federal* majority, wins.

Electoral College critics cannot accept the legitimacy of popular vote loser Presidents, partly because they have assumed the need for the very matter in question.[9] Must a presidential election process require presidential candidates to obtain support from a majority of individuals? Or can the process legitimately require that candidates obtain support from a majority of some other aggregate of individuals, such as states, counties, or families? Many today may avoid these questions, but the Framers evaluated them at length. They concluded that freedom would best be protected if presidential candidates were required to win a majority of state electoral votes. Such a system, they believed, would be successful because it combines the best elements of federalism and democracy.

All that can be expected of a presidential election system is that the rules are fair and lead to their stated objectives. The Electoral College has succeeded in this regard for over 200 years. Similarly, all that can be expected of a presidential candidate is that he plays by the rules of the game then in effect. If he wins under the existing set of rules, then he is the legitimate winner.

Voters' Perceptions

Some argue that the crux of the problem is not whether candidates are or are not playing by the rules—or even whether those rules are fair. Instead, they contend that the problem centers on voters with negative perceptions. Pursuant to this focus, voters are predisposed to value democratic outcomes and will not accept a President who did not win the popular vote. Electoral College critics Neal Peirce and Lawrence Longley stated prior to the 2000 election that people may "find a way to live with" a popular vote loser, but the "authority of the presidency and the quality of American democracy would certainly be undermined" by such an outcome.[10]

The degree to which voters question the legitimacy of Presidents who gained the majority of states' electoral votes, but not the majority of individuals' votes, must be questioned in the aftermath of the 2000 election. Despite dire predictions, the election of George W. Bush was accepted by Americans with relative ease. What is perhaps most striking about the weeks of uncertainty in 2000 is the readiness with which voters accepted that the winner of Florida would be the winner of the Electoral College and, hence, the presidential election. Most of the unrest that occurred revolved around the recounts in Florida, rather than the nationwide popular vote totals. Once the election was decided, calls for Electoral College reform did not last for more than a few weeks. Indeed, as early as February 2001, one columnist remarked,

> Before the election, I wrote in this column that "several possible squeaker scenarios could produce some strange political dynamics after November 7." . . . But where I really went wrong was in saying that if the popular vote went one way and the electoral college another, there could be a "crisis of presidential legitimacy."
>
> Perhaps the strangest aspect of the election's aftermath is that none of what happened, nationally or in Florida, seems to make any difference now.[11]

The electorate accepted Bush so easily that a *L.A. Times* book review declared in 2003 that the "significance of the election . . . now seems diminished to a level inconceivable two years ago. The legitimacy of George W. Bush's reign as President has rarely been questioned; the election reform laws passed by Congress were so slight as to barely merit notice; the electoral college is still with us."[12]

Obviously, a handful of people still vehemently object to the outcome of the 2000 election. Yet this bitterness is not directed primarily at the Electoral College. Many protestors instead emphasize the fact that recounting of Florida votes was stopped; they claim that Gore really won Florida. The implication of such complaints seems to be that the Electoral College is legitimate, but Gore, not Bush, should have won the electoral vote.[13]

Of course, some protestors do complain about the legitimacy of the Electoral College itself. It is fair to say that at least some of these people have political, rather than philosophical, motivations. Al Gore's campaign passionately defended the sanctity of the popular vote during November and December of 2000; however, this position was at least partially one of convenience. Prior to the election, predictions abounded that Gore, not Bush, would win the election without winning the popular vote.[14] Indeed, Gore's campaign reportedly sought in advance to prepare itself for a public relations battle to convince the American public that the winner of the Electoral College, rather than the popular vote, is the legitimate President.[15]

Voters' perceptions are certainly important as a public relations matter. However, Electoral College opponents have once again failed to acknowledge the full spectrum of consequences that could result from a modification to the presidential election system. Perhaps some Americans are so predisposed to value democratic outcomes that they do have a problem with a President who did not win the national popular vote. Would this situation really improve under a direct election system? Are direct elections really the best cure for any perception problems, or is not education a more direct and effective manner of curing any problems that may exist?

Under a direct election system, as has been discussed in other chapters, the likely result is that general elections will devolve into races among multiple candidates. Multiple candidacies mean that one of two situations will likely occur each election year. First, one contender will still be able to attain a large plurality of votes—enough to win even if there is a minimum plurality requirement. Assume this candidate gets the 40 percent often suggested as a threshold. What makes this candidate more legitimate than a President elected under the Electoral College system? This candidate, although democratically elected, did not win a majority of votes, nor did he win a broad coalition of states. He won a minimal plurality of votes. Sixty percent of the populace could easily complain that the majority of voters did not vote for the winning candidate.

A second situation is perhaps more likely to occur. As multiple candidacies become the norm, candidates will achieve fewer and fewer votes in the general election. Under NPV, a candidate could win the presidency with *any* plurality, whether that plurality is 15, 25 or 35 percent of the vote: NPV does not require candidates to achieve a minimum plurality. Even if provision is made for runoffs when vote totals are low, two candidates could obtain their place on the runoff ballot with similar small pluralities. Sure, if a runoff is conducted, then one of these two candidates could win "a majority" of votes in the runoff, but they will do so only because the voters have limited options. These candidates will not be the first choice of a large majority of the population, who voted for a different candidate in the general election. What would make this President legitimate, while the candidate elected through the Electoral College is not? Voters who once complained about "popular vote loser" Presidents may suddenly find themselves wishing for the days when presidential candidates had to at least obtain a majority of the states' electoral votes.

Those who back direct popular elections have a good sound bite to throw at a public that, by and large, does not know much about the origins of its presidential election system. Naturally, these critics' arguments sound irrefutable when they call for election of a President by "the majority of the people." The reality, however, is that (absent a two-party system) election systems are unlikely to produce presidential candidates who are able to gain support from 50.1 percent of the people. Voters' opinions vary too widely. Given the opportunity for a purely democratic vote, the most likely result is a fracturing of the electorate into many groups. The Electoral College system seeks a better method. It produces a candidate who has gained the support of most voters in a broad cross-section of states.

Voters obviously can be satisfied with candidates who have not gained support from a majority of individuals. Judith Best points out that 15 "minority" Presidents governed the country from 1824 through 1971.[16] (Two more minority Presidents have been elected since Professor Best's observation: Bill Clinton and George W. Bush.) Included among these minority Presidents is Abraham Lincoln, who was elected to the presidency with the lowest popular vote percentage in the nation's history.[17] Lincoln is not today considered illegitimate; instead, he is generally regarded as one of the nation's greatest Presidents.[18]

※ ※ ※

The winner of the presidency has legitimacy if he played under the rules then in effect. These rules, in turn, can have legitimacy even if they require winning candidates to obtain a majority of something besides individual votes. Requiring a majority of electoral votes serves several purposes that uphold the federalist nature of America's republican democracy.

Moreover, in any given election, no one can say with certainty what the outcome would have been under a different set of rules. Candidates strategize differently when the rules are changed. Had a direct popular vote system been in effect in 2000, maybe Bush would have won that election, too. He probably would have spent more time racking up votes in Texas and other southern states. Bush, however, was not trying to win the popular vote in 2000. Both Bush and Gore were striving to win the most electoral votes. Bush succeeded. Gore did not. The truth of this observation was confirmed by former Clinton Solicitor General Walter Dellinger while the 2000 election was being decided. He observed, "There's no real legitimacy argument. If the presidency was decided by the popular vote, the two candidates would have run different races. We simply don't know who would have won."[19]

Americans accept the winner of the World Series, even when the winner does not score the most runs during the baseball season. They accept the winner because they understand and accept the validity of the rules. Similarly, voters will accept the legitimacy of the Electoral College winner, even when he loses the popular vote, if they understand the rules of the game. Education is the key to any legitimacy problem that may exist.

The Electoral College has a history of more than 200 years of electoral stability and success. Lack of understanding alone, on the part of some of the populace, is an insufficient reason for abolishing the system. A better solution is to educate voters as to the importance and benefits of a federal election system.

Chapter Eleven

Alternative
Proposals

Direct popular election is not the only alternative to the Electoral College that has been proposed. Critics of the Electoral College argue that any one of several other alternatives would be an improvement upon the current system: (1) The "Bonus Plan" would retain the Electoral College, but award a large electoral bonus to the popular vote winner; (2) The "District Plan" would award electoral votes by congressional district, rather than by state; and (3) The "Proportional Plan" would divide electoral votes proportionally, according to the popular vote outcome within the state. The first plan would require a constitutional amendment. The latter two plans could be adopted either nationally, via constitutional amendment, or by individual states that wish to implement the idea within only their own borders.

Finally, the "National Popular Vote" plan, a recent legislative effort, would attempt to impose change nationally, across all the states, even as it sidesteps the constitutional amendment process. NPV has had a fair amount of legislative success and thus requires a more in-depth discussion. It will be discussed in Part Four of this book.

Some of these plans sound plausible at first glance, but a deeper analysis shows that none truly constitutes an improvement upon the country's existing federalist presidential election process.

Bonus Plan

Some academics acknowledge that the Electoral College, with its state-by-state voting, has encouraged stability and a two-party system in American politics. They seek an alternative that will maintain this stability and prevent the rise to power of extremist factions, yet which will nevertheless award the presidency to the popular vote winner. They propose that the presidential election system remain more or less as it is, but that a 102-electoral vote "bonus" (two votes per state, plus the District of Columbia) be awarded to the popular vote winner.[1] The Bonus Plan could still technically allow a candidate to win the presidency without winning the popular vote, but that possibility would be exceedingly remote.

The Bonus Plan might sound appealing at first, but it is likely that America's stable presidential election system would deteriorate under such a plan, just as surely as it would under a direct election system. One major problem with the Bonus Plan is that it lowers the total number of (pre-bonus) electoral votes needed for victory. Presidential candidates would no longer need 270 electoral votes to win; 219 plus the 102-vote bonus would be sufficient.[2] Under the current system, as few as 11 states can deliver the presidency to a candidate (if the 11 most populous states vote for the same candidate; historically, this has never happened, as discussed in Chapter Fifteen). Under the Bonus Plan, as few as *eight of 50 states* could deliver the presidency to a candidate. When candidates need the support of fewer states to win, they also have less incentive to build national coalitions.

The primary focus of candidates under the Bonus Plan would be on popular vote totals: The biggest prize goes to the candidate who wins the popular vote, regardless of where the votes are captured. Campaigning in California could not only garner 55 electoral votes for a candidate, but it could also make a significant contribution toward collecting the 102-vote bonus. What hope does Wyoming have under such a system? Once the focus turns to popular vote totals, rather than coalition-building, the delicate balance of the American presidential system is thrown out of whack.

The Founding Fathers created a presidential election plan that would deliberately inflate the voting power of small states. The Bonus Plan instead dilutes the importance of small states, leaving them in essentially the same position that they would be in if the country implemented a direct election system. If the 2012 or 2016 elections were held under the Bonus Plan, the results would be reasonably predictable, just as they would be with direct election. Democratic candidates would run up their popular vote totals in California and New York, and Republicans would camp out in the South, so as to run up their popular vote totals there.

Over time, the Bonus Plan would lead to a deterioration of America's otherwise stable political system. In a "best case" scenario, the Bonus Plan allows the two-party system to be maintained, but at great cost: Large regions of the country feel neglected as the two major parties focus on the large population centers along the coasts and in the South. Hardly a good state of affairs. In a "worst case" scenario, these sparsely populated regions feel so neglected that they throw their support behind a regional third-party candidate or candidates. If enough third-party candidates are motivated to jump into the fray, the danger of multi-candidate races, runoffs, and a fractured electorate arise, just as they would under a simple direct popular election plan. In either situation, the possibility of nationwide recounts is heightened. After all, a 102-electoral vote bonus is quite a prize for any candidate.

The Bonus Plan appears to maintain federalist principles at first glance, given that it maintains state-by-state voting. But, in practice, it would be unlikely to do so. Professor Paul Schumaker summarizes the problems inherent in this presidential election alternative: "[The Bonus Plan] would be susceptible to the flaws of a popular-vote-plurality system because its outcome would always hinge on the national popular vote."[3]

District Plan

A second alternative to the Electoral College would award electoral votes based upon congressional district. The candidate with the most votes in any congressional district would win that district's one electoral vote. The two Senate "add-on" votes in each state would then be treated as "at-large" votes and awarded to the state's popular vote winner. Maine and Nebraska already operate under this system. If implemented by constitutional amendment, other states would be required to join them.

Proponents of the plan argue that the District Plan will preserve the small state advantage, while allowing diversity within the states to be reflected in the national election totals.[4] Moreover, they add, campaigning would no longer focus on "swing states"; instead, candidates would be encouraged to campaign in states previously considered "safe." As this argument goes, the District Plan would not only encourage presidential candidates to campaign more widely, but it would also promote greater voter participation, because every voter would feel that his vote counts. Other Electoral College critics dismiss the District Plan, however, arguing that inequality of individual votes remain and the plan fails to address the "problem" of a popular vote winner failing to win the presidency.[5] Indeed, Bush's margin of victory in the Electoral College would have been *greater* under the District Plan, despite his popular vote loss.[6]

In a perfect world, the District Plan could be a good idea. America's presidential election system should encourage national coalition-building, and campaigning by districts would ideally work toward this goal.[7] But the plan is unlikely to work out as hoped. Instead, it will create at least two serious new problems.

First, the primary incentive created by the District Plan is an increased motivation to draw congressional boundaries in such a way as to benefit one political party. (Partisan drawing of congressional lines is a political tactic often referred to as "gerrymandering.") Congressional districts are already seriously gerrymandered today, when only the outcome of congressional elections hinges on the drawing of the boundaries. Imagine the ferocity that would accompany redistricting battles every ten years if presidential elections also turned on where these boundaries lie. To the extent that districts' boundaries can be contrived and controlled by those in power, election outcomes will always be influenced as well. State boundaries have one significant advantage over congressional district boundaries: They are permanent and cannot be changed by an incumbent class of officials.[8]

Second, the District Plan could actually *depress* voter participation and narrow the playing field for presidential campaigns, despite the hopes of its proponents that the opposite would happen. Most congressional districts are specifically drawn to be "safe" for one political party or the other. Increased voter participation in these safe districts is improbable. The District Plan's so-called reform could actually have the opposite effect from what was intended in states that are close overall but have congressional districts that are not. In general, the focus of presidential campaigns would shift from a battle over contested states—"swing states"—to a battle over the handful of contested congressional districts—"swing districts." Candidates could be discouraged from addressing issues that appeal to the state as a whole and might instead be motivated to address the concerns of district rich, high-population centers to the exclusion of rural districts. Moreover, if a state votes in pieces, consequential issues would fall out of the larger debate in favor of local grievances. Attention would be further diverted from statewide and national issues and the federal government could become even more entangled in matters that should have remained purely local.

Despite these arguments against the District Plan, the current system allows a state (acting through its state legislature) to switch to the District Plan if it decides that doing so would be beneficial within its borders—and it may do so without the necessity of passing a constitutional amendment. Indeed, some California and Pennsylvania legislators recently proposed to do just that.[9] Moreover, the state can switch back to a winner-take-all system if implementing the District Plan causes more problems than it solved (as it is likely to do). Constitutional amendments are not completed—or undone—nearly as easily. Today, states are free to change their election system every year, if they choose. No reason exists to pass a constitutional amendment requiring all states to permanently implement the District Plan.

Proportional Plan

Under the Proportional Plan, the Electoral College would be retained, but the electoral votes in each state would be allocated based upon the percentage of the popular vote won. If implemented nationwide via constitutional amendment, some versions of the Plan call for whole electoral votes to be divided in the interest of accuracy.[10] Others also propose that the total number of electoral votes needed to win should be lowered to a 40 percent threshold.[11]

Proponents argue that the plan would preserve the states' Electoral College strength, but that the results would be closer to the national popular vote outcome.[12] Further, they argue, the voices of minority voting groups would be reflected in the final election tally because even ballots cast for third-party candidates could be reflected in the national results. Presidents could be elected without winning the popular vote, but such an outcome would be less likely than under the current system. Many Electoral College opponents consider the Proportional Plan to be an improvement, but others deem even the small remaining possibility of a "popular vote loser" President to be unacceptable.[13]

The Proportional Plan is yet another option that sounds good on the surface, but that creates problems in practice. First, constant fighting would erupt over election tallies. After all, a swing of a mere decimal point or two in one or several states could change the outcome of the election. In her book, *The Choice of the People? Debating the Electoral College*, Dr. Judith Best discusses the multiple difficulties with calculating election tallies under such a system. Should electoral votes be rounded to a tenth of a vote? A hundredth or a thousandth of a vote?[14] In any of these circumstances, the potential exists for at least one electoral vote in each of the 50 states, plus the District of Columbia, to be open to dispute. Even small differences in the popular vote could determine how that electoral vote is divided or whether it is awarded to one candidate or another.[15]

Worse, because national implementation of this system is so similar to a direct popular election system, it contains many of the downfalls that have been reiterated throughout this book: Multiple candidacies, close elections, runoffs, and few disincentives for extremist candidates who wish to join the fray. Definitive election outcomes are discouraged. Close vote totals and challenges to election outcomes become the norm.

As this book has argued, one of the great strengths of the current system is that a state legislature can already choose to change its manner of allocating electoral votes, effective immediately. Any state legislature can enact a proportional method of electoral vote allocation if it deems such a method to be in the best interest of its state. However, if one state acting on its own (particularly a small state) were to enact a proportional method of allocating electoral votes, the primary effect of its action would be to significantly dilute its voting strength as compared to the other states. State legislatures may be authorized to change their methods of electoral vote allocation, but they will avoid election disputes and better serve their citizens if they leave the winner-take-all system in place.

If It Be Not Perfect, It Is at Least Excellent

The Electoral College is not perfect, nor is it realistic to expect perfection out of a presidential election process. A flawless presidential election system is surely impossible in an imperfect world. The Electoral College system, however, is unusually clever. It is certainly better than the other options, which often sound reasonable but work out poorly in practice.

The direct election option, for instance, appears to result in a President who is the choice of the majority of the people. In practice, a majority of people will never agree on one person. The electorate consists of a variety of people with an assortment of opinions. The best that can be hoped for is that the presidential election process will provide a method whereby compromise can be achieved. The President may not be the first choice of the majority, but most Americans, as represented by their states, recognize and vote for him as a good choice.

The Bonus Plan sounds as if it should uphold federalist principles because the states still cast votes. In reality, the Bonus Plan has all the downfalls of the direct election plan because the single biggest prize in the election is a 102-electoral vote bonus. The focus is on popular votes. Developing a national coalition is merely a secondary goal. The Electoral College, by contrast, requires presidential candidates to create national coalitions.

The District Plan, in an ideal world, would encourage national coalition building. Practically speaking, it will result in even more intense gerrymandering of districts. The Electoral College relies upon permanent state boundaries. The District Plan will also inappropriately encourage a national focus on purely local issues, as needed to win swing districts.

The Proportional Plan appears to retain the small state advantage, while giving greater weight to the popular vote. In reality, it would devolve into constant disputes about who gets the last electoral vote in each state. The Electoral College, by contrast, tends to magnify margins of victory and give certain election outcomes.

Alexander Hamilton was right when he described the Electoral College in *The Federalist No. 68*. Perhaps the Electoral College is imperfect—but a perfect solution is doubtless unachievable. Nevertheless, the presidential election process devised by the Framers is certainly excellent.

Part Four

The National Popular
Vote Plan

Chapter Twelve

NPV's Attack
on the Electoral College

Shortly after the 2000 election, several academics proposed an idea that would purportedly allow a direct popular election, without the bother of a constitutional amendment.[1] Such creativity is necessary, one professor argued, because public discussion regarding a direct popular vote is likely to be "stifled" by the difficulty of effecting an amendment.[2] A formal amendment requires the support of two-thirds of the House and the Senate; it must then be ratified by 38 states.[3] Quite an uphill battle. The professors' alternative plan would allow a handful of states to do an end-run around the amendment process, implementing a "De Facto Direct Election" (as it was then called) until support for an amendment can be found.[4]

In 2006, a California-based group decided to take the idea and run with it: National Popular Vote, Inc. (NPV) was born.[5] It is the most direct threat to the Electoral College that the country has ever seen, and it stands a great chance of success unless voters nationwide learn about the effort and fight back against it.

Mechanics of the Legislation

NPV's proposal relies heavily on the states' role in our current presidential election system.[6] Article II of the Constitution provides:

"Each State shall appoint, in such Manner as the Legislature thereof may direct, a Number of Electors . . . ."[7] As this book has discussed, most states have chosen to allocate their electors to the winner of the *statewide* popular vote. NPV seeks to change this. It instead asks states to allocate their electors to the winner of the *national* popular vote. If states with a majority of electors (currently 270) were to agree, then the presidential election system would operate as a national popular referendum rather than a federalist, state-by-state process. To ensure that no state is left alone in its decision, NPV operates through an interstate compact. States do not have to allocate their electors to the winner of the national popular vote until a critical mass of states has agreed to join the effort—then they will all do it together.

Put differently, the majority of electors can dictate the outcome of any presidential election. Thus, if those electors are committed to the winner of the national popular vote, then the nation is, in effect, relying upon a national direct election system. The Electoral College would still exist, but only on paper. It would have no practical effect on presidential campaigns. As one legal scholar explains, the compact reduces "the Electoral College to an empty shell."[8]

Technically, NPV's proposal could be enacted by only 11 states—the 11 largest states. Following the 2010 Census, these states hold exactly 270 electors, just enough to win a presidential election. Therefore, if these states were to choose to award their electors in accordance with the national popular vote total, they could determine the outcome of the election.[9] Their decision would hold even if the other 39 states voted for the other presidential candidate. By contrast, remember, a constitutional amendment requires the approval of three-quarters of the states (currently 38).

Practically speaking, the 11 largest states are unlikely to cooperate for purposes of implementing NPV. Unfortunately, the support of a relatively small number of states is already guaranteeing NPV some measure of success.

Legislative Efforts

Since its launch in 2006, NPV has won several legislative victories. As this book goes to press, eight states have adopted NPV's proposed legislation: California, Hawaii, Illinois, Maryland, Massachusetts, New Jersey, Vermont, and Washington (129 electoral votes).[10] The District of Columbia, with three electoral votes, has also approved NPV (bringing the total to 132 participating electoral votes). The Rhode Island legislature approved the plan in 2008, but then-Governor Donald Carcieri vetoed it.[11] Such vetoes remain important: A reasonable argument can be made that the vetoes are irrelevant and that the legislative decision trumps the gubernatorial one (see Chapter Fourteen). The support of Rhode Island would bring NPV's electoral vote total to 136 electoral votes—more than half of the votes needed—despite the fact that NPV's plan would have been approved by only nine state legislatures plus D.C.

NPV's success stems from several factors: First, its effort is well-funded by a few liberal billionaires,[12] and the group is thus able to make a serious push in every state. NPV has hired both Republicans and Democrats to travel the country and pitch its idea before legislative committees. (These individuals don't usually broadcast the fact that they are being paid, although they sometimes admit it when asked directly during legislative hearings.[13]) By contrast, Electoral College supporters have so far been necessarily limited by the fact that they are mostly volunteers, acting largely in reliance on their own time and resources and without a national support network of lobbyists. At least one pro-Electoral College group is working to raise money,[14] but it seems unlikely to match the tens of millions so far pledged to NPV.[15]

Second, NPV benefits from the fact that most voters have no idea that the Electoral College is under attack. NPV has been debated largely behind the scenes, without fanfare, in state legislative committees. For the average voter, the headlines are dominated by other matters—the economy, health care, and turmoil in the Middle East. The Electoral College is often not known to be in danger, and its defense is relegated to the back burner.

Third, NPV benefits from the fact that state legislators do not always understand the current Electoral College system. Their lack of background on the matter doubtless causes some of them to accept the simplistic sound bites thrown their way by NPV's lobbyists. Fortunately, many legislators have also been honest enough to reverse course—pulling support from the legislation or removing their names as sponsors—once they obtain more information.[16] Unfortunately, other legislators are less principled. They believe NPV will benefit their political party, and they act accordingly. Finally, many other legislators do not have the time to be fully informed about every single matter on the legislative agenda. When it comes to the Electoral College, they simply vote how their party leadership tells them to vote.

Voters must reverse this trend by insisting that the matter be more fully explored and debated.

Philosophical Problems with the Legislation

Those who support NPV typically come at the issue from one of two perspectives: The first type of supporter is simply acting out of partisan interest. These individuals believe that elimination of the Electoral College will deliver the presidency to their political party in future years. Thus, they work to get rid of the system. Other supporters are more ideological. They don't believe in the Electoral College, but they know that a constitutional amendment will be difficult to achieve. They simply want a quicker, easier way to move to a direct election procedure; any route will do. Both perspectives are equally flawed.

First, it is wrong to eliminate the Electoral College based purely on temporary, partisan gain. The Electoral College and other safeguards in our Constitution were created to serve the entire country on a permanent basis. They were intended to protect freedom over the course of decades. It is destructive to change them simply to serve one person or party at one moment in time. The founding generation would never have understood tampering with fundamental law for such short-sighted reasons. The Electoral College serves all of us by ensuring that presidential candidates must always take into account the needs of a wide variety of Americans. They can't cater to one region, state, or special interest group. Small and less densely populated states have a particular interest in preserving the Electoral College, which prevents them from being tyrannized by the majority in large cities and states.

Second, no one can know which political party will benefit more if the Electoral College is abolished. As this book has argued, eliminating the system would probably have two immediate results: Elections will become easier to steal, and the two-party system will be undermined. Thus, it follows that two types of political parties would benefit the most: Those that don't mind stealing elections and third parties. Unfortunately, extremist third parties and special interest groups will benefit the most if the two-party system is eradicated. Surely no one really wants to encourage such a situation.

But let's assume that the two-party system remains relatively stable after the Electoral College is gone. Many NPV supporters have jumped to questionable conclusions about what is likely to follow. A few Republicans have argued that their party will benefit from NPV because it will allegedly make candidates more likely to campaign outside of the big, left-leaning cities.[17] One Republican notes that small states and rural areas have cheaper media markets. In a direct election, he argues that candidates would thus be motivated to reach out to these less densely populated areas; they would not spend all their money in expensive media markets such as Los Angeles or New York.[18] He is forgetting the simple rules of supply and demand. These latter media markets are expensive because advertisers can reach so many people with their message. Presidential candidates will respond to these incentives as well as anyone else. Since their goal is to amass large numbers of individual votes, they will spend their money where they can reach the most people at once: the big cities.

Other Democrats doubtless believe that the partisan gain will be for their own party.[19] Candidates who are striving for individual votes campaign most efficiently when they focus on big cities and densely populated areas—currently a Democratic strength. These Democrats are being short-sighted. Even assuming they are correct about the immediate political gain, they can't assume that they will always have strength in urban areas. Political winds are constantly shifting. A Democratic strength today can easily be a Democratic weakness tomorrow. Remember how quickly and completely a state like Texas switched from "blue" to "red" in the 80s and early 90s.[20]

Finally, Republicans and Democrats alike should be wary of the roundabout manner in which NPV is seeking its goal. The Electoral College has a long and successful history. It should be kept. But if it is to be eliminated, respect for the Constitution requires use of the formal constitutional amendment process.

NPV proponents fail to address an important question: Why should a mere 11 states have the power to implement its change? True, the Electoral College technically allows the 11 largest states to elect a President. This never happens for a variety of practical reasons (see Chapter Fifteen), but even if it were to happen, such an occurrence would be rare; it would determine only the identity of one President in one election year. By contrast, NPV would allow 11 states to make a far more serious decision: They would dictate the very method by which we elect Presidents. They would effect constitutional change without bothering to get the consent of at least 27 additional states, as required by Article V of the Constitution.

The Constitution is set up as a system of checks and balances. The constitutional amendment process requires the approval of three-quarters of the states so the large states cannot bully the small states, yet that is exactly what NPV's proposal attempts to do. Eleven populous states would implement change with or without the approval of their smaller neighbors.

True, the amendment process is an uphill battle. *It was intended as such.* Constitutional principles should be changed only after great thought and consent from the vast majority of the country. Difficulty in changing the Constitution protects Americans' freedom.

NPV takes the precise opposite approach from the Founders' intent. It relies on a handful of states to change the presidential election system for the whole country, with minimal debate and even less agreement. Such a situation will do nothing more than to create unhealthy division and resentment among voters.

Chapter Thirteen

Logistical Problems
with NPV

The current presidential election process is a unique blend of federalist and democratic principles.[1] America holds 51 completely separate, purely democratic elections each presidential election year (one in each of the states, plus one in the District of Columbia). Local election laws impact the manner in which any one of these elections is held, but any differences among the states' election codes don't matter. The unique laws of any particular state impact only voters within that state. The country holds 51 completely separate presidential elections, and it achieves 51 different sets of results. Each state's single goal is to select a slate of electors that will represent it in the later, national election among the states.

NPV would entirely change this system. America would still hold 51 completely separate elections, but NPV would attempt to derive one single result from these various election processes. Suddenly, internal variances among states' processes—previously irrelevant—would matter a great deal. Indeed, the group that prides itself on "every vote equal" would *ensure* that voters are never treated equally across states. This chapter will discuss the numerous logistical issues that arise from such a situation. The next chapter will discuss the legal ramifications of treating voters unequally.

Differing States' Laws

Federal election law controls many aspects of the presidential election. For instance, federal law requires states' electors to meet on a certain day and to submit their votes to various officials in Washington, D.C., as described in Chapter Three. But other issues are purely matters of state law. For instance, states have different criteria for what does (or does not) trigger recounts within their borders. The states have made different decisions about whether felons may vote. They have different early voting procedures. They have different methods of qualifying for the ballot.

Such differences among state election codes are irrelevant in the current system. A voter in Oklahoma has no reason to care about the law in Minnesota. He cares only that he is treated equally with other Oklahomans: He must compete against them to determine the identity of Oklahoma's electors. Similarly, voters in Minnesota need only be treated equally with each other; they compose the relevant election pool for determining the identity of Minnesota's electors. NPV would change all of this. Suddenly, voters in Minnesota and Oklahoma would be thrown into the same election pool. In this new world, the identity of a Minnesota elector could be changed by a vote cast in Oklahoma—or any other state. Differing state election codes would wreak havoc. Indeed, the situation carries the potential for Equal Protection problems (as discussed in the next chapter). It also creates the potential for chaotic, logistically difficult presidential elections. Among the worst of these problems would be the issue of recounts.[2]

NPV's interstate compact requires the chief election official in each member state to "determine the number of votes for each presidential slate in each State of the United States and in the District of Columbia in which votes have been cast in a statewide popular election."[3] These votes are to be added together to determine which candidate won the "largest national popular vote total."[4] The official then certifies the appointment of the slate of electors associated with that "national popular vote winner."[5]

Sounds easy enough, but what if this calculation reveals that the national total is close—close enough to warrant a recount? If each vote is to be "equal," then every individual vote in the country must be included in such a recount. Moreover, recounts in all 51 jurisdictions must be completed quickly: As Florida learned in 2000, a state must certify its slate of electors before the federal "safe harbor" deadline in mid-December.[6] Otherwise, Congress may not consider the state's decision about its own electors to be conclusive.[7] Unfortunately, NPV cannot promise a full and fair nationwide recount, much less a timely one.

Remember that each state must individually satisfy the recount standard in its own election code before it may legally participate in a recount. Potentially, a recount would not be conducted—at all— because the margins in individual states are not close, despite the close national totals. Or perhaps a recount is mandatory in a handful of states, in which state recount criteria were satisfied, but wide margins in the remaining states would otherwise prevent the others from also participating in the recount.[8]

Imagine that Florida, Ohio, and Pennsylvania are each conducting recounts due to the close margins within their own states. The rest of the nation is forced to watch. Maybe each of these three states has a different idea of how to count a hanging chad. Perhaps a fourth state, Nevada, sees what is going on and chooses to conduct a recount that its statutes previously deemed optional. Maybe Nevada has a different definition of "hanging chad," and its sole purpose is to counteract the efforts of the other states.[9] In fact, a few dozen states could jump into the recount, relying on "optional" recount provisions, because they have the same, partisan motivation. Such a situation will result in numerous court challenges and protracted proceedings that will make Florida 2000 look like a picnic.

To be fair, if NPV were implemented, then many state legislatures would probably work to make their recount statutes more lenient. Even if these states otherwise disagree with NPV, they would not want to be caught in a situation where they could not participate in a national recount. Moreover, as alluded to previously, many states already provide "optional recount" statutes that allow recounts to be requested by candidates or voters even without a close margin.[10] On the other hand, some of these optional recounts can't be conducted without approval from some governmental entity; thus, the process contains the potential to be manipulated for partisan purposes. Perhaps government officers would not always approve the recount requests—for instance, if it is feared that the wrong political party would be hurt or helped by the recount. On the flip side, perhaps some states would be motivated to make their recount standards *very* lenient—constantly trying to be more lenient than their neighboring states—in an effort to have more sway over election outcomes.[11]

At the end of the day, 51 separate sets of rules for recounts can't be fairly relied on in the conduct of one national election. Such a situation provides too much opportunity for partisanship to creep into the process of resolving post-election disputes. Such logistical chaos and partisanship can be minimized in one of two ways: Leave the current system that relies on 51 sets of recount rules for 51 different elections (as this book advocates) or change the system via constitutional amendment. Such an amendment would allow one set of recount standards to be created and relied upon in the conduct of one national election. NPV's halfway measure will not work.

Unfortunately, recounts are just the tip of the iceberg. States that have agreed to participate in NPV can't force the other states to take any particular action—including a runoff or other secondary election procedure. Thus, NPV's compact awards the presidency to the candidate winning the "*largest* national popular vote total."[12] The compact does not require a majority winner. It does not even require a minimum plurality. Practically speaking, it cannot. Thus, with NPV's compact in place, a candidate could win even with a very small plurality, such as 15 or 20 percent of voters. Is it "fair" or "better" if an American President is elected with a large majority of people opposed to him?

But the logistical difficulties could get even worse. A participating state could be forced to award its entire slate of electors to a candidate who was not even on its own ballot. Imagine, for instance, that Ron Paul qualifies for the ballot in Texas and perhaps a few other southern states. He obtains a winning plurality solely from this regional constituency. Paul did not bother to qualify for the ballot in a place like New Jersey. Voters in that state did not have the chance to vote for—or against—him. Yet, as a signatory to NPV's compact, New Jersey would be forced to award its entire slate of electors to the choice of southern voters. New Jersey probably did not nominate a slate of electors for Paul because he was not on its ballot. NPV's compact offers a solution, but it is doubtful that voters in New Jersey will like it. Paul would be entitled to personally appoint the 14 electors who will represent New Jersey in the Electoral College vote.[13] In all likelihood, he would select loyal Texans to represent New Jersey in the presidential election. Why would Paul appoint individuals from New Jersey? He would run the risk that such electors will be "faithless": These local electors could very well vote for the choice of New Jersey's voters, instead of Paul.

And yet there is more. As mentioned, other inconsistencies among states' ballots could skew the election results. Some states allow felons to vote. Others do not. States differ in their requirements to qualify for the ballot. They have different early voting rules. States would be forced to abide by national election results derived from policies with which they disagree. Worse, states would almost certainly amend their election codes, competing to have the biggest impact on national totals.[14] In combination with the race to create lenient recount standards, such a situation creates the danger of a "race to the bottom" as the administration of elections becomes more and more politicized.

NPV could avoid these problems if it instead sought orderly change through a constitutional amendment. Such an amendment would help to establish one set of federal laws to govern one national election.

NPV's Counter-Arguments

The problems discussed above are serious, but NPV typically ignores them or lightly brushes them aside. To the degree these issues are discussed, NPV has a tendency to treat them as pure melodrama, created by Electoral College advocates as mere scare tactics. Such chaotic proceedings are theoretically possible, NPV might admit, but such outcomes will never actually happen.

Take the issue of recounts, which are brushed aside as a non-issue by the authors of *Every Vote Equal*. It simply notes that "the personnel and procedures for a nationwide recount are already in place because every state is always prepared to conduct a statewide recount after any election."[15] NPV has not addressed the problem inherent within its own statement. True, states have personnel and procedures in place for recounts—51 of them. Fifty-one different statutory schemes can't govern one (allegedly) national election. The authors do not address this problem and instead assume that recounts won't be needed very often anyway. *Every Vote Equal* contends that "there would be less opportunity for a close election under nationwide popular election of the President than under the prevailing statewide winner-take-all system" because a "a close outcome is less likely in a single pool of 122,000,000 popular votes than in 51 separate pools each averaging 2,392,159 votes."[16] NPV may regret jumping to this conclusion so quickly. It is not safe to assume that recounts will be few and far between with a national popular vote system in place. To the contrary, there are at least two reasons to believe that recounts will become more frequent.

First, America's presidential campaigns would certainly change if the rules of the game change. In any game, rule changes regularly impact strategy, motivations, and incentives. In presidential elections, the changed rules of the game would seriously undermine America's stable, two-party system, as discussed in Chapter Six.[17] Without the Electoral College and the winner-take-all allocation of electoral votes within states, presidential campaigns could easily devolve into European-style, multi-candidate races. In the context of recounts, this is important. As more candidates enter the field, individual votes will necessarily be divided among an ever-increasing number of candidates. The result will be lower vote totals per candidate and an increased likelihood that two or more candidates will have close popular vote totals. In short, recounts will be needed more often than NPV anticipates.

Second, the authors of *Every Vote Equal* do not adequately address the historical record. Even assuming, *arguendo*, that America maintains its relatively stable two-party system, past election results show that recounts would be more likely without the Electoral College. Popular vote totals are usually closer than electoral vote totals, as discussed in Chapter Seven. Indeed, former FEC chairman

Bradley Smith points out that recounts may have been necessary in as many as six presidential elections since 1880, if a national popular vote system had been used.[18] That's nearly one out of every six elections! It is not safe to assume that recounts will be a rarity with NPV in place.

NPV similarly brushes off other concerns about logistical problems with its legislation, without adequately addressing them. In a Senate Judiciary Committee meeting in Alaska, for instance, NPV proponent Laura Brod laughed off the idea that a state would be forced to award its electors to a candidate who was not on its ballot, deeming such a contention to be no more than an "interesting conceptual exercise."[19] Instead, she summarily concluded that "a serious candidate will be on the ballot in all 50 states."[20] But her statement ignores the very real possibility that the two-party system could be weakened without the Electoral College in place. And certainly a "serious candidate" does not have to be on the ballot in every single state, if the race is a multi-candidate one. Unfortunately, Brod's faulty logic continued into another area, as she similarly dismissed the idea that presidential candidates could appoint electors from outside the state (per the Ron Paul example in the previous section). "That's just a scenario that would be very, very, very extremely unlikely," she testified.

> And to suggest, which has been suggested before, that a candidate would choose an elector from outside the state is ridiculous. If the candidate is in that state working hard for those votes, they would certainly do just like every other candidate does, which is grab a slate of electors that represents that state.[21]

Of course, in the Paul example, he was *not* "in that state" and was *not* "working hard for those votes," which is why no slate of electors was available for him in the first place. But it is easier for NPV to laugh off claims as "ridiculous" than to address them on the merits. Sadly, the Alaska committee before which Brod testified did not dig deeper into the question, but accepted her explanation at face value.[22]

In reality, it appears that NPV advocates are not too worried about the manner in which their plan undermines federalism and creates logistical difficulties. In honest moments, advocates let slip what they really want and expect: A one-size-fits-all national solution to presidential elections. John Koza, the founder of NPV, claims that a constitutional amendment to eliminate the Electoral College is something that should have happened long ago. "The public has been behind this concept for a long time," Koza claims, "[w]e're just trying to get past the initial inertia."[23] He predicts that a constitutional amendment will be the logical consequence of NPV.[24] Other NPV advocates hold similar views. Robert Bennett, one of the academics who originally floated the plan behind NPV, notes: "Over time pressure to regularize requirements across states would likely build . . . . Such regularization would presumably require constitutional amendment."[25]

Others predict that, even if the amendment is not ultimately adopted, federal election statutes will replace state election statutes. In sharp contrast to the testimony offered by NPV lobbyists such as Brod, Professor Vikram David Amar acknowledges a "problem I see in the current National Popular Vote bill is that it does not guarantee a true national election with uniform voter qualification, voter mechanics, and vote-counting standards. Absent such uniformity, some states might have incentives to obstruct or manipulate vote counts." The solution he offers is "Congressional action."[26] Such congressional action opens up a whole can of worms: Does Congress have the authority to trump state election laws?[27] Even if Congress does have this authority, why should states that have rejected NPV be forced into cooperating with an effort to create such a federal election code? The fact that such solutions are being assumed smacks of arrogance.

If NPV advocates were being honest, they would acknowledge the existence of these issues in state legislative hearings, rather than disingenuously blowing off such concerns as "ridiculous" and "scare tactics."

Non-participating States

NPV faces further logistical difficulties in its attempts to deal with states that reject the plan—or with states that change their mind about participating in the compact. Indeed, a non-participating state could easily undermine NPV's attempt to implement a national direct election. It would simply need to change the manner in which electors are (or are not) listed on its ballot.

Recall from Chapter Eight that states today generally use the presidential short ballot, which lists only the names of presidential candidates. Electors' names don't typically appear.[28] States do not have to use this short ballot. In fact, its use is a relatively recent phenomenon. Non-participating states could revert to an older form of ballot, thereby undermining NPV's attempt to implement a national direct election.[29] One past election shows the ease with which a state could make it impossible for NPV to obtain a "national popular vote total," as its interstate compact demands. Of course, this election also shows the continuing chaos created by an election system that pretends to implement one national election, even as it leaves 51 different sets of state election codes in place.

In 1960, the state of Alabama relied upon a ballot that listed individual electors, rather than presidential candidates.[30] Such a decision was not a particularly unusual one for a state to make at that point in time. But matters that year were made more confusing by the state's Democratic Party. That party nominated a split slate of electors. Five electors were pledged to vote for the eventual Democratic nominee, John Kennedy, but six electors were unpledged. (They ultimately cast their ballots for Harry F. Byrd.) Voters in Alabama could not vote for 11 Kennedy electors, even if they wanted to. They could vote for a pledged Kennedy elector and an unpledged Democratic elector simultaneously. Or they could vote for only unpledged electors or only Kennedy electors. Given the many various ways in which a voter could cast his ballot—to say nothing of the fact that these were secret ballots—an official popular vote total in Alabama would have been impossible to definitively tabulate if NPV had been in place that year.

Now imagine that a state such as Texas were to attempt to undermine NPV by deliberately recreating the 1960 situation.[31] Its legislature would simply replace the state's winner-take-all system with direct elections for individual electors. Texans would go to the polls and cast up to 38 votes for individual electors on the Texas ballot. They could vote for 38 Republican electors or 38 Democratic electors—they could even vote for some of each. They could vote for a few third-party electors. At the end of Election Day, no one would be able to say which presidential candidate won the "most" votes in Texas. Yet Texas would still be fully and fairly represented in the Electoral College vote by the 38 electors who received the highest number of votes.[32]

Non-participating states could further complicate NPV's efforts simply by refusing to make their Election Day vote totals known until after the meetings of the Electoral College.[33] In an age where transparency in government is valued, perhaps such a solution would be rejected. On the other hand, a state statute might provide that release of its vote totals can be delayed only in certain circumstances; for instance, if the winning candidate achieved a certain (landslide) margin and the NPV compact was then in effect.[34]

In either of these situations, NPV's compact should fail because the national popular vote total would be unknowable—although NPV advocates could conceivably seek to explicitly exclude such a state from the presidential election. Presumably, it would be politically difficult for them to take such action, but similar solutions have been suggested by at least some academics.[35]

Finally, remember that states might change their mind about the wisdom of joining NPV—or perhaps they would simply want to opt out for purely partisan reasons in a particular election year. NPV's compact is a temporary solution—easy to join and easy to leave, by its own terms—as opposed to a constitutional amendment, which would be a relatively permanent solution.

Imagine that NPV has just enough states to be operable during the 2016 election. The presidential campaigns are proceeding on the assumption that a national direct election will be in place on Election Day. But in late June, Massachusetts gets worried that the Republican will win the national popular vote. In disgust, its legislature decides to pull out of NPV's compact. Suddenly, NPV no longer has enough states to proceed. The country is again hosting a normal presidential election with the Electoral College in place. Well, unless some other state like Texas changes its mind and swiftly adopts NPV for purely political reasons—Texas, after all, *does* want the Republican to win. The Texas legislature is not normally in session during a presidential election year, but the Governor could call it into special session. Imagine a Texas Governor such as former presidential candidate Rick Perry calling a special session in the hopes that NPV will be approved and he can get himself elected! Such examples show the degree to which partisanship and self-interest will almost inevitably flow from NPV's plan. Moreover, this kind of flip-flopping back and forth is not good for the stability of the country or its presidential election system.

NPV insists that the ability of states to withdraw from the compact is a benefit, not a problem. If its proposal proves to be a mistake, then a state can undo its actions much easier and faster than if a constitutional amendment had been enacted. NPV correctly notes that an amendment would be difficult to undo (which is why *any* amendment should not be undertaken flippantly), but it incorrectly jumps to the conclusion that its alternative is better. If a state attempts to withdraw from NPV, the ramifications of its actions will differ, depending on when it attempts to withdraw.

No one disputes that a state may withdraw anytime before July 20 in a presidential election year, as explicitly provided by NPV's compact.[36] In the example above, there is no reason that Massachusetts could not bow out of the compact in June—and no reason that Texas couldn't swiftly join the compact in response, all for partisan advantage. Potentially, such partisanship could cause NPV's compact to bounce back and forth—in effect one month or year, but not the next. Perhaps states would opt in and out based on their perception of whether the compact would play to its benefit in any particular presidential election year.[37] Consistency in America's presidential election system is impossible in such circumstances.

A second issue is whether a state may bow out after July 20 in a presidential election year, but before Election Day and the meetings of the electors have occurred. What if a state attempts to pull out of the compact in violation of its terms? Can compliance be enforced? How much litigation would ensue before the presidential election could be resolved? NPV answers these questions by insisting that states are bound to the compact by Article I, section 10, clause 1 of the Constitution: "No State shall . . . pass any . . . Law impairing the Obligation of Contracts."[38] But NPV's response is too simplistic.

Obviously any state that wants out of the compact will do more than simply say "please" and hope that it will be released from a contractual obligation. Such a disgruntled state will instead go to court and argue that NPV's compact is unconstitutional.[39] If the compact is unconstitutional, then the state can't be bound. The legal issues surrounding the constitutionality of the compact will be discussed more in the next chapter. For now, it is worth noting that NPV's plan runs the unnecessary risk of encouraging litigation in the days and weeks immediately prior to a presidential election.

⁂ ⁂ ⁂

NPV proponents act as if they can successfully avoid the constitutional amendment process through their interstate compact. Their idea is admittedly imaginative, but it would create a whole host of logistical problems.

One national election cannot be conducted in reliance on 51 sets of election codes. Chaos will result from the varying recount requirements and ballot qualification laws, among other issues. Moreover, problems result from NPV's inability to control non-participating states. Because it can't force these states to conduct a runoff, it must instead accept any plurality winner as the winner of the presidency. America could be forced to accept the winner of a very small plurality as its new President. In addition, NPV has no adequate solution if a state changes its laws in such a way as to confuse tabulation of the national popular vote total.

These many logistical problems have as yet to be seriously addressed. Instead, NPV supporters continue to act as if one internally consistent nationwide outcome can be derived from 51 separate state and local processes. Their position is nothing more than wishful thinking.

Chapter Fourteen

Legal Problems with NPV

S etting aside the question of whether NPV is a good idea from a logistical or policy perspective, voters and legislators obviously must consider the more basic question of NPV's constitutionality.[1] To listen to NPV advocates talk, one would think that the Founders practically *wanted* something like NPV to come along someday. Indeed, NPV not only defends its plan as constitutional, but even implies that its idea is *more* in line with the Constitution than the status quo.

The hyperbole is astonishing. NPV is "not in conflict with the Constitution and not an end run around the Constitution. In actuality, the legislation is an exercise of power by the states that is explicitly granted through the Constitution."[2] Another advocate bashes those who propose a constitutional amendment as the only legitimate method of changing the presidential election process: Such a position "misunderstand[s] the purpose of the Electoral College and the important principal [sic] of federalism it represents."[3] NPV "preserves the Electoral College" and protects "a basic state right specifically enshrined by our Founders in Article II of the United States Constitution."[4] Another political consultant resorts to the claim that our "Founding Fathers did not oppose or support a national popular vote or any other method of electing our president, instead leaving it to the states to award electors in a manner that is in the best interest of the people that they serve."[5] Robert Bennett tries to put NPV on par with other exercises of state authority:

> Justice Louis Brandeis once famously sang the praises of the states as the engines of experimentation to meet "changing social and economic needs." A "single courageous state," he urged "may . . . serve as a laboratory." In the case of the electoral college, the invitation to experiment is especially clear, as the Constitution—fortified by Supreme Court decisions—vests the states with wide-ranging control over the "manner" of selection of its electors.[6]

Of course, NPV is more than a decision by a single state, the ramifications of which will impact only residents of that state. It is a unilateral decision, made by a minority of states, to force the entire country into a new presidential election experiment. No state will be able to opt out.

The attempt to pretend that NPV is in line with the Constitution is puzzling, to say the least. At the Constitutional Convention, small state delegates were adamantly opposed to a national direct election system for the President. They voted against the prospect. Delegates such as Hugh Williamson of North Carolina believed that "[t]he people will be sure to vote for some man in their own State, and the largest State will be sure to succeed."[7] Roger Sherman of Connecticut agreed,[8] as did Charles Pinckney of South Carolina who noted that "[t]he most populous States by combining in favor of the same individual will be able to carry their points."[9] Gunning Bedford of Delaware was perhaps even blunter. He spoke of the need for small states to protect themselves against their larger neighbors:

> I do not, gentlemen, trust you. If you possess the power, the abuse of it could not be checked; and what then would prevent you from exercising it to our destruction? You gravely allege that there is no danger of combination . . . ? This, I repeat, is language calculated only to amuse us. Yes, sir, the

larger States will be rivals, but not against each other—they will be rivals against the rest of the States.[10]

The small states never would have joined the union if a national direct election provision had been included in its founding charter. NPV is being disingenuous when it seeks to implement a system that was specifically rejected by Convention delegates yet innocently refers to it as just another exercise of "states' rights."

A more balanced approach would acknowledge that NPV's plan is not in line with the discussions that were held at the Constitutional Convention. The direct election process that it implements was not only considered, but also rejected, by Convention delegates. Non-participating states and voters are rightfully outraged by NPV's attempt to force a new election process upon the country without first going through the formal amendment process.

Many legal challenges can and will be filed against NPV's compact. If NPV survives these challenges, it will not be because it is a clearly permissible exercise of constitutional power. It will be only because NPV proponents have found and are exploiting a loophole in the law.

The Use of an Interstate Compact

The NPV proposal relies on its use of an interstate compact—basically, a contract signed by any state that wants to participate in the move to a direct popular election. When a state approves NPV's legislation, it is simply indicating that it will sign the contract.[11] By the terms of the contract, member states are required to allocate their electors to the winner of the national popular vote. The contract becomes binding when states holding a majority of electoral votes (270) have agreed to sign. Until then, each state maintains its status quo—usually a winner-take-all system within the state.

Why implement NPV through an interstate compact? Because NPV knows that states will be more likely to join the effort if they can do so in concert with other states. The compact shields those state legislators who generally like the idea of a national popular vote, but who don't want their states left out in the cold if other state legislatures choose not to take similar action. For instance, perhaps Massachusetts legislators want to move to a direct election, but they do not want to allocate their electors to the winner of the national popular vote when every other state is still allocating its electors to the winner of the states' popular votes. Why would a blue state like Massachusetts give its electors to someone like Tea Party favorite Sarah Palin, helping her to win the presidency, if every other state is still voting in accordance with its own citizens' desires? Perhaps Palin would have won without Massachusetts' electors, but voters in that state would probably be pretty unhappy with the situation anyway. The compact ensures that participating states can act only when they are guaranteed the ability to do so with other, like-minded states.[12]

Use of a compact might serve practical political purposes, but it also creates constitutional problems, as even NPV proponents occasionally concede.[13] Article I, Section 10 of the Constitution provides that "No State shall enter into any Treaty, Alliance, or Confederation" and "No State shall, without the Consent of the Congress, . . . enter into any Agreement or Compact with another State."[14] The text of this Compact Clause would seem to be clear that some agreements (treaties) are completely forbidden and that others (agreements and compacts) are permissible only with congressional approval, but the Supreme Court has held otherwise.

As early as 1893, the Court declined to focus on the simple text of Article I, instead looking to the "object of the constitutional provision."[15] The Court's decision to engage in subjective analysis unsurprisingly changed the direction of its jurisprudence. Today, the Court effectively assumes that all agreements among states are permissible, and it will consider only whether additional congressional approval is required.[16]

The Court's position benefits NPV. Despite the apparently plain text of the Constitution, congressional approval is not required for many agreements among states;[17] instead, the Court will require approval only for certain political agreements that affect the balance of power among federal and state governments.[18] Indeed, NPV takes this watering down of interstate compact law a step further. In heavy reliance on a 1978 case, *United States Steel Corp. v. Multistate Tax*

Commission, it claims that only impacts on the vertical relationship between federal and state levels of government should be taken into consideration.[19] Because NPV's compact allegedly has no impact on this vertical relationship, NPV considers its compact legal and binding, with or without congressional approval.[20]

NPV conveniently ignores part of *U.S. Steel* to reach this conclusion. The Court did spend most of its opinion evaluating the vertical relationship between the federal and state governments, but it also acknowledged that a compact's impact on non-participating states—horizontal relationships among states—must be considered.[21] The Court further left open the possibility that a future compact implicating the "federal structure" could be problematic.[22] This portion of the case was admittedly brief because the Court determined that the non-member states in *U.S. Steel* were not unfairly impacted. It has particular importance when assessing NPV's compact, however. A more reasonable evaluation shows that both the vertical and horizontal relationships among federal and state governments are impacted by NPV.

The federal government has at least one important interest at stake: It has a vested interest in protecting its constitutional amendment process.[23] If the NPV compact goes into effect, its proponents will have effectively changed the presidential election procedure described in the Constitution, without the bother of obtaining a constitutional amendment. Indeed, NPV proponents cite the relative ease of enacting the compact as a selling point. The compact could be implemented with the consent of as few as 11 states, whereas an amendment requires the ratification of 38 states. But supermajority requirements for certain actions provide important protections for Americans' freedom, and it is the prerogative of the federal government to protect the Constitution's amendment process.[24]

Moreover, NPV supporters may have already conceded that NPV's compact is not entirely about a state's discretion in allocating its electors. NPV claims its compact "would not 'encroach upon or interfere with'" federal power or supremacy "because there is simply no federal power—much less federal supremacy—in the area of awarding of electoral votes."[25] If that is so, then why was it necessary for California to seek federal approval for enactment of its legislation in late 2011? In November of that year, the state submitted a request to the Department of Justice, asking for preclearance for NPV, as required by the Voting Rights Act.[26] Such federal approval would not be needed if there was "simply no federal power—much less supremacy" at stake.

Non-compacting states have interests that are at least as important as the federal interests. First, NPV deprives these states of their opportunity, under the Constitution's amendment process, to participate in any decision made about changing the nation's presidential election system. They are also deprived of the protections provided by the supermajority requirements of the constitutional amendment process laid out in Article V. Second, the compact grants new authority for some states to control other states in certain situations: Specifically, if a member state changes its mind about joining the compact, other member states claim the ability to enforce compliance, thus compromising that state legislature's broad authority to determine the manner of elector allocation. Finally, the voting power of states relative to other states is changed. NPV is the first to bemoan the fact that "every vote is not equal" in the presidential election and that the weight of a voters' ballot depends on the state in which he lives. In equalizing the legal weight of votes,[27] NPV is by definition increasing the political power of some states and decreasing the political power of other states.[28]

NPV contends that non-compacting states are not affected and that every state is treated equally under its plan because all votes are counted and given equal weight—even those cast in non-participating states.[29] And, proponents add, the compacting states are merely doing something that they are entitled to do anyway.[30] The Court has held that "the State legislature's power to select the manner for appointing electors is plenary; it may, if it so chooses, select the electors itself."[31] A state's decision to sign on to the compact is thus not unconstitutional or problematic; it is simply an exercise of states' rights.

Yes, Article II of the Constitution is quite clear that "[e]ach State shall appoint, in such Manner as the Legislature thereof may direct, a Number of Electors . . . ."[32] State legislatures are given responsibility to decide the best manner of elector allocation for their states, and they are given great discretion in what method each legislature chooses. And if a state such as New Jersey feels so strongly about the wisdom of giving its 14 electors to the winner of the national popular vote, then perhaps it should vote to do so. Immediately. Alone. Without the protections afforded by NPV's interstate compact.

New Jersey won't take such a step, however. No state legislator wants to make such a leap unless he is guaranteed that a critical mass of legislators in other states will jump with him. Proponents want NPV in its entirety—complete and radical change to the presidential election system. They are not aiming for a simple change in elector allocation that impacts the voters of only one state. Indeed, no state legislator thinks that such a method of elector allocation in his state's best interest unless everyone else does it, too. NPV admits as much when it explains the need for its compact in *Every Vote Equal*:

> No single state would be likely to alone enact a law awarding its electoral votes to the nationwide winner. For one thing, such an action would give the voters of all the other states a voice in the selection of the state's own presidential electors, while not giving the state a voice in the selection of presidential electors in other states and would not alone guarantee achievement of the goal of nationwide popular election of the President.[33]

NPV is not an exercise of states' rights that serves the voters of a particular state. It is an abuse of state discretion that attempts to subvert the constitutional amendment process. And, because a handful of states can put the compact into force even if the rest of the states disagree, NPV could actively deprive the majority of states of their constitutionally protected right to participate in any discussion about such a radical change to the nation's presidential election system.

Finally, NPV's compact leads to serious, unanswered constitutional questions: Is this power of state legislators *completely* unrestricted?[34] Can a state allocate its electors in such a way that it not only appoints electors for the state, but it also changes the method by which the nation elects Presidents? Can one state let the citizens of other states (or any other entity) determine the identity of its electors? If so, then Rhode Island could decide to allocate its electors to the winner of the Vermont election. Or New York could give the United Nations a say in the allocation of its electors. Arguably, such decisions are not permissible because the Constitution presupposes that the electors belong to each individual state and the state may not delegate this responsibility outside of state borders.[35] Such an argument gives state legislatures great discretion in allocating their electors, but not completely unfettered discretion.

NPV's best counter-argument is that none of these scenarios ever occurred to the Founders, and they thus did not place sufficient restrictions on the legislature's discretion. Members of the founding generation were distrustful of other states and the national government, and they almost certainly could not conceive that future state legislators would so thoughtlessly betray their own states' interests. In this scenario, NPV is the opposite of what the Founders wanted, but failure of imagination prevented the Founders from explicitly prohibiting this particular manner of allocating electors.[36]

But even if NPV has found a loophole and proves that states could take such action alone, Article I, Section 10 forbids them from doing so jointly unless they first submit their compact to Congress. If ever a compact encroached on federal and state sovereignty, this is it.

Violation of the Equal Protection Clause

NPV's use of an interstate compact is just the tip of the iceberg. Its end run around the constitutional amendment process is likely to result in court challenges on a variety of fronts, including claims that voters are being treated unequally and thus are being disenfranchised.[37]

The previous chapter discussed the logistical ramifications of conducting one national presidential election in reliance on 51 different sets of local election codes. Today, the variances in these election processes are irrelevant. A voter in Oklahoma, for instance, participates in elections that determine the identities of Oklahoma's electors. A vote cast in Oklahoma does not impact the identities of electors in other states. NPV would change this. Suddenly, a vote cast in Oklahoma could change the identity of an elector in Minnesota. Oklahoma and Minnesotan voters would be in the same election pool, despite the fact that they are voting under different sets of laws. Some voters could be disenfranchised by the inequities created.

The 14th Amendment provides: "No State shall . . . deny to any person within its jurisdiction the equal protection of the laws."[38] In 2000, the nation watched as this clause—often referred to as the Equal Protection Clause—became a point of contention for lawyers in the George W. Bush and Al Gore camps. Lawyers haggled over small differences in how hanging chads were counted in various Florida counties and argued about whether an Equal Protection violation had resulted. The issue boiled down to a simple question: If a vote is counted one way in one county and another way in a second county, are voters being treated fairly and equally?

The Supreme Court summarized the dispute:

> The right to vote is protected in more than the initial allocation of the franchise. Equal protection applies as well to the manner of its exercise. Having once granted the right to vote on equal terms, the State may not, by later arbitrary and disparate treatment, value one person's vote over that of another. . . .
>
> . . . The question before us, however, is whether the recount procedures the Florida Supreme Court has adopted are consistent with its obligation to avoid arbitrary and disparate treatment of the members of its electorate.[39]

Ultimately, the Court put a stop to the recount in Florida, determining that the "recount cannot be conducted in compliance with the requirements of equal protection and due process without substantial additional work."[40]

However difficult these legal challenges may have been, they would pale in comparison to the challenges that could arise if NPV's plan were enacted. NPV claims that its change to a direct election system is needed in order to guarantee "Every Vote Equal." Oddly, its proposal guarantees the exact opposite.[41] It would cram voters from across the country into one election pool, despite the fact that different election laws apply to different voters. *Voters would not be more equal. They would be more unequal.* Lawsuits claiming Equal Protection problems would certainly follow.

Consider the issue of early voting.[42] Voters in Alaska have one set of laws regarding early voting. Other states might have different provisions regarding when early voting starts, how long it lasts, or who may early vote and how they may early vote. These differences in laws do not matter when Alaskans are participating in their own election only with other Alaskans—all voters are treated equitably with other members of the same election pool. However, if NPV throws Alaskans into another, national electorate, then the differences in laws begin to create many inequities. Some voters in this election pool, for instance, may have more time to vote than the Alaskan voters. Or maybe others have an easier time registering to early vote. Alaskans are not treated equitably with other members of the national election pool if they must abide by a more restrictive— or even a less restrictive!—set of election laws.

A multitude of differences among states' election codes would magnify this problem still more: States differ in whether they allow felons to vote. They vary in what they require before a candidate may qualify for the ballot. They have different triggers for recounts. They may have various methods for handling provisional ballots. Each and every one of these differences is a lawsuit waiting to happen if NPV's compact goes into effect. Indeed, more problems could arise as courts struggle to figure out *which* court has jurisdiction. Can a voter in Alaska sue in an Alaskan state or federal court if he believes his rights are being violated in Tennessee?[43]

NPV defends itself by noting that the Equal Protection Clause of the 14th Amendment is a restriction on states *only* to the degree that a voter lives "within its jurisdiction."[44] In other words, a state like Massachusetts is legally required to make sure that its voters are treated equally with other Massachusetts voters. But if Massachusetts wants to implement laws that will cause its voters to be treated unequally as compared to New Jersey voters—even if it does so knowingly or deliberately—then such action is constitutionally permissible because New Jersey is not "within its jurisdiction."

NPV is too quick to dismiss the possibility of Equal Protection problems. Its compact creates an electoral situation that has never existed in America. No other election could possibly require Massachusetts and New Jersey voters to both participate in the same pool of voters. Every other election is conducted only among the voters of one state—a New Jersey voter will never vote for a Massachusetts Senator, Governor, or Mayor. Thus, a court has never addressed the inequities that might exist if a voter in Massachusetts is being disenfranchised by New Jersey's laws.[45]

When the matter comes before a court, the question will be whether states can combine to do something that they could not do on their own. Acting alone on a matter that affects only its own voters, a state cannot, by "arbitrary and disparate treatment, value one person's vote over that of another."[46] Does NPV's compact give states an excuse to do in combination what they could not do alone? NPV hopes to have its cake and eat it, too. It strives to use out-of-state voters for one purpose (vote tabulation) and disavow them for another purpose (Equal Protection). A court may see through the ruse.[47]

NPV's position is an odd one for an organization that claims its goal is to make "every vote equal." NPV acknowledges that voters will be treated unequally but hopes to get off on a technicality. It looks for one loophole in the law to get around the constitutional amendment process, and it looks for another loophole to get around Equal Protection requirements. Even if NPV manages to satisfy these legal requirements, such elaborate maneuvering suggests that their idea is a terrible one, as a matter of public policy.

"Passing Muster" Under Articles IV and V

NPV relies on the "plenary" power of state legislatures to select the manner in which its state will appoint electors.[48] In doing so, it correctly cites Court statements that the "appointment and mode of appointment of electors belong exclusively to the states under the Constitution of the United States"[49] and that each state has "absolute power to appoint electors in such manner as it may see fit, without any interference or control on the part of the Federal Government."[50] However, NPV forgets that just because the Constitution grants a broad power, it does not necessarily follow that this power is *limitless*. Even NPV acknowledges that states may not flagrantly violate the Constitution by appointing electors in a manner that discriminates based on race, color, or previous condition of servitude.[51]

A reasonable argument can be made that the states' power, while sweeping, is not completely without limit. Justice Clarence Thomas once alluded to these potential limits as he described the states' power to determine a method of allocating electors: "States may establish qualifications for their delegates to the electoral college," he noted, "as long as those qualifications pass muster under other constitutional provisions."[52]

Does NPV "pass muster" under Article IV of the Constitution, which "guarantee[s] to every State in this Union a Republican Form of Government"?[53] Does it "pass muster" under Article V, which does not allow constitutional provisions to be altered without approval by "the Legislatures of three fourths of the several States, or by Conventions in three fourths thereof"?[54] To the latter question, NPV argues "yes" because its proposal does not technically alter the text of Article II and the 12th Amendment. Instead, it asks state legislatures to use the text in a unique way. As discussed above, the argument is not completely without merit, but it is at best a loophole—a scenario completely unanticipated (and thus not explicitly prohibited) by the Founders. Moreover, such an assessment of NPV seems a bit disingenuous. As CATO scholar John Samples has observed: "NPV offers a way to institute a means of electing the president that was rejected by the Framers of the Constitution. It does so while circumventing the Constitution's amendment procedures."[55] If NPV is enacted, a court will almost certainly be asked to decide if it unconstitutionally alters America's presidential election process without first obtaining approval from the requisite number of states.

The Court has previously struck down statutes that were said to upset the compromises struck and the delicate balances achieved during the Constitutional Convention: It struck down the federal Line Item Veto Act,[56] and it struck down a state's attempt to impose term limits on its own senators and congressmen.[57] Justice Stevens's conclusion in the latter seems especially appropriate in the context of NPV; he noted that a state provision "with the avowed purpose and obvious effect of evading the requirements of the Qualifications Clauses . . . cannot stand. To argue otherwise is to suggest that the Framers spent significant time and energy in debating and crafting Clauses that could be easily evaded."[58] Stevens's words repeated a concern expressed by the Court in a 1992 case: "A departure from the Constitution's plan . . . cannot be ratified by the 'consent' of state officials."[59]

These Court statements echo the concerns of Electoral College supporters who worry that NPV is simply an "end run" around the constitutional amendment process. The Founders spent months debating the appropriate presidential election process for the new American nation. NPV asserts that a handful of states can now "easily evade" the compromises and provisions that resulted from that debate, but its claims fall flat. The NPV compact is more than a creative way to use the Electoral College. It turns the current presidential election system on its head. The Court may treat it as such. The Constitution was the product of much give and take among the delegates. It is dangerous to forget that it would never have been ratified, at least by the small states, but for these compromises.

The Definition of "Legislature"

More lawsuits could be filed over the precise meaning of the word "Legislature" in Article II. NPV relies heavily on this clause, which provides: "Each State shall appoint, in such Manner as the Legislature thereof may direct, a Number of Electors . . . ."[60] The meaning of "Legislature" is important. It could influence if and when NPV goes into effect because of its bearing on two questions: First, must a state legislature itself approve the NPV plan or can it be adopted by citizen initiative? Second, if a governor vetoes the plan, is the veto legally binding? If "Legislature" refers specifically to the lawmaking body and not to a state's lawmaking process, then the answer to both of these questions is "no."

Litigation on this matter is already a possibility. Several state governors have vetoed NPV (although some of these vetoes have been overturned by subsequent events).[61] In addition, at least two states have considered a change to their method of elector allocation via initiative, rather than by legislative enactment.[62] Conceivably, voters in more states could attempt to implement NPV by citizen referendum or initiative in the future.

The Supreme Court has never definitively addressed the Article II use of the word "Legislature," and legal scholars remain split on how it should be interpreted. If the plain meaning of the text is used, then it should be read as a reference to the lawmaking body, not the lawmaking process. Article II distinguishes between the responsibility of the state (to "appoint") and the legislature (to "direct"). Why delineate separate responsibilities if the general state lawmaking process could regulate the entire process of appointing electors? The closest the Court has come to expressing an opinion on this subject was during the *Bush v. Gore* litigation. Justices William Rehnquist, Antonin Scalia, and Clarence Thomas issued a non-binding opinion that seemed to lean toward a plain reading of the word "Legislature" in Article II. They determined that the judiciary could not trump the "constitutionally prescribed role of state *legislatures*" in Article II.[63] The other six Justices either rejected the statement or expressed no opinion on the matter.[64] The Court has addressed the definition of "Legislature" in other contexts, but with mixed results.[65]

NPV makes some reasonable historical arguments for accepting the broader definition of "Legislature." *Every Vote Equal* notes that two states had gubernatorial vetoes at the time the Constitution was adopted. During early presidential elections, both states considered the elector appointment issue just as they would have any other piece of legislation, including submitting their bills for gubernatorial action.[66] Such action indicates that these two state legislatures understood the word "Legislature" to mean "lawmaking process."[67] On the other hand, it is just as possible that they submitted the bills to the governors out of habit.[68]

It would be ironic if NPV's point ends up carrying the day, requiring that the Article II use of "Legislature" be defined as "lawmaking process." NPV's objective in making such arguments was to ensure that its plan could be enacted through initiative. But winning that argument may also necessitate acceptance of at least one gubernatorial veto in Rhode Island;[69] it may mean accepting vetoes in other states in the future. NPV would lose votes that could otherwise have been used to help implement its interstate compact.

⚜ ⚜ ⚜

Several aspects of the NPV proposal will inevitably be the subject of litigation if a significant number of states approve the NPV compact. Any one of these questions requires serious thought and discussion—and probably lengthy litigation. Unfortunately, the list of issues discussed in this chapter is by no means exhaustive. Creative lawyers are likely to come up with even more potential questions.[70] Matters could also get interesting if one state were to try and defend itself against the NPV compact, as discussed in Chapter Thirteen.

The Article V constitutional amendment process exists for important reasons. American liberty is protected when that process is respected. The NPV debate, which is occurring in only a handful of states, is not healthy for the country. Those who wish to eliminate the Electoral College would serve their country better if they instead introduced a constitutional amendment to that effect. The national discussion and education that would ensue would be healthy for this country.

Part Five

The Electoral
College in Action

Chapter Fifteen

Successful Results
Over the Years

Opponents of the Electoral College seem to live in constant fear that the next election will be the one that produces a constitutional crisis of astronomical proportions. Apparently, 200 years of a smoothly functioning presidential election system are insufficient to convince these critics that the country is not constantly on the edge of an election "mistake" or disaster. Yes, electoral issues occasionally occur (as in 2000 or 1876), but none of these elections have degenerated into the crisis that opponents fear. Instead, any issues tend to be relatively short-lived, at least in part because the Electoral College isolates problems to one or a handful of states and gives the country an easily identifiable set of issues to resolve.

Detractors of the current system refuse to acknowledge the relative ease with which American presidential elections have been conducted. Instead, they point in horror to the potential crises that are "sure" to come in a future presidential election year. For instance, they cite the fact that, technically speaking, a candidate could win the 11 largest states, each by a mere plurality, and thus be elected—despite the fact that he was not the preferred candidate of more than 75 percent of the states. Of course, such a situation is unlikely to occur. The 11 most populous states are scattered across different regions of the country. The political concerns expressed by the voters in these states are fairly diverse. A candidate could not obtain the votes of each of these 11 states without first generating some degree of cross-regional and cross-ideological appeal. It is hard to imagine liberal, Democratic California and conservative, Republican Texas voting for the same candidate while the majority of the states vote for someone else.

Electoral College opponents also point out, in dismay, the multiple elections in which a swing of "only" X thousand votes in State A could have caused the election of a "popular vote loser President." It seems the country has been on the brink of disaster multiple times, and nothing but good luck has kept the country running for so long. These claims, however, are mere manipulation of statistical data and do not take other, practical, factors into consideration.

America's election systems have operated smoothly for more than 200 years because the Electoral College accomplishes its intended purposes. America's presidential election process preserves federalism, prevents chaos, grants definitive electoral outcomes, and prevents tyrannical or unreasonable rule. A review of the dynamics in four elections—two resulting in Presidents who did not win the popular vote and two resulting in "electoral landslide winners"—will show that the Electoral College is a well-designed machine serving its purpose well, election after election.

Smooth Operations, Election After Election

In theory, the votes of the 11 largest states, alone, can deliver an election to a presidential candidate—their electoral votes, taken together, currently constitute a bare majority of the Electoral College.[1] Critics of the current presidential election process find this prospect horrifying. They shudder at the thought of an election decided by 11 states while the other 39 are ignored. Well, at least, they shudder at the thought of a decision made by 11 states under the Electoral College system. If the 11 states want to unilaterally redirect the country toward direct election (via the National Popular

Vote plan, as discussed in Part Four), some critics apparently have no problem with *that* decision made on behalf of the other 39 states.[2]

An evaluation of the historical evidence provides a strong indication that the one-sided outcomes pictured by Electoral College opponents are more theoretical than real. The 11 most populous states are composed of voters from various regions of the country. These voters have diverse interests, and they cast their ballots for a wide range of reasons. If a presidential candidate managed to earn the support of these 11 quite different states, then he undoubtedly managed to obtain the support of many other states in the Union as well.

The last candidate to win all 11 of these states was Ronald Reagan. In 1984, Reagan won every state except Walter Mondale's home state of Minnesota. (He also lost the District of Columbia.) Reagan achieved the support of these 11 states because he successfully built a national coalition, a goal that the Electoral College seeks to encourage. A Senate minority report effectively made a similar point in 1970:

> A commonly heard indictment of the electoral college . . . is that the 11 largest States (plus another small State or the District of Columbia) would suffice to carry a candidate into office. The conclusion one is supposed to draw from this argument is that the 11 largest States are therefore in a position to dictate to the other 39. But what those who use this essentially emotional argument always conveniently forget to add is that the very compromises which enable a candidate to carry the 11 largest States also enable him to carry many others as well. And that is precisely why no candidate has ever won with anything like 11 States. In point of fact, only one President in this century (John F. Kennedy) was ever elected with less than a *majority* of the States supporting him. That exception excluded, no one in this century has ever won with less than 29 States, and the average number carried by the winner has been nearly 37.[3]

Since the time of that Senate report, only two other Presidents have won with less than 29 states: Jimmy Carter won the presidency with the support of 23 states and the District of Columbia in the close election of 1976; Barack Obama was elected with the support of 28 states, D.C., and one vote from Nebraska.[4] Moreover, since 1970, the average number of states carried by the winning candidate has remained high: nearly 36. The strength of this dynamic caused some Democrats to criticize John Kerry in the wake of his failed 2004 presidential campaign: As one commentator explained, his "'18-state strategy' aimed at winning the Electoral College rather than a '50 state strategy' aimed at winning the allegiance of the American people" was doomed to failure.[5]

The next argument of Electoral College detractors concerns another "nightmare" scenario, which is also unlikely to occur. They comment on the many elections that have "nearly" ended in the election of a President who lost the popular vote.[6] (An event that would supposedly lead to rioting in the streets.) It would appear that the country has come close to calamity repeatedly, and only the best of luck has kept the country operating smoothly year after year.

Putting aside the fact that the "perfect storm" hit in 2000 without causing any discernible damage, one could find examples of several "near misses" in the last century. The election of 1916 between Charles Evans Hughes and Woodrow Wilson is often cited as one example of an election nearly gone awry. Hughes would have won if about 2,000 more votes in California had gone his way. Had he gained these extra votes, a Hughes victory would have occurred despite the fact that Wilson led in the popular vote by more than 500,000 votes.[7] In 1948, Thomas Dewey could have won the election with a shift of less than 30,000 votes across three states, despite the fact that Harry Truman received 2.1 million more votes than Dewey nationwide.[8] Jimmy Carter would have been denied victory in 1976 if Gerald Ford had obtained just 9,300 more votes in two states, although Carter received nearly 1.7 million more votes overall.[9] And, more recently, John Kerry could have won the 2004 election if 59,300 people in Ohio had voted for him instead of George W. Bush, despite the fact that Bush led the national tally by more than 3 million votes.[10]

As a mathematical matter, these observations of Electoral College critics may be true. However, in most of these examples, a candidate could not have gained the extra votes he needed in one state without losing more votes in another state or states. Judith Best has completed an analysis of several of these so-called electoral disasters.[11] In discussing each of these elections, she identifies the policy issue that would have, in all likelihood, swung extra votes in one state, obtaining an Electoral College victory for one candidate despite his loss of the popular vote. In each instance, she notes, the "[shift-in-votes argument] fails because it abstracts from political realities."[12]

For example, the election of 1844 is often cited by Electoral College opponents as a near-electoral disaster.[13] In that election, a shift of 2,555 votes in New York would have swung the election in Henry Clay's favor from James Polk. As a purely theoretical matter, this consequence appears accurate. In the real election, obtaining those votes was not quite so easy. Clay might have been able to win New York, but he likely would have had to change his position on the annexation of Texas. Modifying his position on this issue to win New York would probably have caused him to lose Tennessee, a state that approved of his position on annexation. Clay's margin of victory in Tennessee was only 113 votes. Gaining New York but losing Tennessee would still have led to an election loss for Clay.

In sum, the scenarios forecast by Electoral College opponents are possible as a purely abstract matter, but in reality, they are unlikely to occur. Although critics correctly note that, as a mathematical matter, the outcome of this or that election could easily have swung in a different direction, they fail to take into account the practical issues and concerns that would realistically have affected the actual campaigns.

Historical results support an assessment of the Electoral College as a successful election device. The American election system encourages presidential candidates to seek national support and build cross-regional coalitions. Presidents who have lost the popular vote are not elected very often, but when they are, the situation usually comes about because the presidential candidate who won the popular vote simply did not work hard enough to amass the support of individuals across state boundaries. Instead, that presidential candidate spent too much time focusing on one region or one special interest group.[14] These candidates, despite winning the popular vote, did not deserve to win the presidency. The President should be an American President; he should not be a regional one.

Presidents Who Lost the Popular Vote

Some disagreement exists regarding how many American Presidents can be fairly characterized as candidates who were elected with an Electoral College win, but a popular vote loss. Some academics argue that the country has had as many as four such Presidents: John Quincy Adams (1824), Rutherford B. Hayes (1876), Benjamin Harrison (1888), and George W. Bush (2000).[15] None of these men garnered either a majority or a plurality of the recorded individual popular vote before being inaugurated. The elections of 1824 and 1876, however, cannot accurately be described as elections in which the clear winner of the popular vote lost the presidency.[16]

In 1824, Andrew Jackson won a plurality of both the popular and the Electoral College votes.[17] Because he did not win a majority of electoral votes, the election was thrown into the House contingent election, where he lost to John Quincy Adams. Jackson spent the next four years claiming that he should have won the election because he won the popular vote. His arguments scored points with the American people, who elected him to the presidency over Adams in 1828.

Jackson's claims, however, were not entirely accurate. He won a plurality of the *recorded* popular vote in 1824, but many individual votes were never recorded.[18] At the time, many states' legislatures were still selecting electors on behalf of citizens.[19] There is no way to know what the popular vote would have been in 1824 if all states had then relied upon a popular vote as their method of elector selection. Adams may or may not have been what Electoral College critics would call a "runner-up" President; it is impossible to know for sure. Either way, the election of 1824 is not representative of today's electoral system, which relies upon popular votes in all the states and a winner-take-all system of appointing electors.

The next election that allegedly produced a President who lost the popular vote is the election of 1876.[20] In that election, Rutherford B. Hayes received approximately 250,000 fewer popular votes than did his opponent, Samuel J. Tilden. The general election was followed by weeks of doubt as 20 electoral votes in Florida, Louisiana, Oregon, and South Carolina were disputed. Three of the states submitted votes from multiple slates of electors; one electoral vote in Oregon was disputed. Hayes needed all 20 of these contested electoral votes to obtain a majority of 185 electoral votes and the presidency; Tilden needed only one.

The Republican-controlled Senate and the Democrat-controlled House had difficulty determining which slates of electors to accept. They eventually agreed to appoint an Electoral Commission to resolve the challenges. The Commission was composed of 15 individuals: seven Republicans, seven Democrats, and one independent Supreme Court Justice. Unexpectedly, the independent Justice, David Davis, was elected to the Senate by the Illinois state legislature. After his election, he declined to serve on the Commission, and he was replaced by Justice Joseph Bradley, a Republican appointee. Perhaps predictably, the Republican-controlled Commission decided all 20 disputed electoral votes in favor of Hayes, throwing the election to him. A Democratic filibuster nearly sidetracked congressional acceptance of the Commission's findings, but eventually Congress declared Hayes the winner of the presidential election.[21]

The Hayes victory in 1876 cannot accurately be characterized as a definitive popular vote loss for Hayes. Elections in the South were not free and blacks were often not allowed to vote. Fraud and dishonesty pervaded the election as the northern and southern portions of the country struggled to reunite after the Civil War. At least one study has concluded that a "fair and free election" would have resulted in a popular vote victory for Hayes.[22] Under such circumstances, many more ballots would likely have been cast for Hayes in states such as Mississippi, Alabama, and North Carolina.

Only two elections can be properly characterized as ones in which a President lost the popular vote but won the electoral vote: the election of Benjamin Harrison in 1888 and the election of George W. Bush in 2000. These elections, however, are not causes for alarm. Instead, they demonstrate that the Electoral College is working as intended. In each case, the victor was able to succeed only because his opponent did not build the national coalition that is required by the Electoral College. In each case, smaller states were protected from their larger neighbors. In each case, the presidential election system functioned effectively to give the country a President with broad-based support. Perhaps most importantly, in each case the Electoral College winner was accepted by the country as a legitimate President—despite dire predictions that a crisis would ensue.

The elections of Harrison and Bush have been unfairly condemned. Although neither of these men garnered popular vote pluralities, their elections illustrate successful results of the Electoral College. Indeed, the most likely result of these elections will be to encourage future presidential candidates to remember small states as well as large states. Candidates will be reminded of the need to understand all the nation's regions, not just one or two of them.

Electoral Landslide Winners

If the Harrison and Bush elections demonstrate the successes encouraged by the Electoral College, then those elections resulting in electoral landslides do as well. As explained in the next chapter, Cleveland (1888) and Gore (2000) lost their bids for the presidency because they were less successful at building national coalitions than their opponents. The two candidates who won by the biggest electoral landslides exemplify the reverse situation. These two candidates were perhaps more successful than any other men in the country's history at generating nationwide support, even across lines that normally divide the electorate.

The two Presidents winning by the greatest electoral landslides were Franklin Delano Roosevelt and Ronald Reagan. (Richard Nixon comes in a close third. He defeated George McGovern by an electoral vote of 520 to 17 in the election of 1972. This was, of course, before Americans knew of Nixon's involvement in Watergate.)[23] In 1936, Roosevelt lost two states, beating his opponent Alfred M. Landon by a vote of 523 to 8. Reagan defeated Walter Mondale in 1984 by a similar margin of victory: 525 to 13. Reagan won every state except Mondale's home state of Minnesota and the District of Columbia.

FDR and Reagan won by huge margins because they attained the objectives encouraged by the Electoral College. These two men established support across the country, and they won their electoral victories easily because voters across regions and partisan lines generally felt that FDR and Reagan understood them and would work to represent their interests. Whether by design or by accident, these candidates managed to embody exactly the type of President that the Electoral College is meant to select. The one characteristic that these two men shared, perhaps better than any modern-day President, was their ability to win the confidence of Americans.

Not coincidentally, these two men were in the news, together, a great deal during June 2004, when Reagan passed away after a long battle with Alzheimer's. Repeatedly, reporters remarked upon the two Presidents who reflected the values of Americans throughout the 1900s: Roosevelt during the first half of the century, and Reagan during the last half of the century. Following Reagan's death, one newspaper described him as "perhaps the most seminal figure in 20th century American politics."[24] It concluded that "only FDR could also be considered" for the title.[25] The same day, historian Richard Norton Smith observed: "FDR shattered the political consensus that he found in place in 1933, and he left behind a new consensus and an army of followers who for 50 years really defined American politics. And Ronald Reagan really followed in his footsteps."[26]

Americans from all over the country flooded to California and the Capitol, where Reagan's body lay in state during the week following his death. The outpouring of affection confirmed the degree to which Reagan had won the hearts of voters across state lines during his time in public life. As the first week of the month-long remembrance beat on, former Reagan speechwriter Peggy Noonan wrote for the *Wall Street Journal*:

> By Friday it was no longer a question, as it had been for years, whether he was one of our top 10 presidents. It was a question only whether he was in the very top five or six—up there with Lincoln and Washington. An agreement had been reached: the 20th century came down to FDR and RWR.[27]

These two Presidents, who won by the largest electoral vote margins in U.S. history, exemplify the purpose of the Electoral College system. Each man campaigned for the support of voters across state lines, and each successfully earned the support not merely of a numeric majority, but also a federal majority. These election outcomes should remind candidates that the greatest success comes when they learn about the diverse needs and interests of voters across the nation. Electoral landslides occur when voters feel that one candidate represents *Americans*, not simply Republicans or Democrats.

❊❊❊

More than an accident of history has kept America's election systems operating smoothly for two centuries. The Founding Fathers created a stable, well-planned and carefully designed system—and it works. Past elections, even the elections of Presidents who lost the popular vote, are testaments to the ingenuity of the Founding Fathers. Those Presidents who won the electoral vote by landslide victories understood perhaps better than many what the Founders were trying to accomplish as they designed a presidential-election process.

In each instance, the Electoral College brought about the intended result, preserved federalism, prevented chaos and uncertainty, or kept an unreasonable or regional majority from trampling the few. The nation's presidential-election system has served America well for more than two centuries. An evaluation of the historical results of the nations' elections confirms that the Electoral College should be preserved at all costs.

Chapter Sixteen

Harrison & Bush:
Narrow Victories

Two American Presidents have been elected to the Oval Office despite losing the nationwide individual popular vote: Benjamin Harrison and George W. Bush. Although these election victories are criticized by some as instances in which the presidential election process failed the American people, they are precisely the opposite. Each election highlights the unique dynamics of the Electoral College, which successfully encourages candidates to attain federal, rather than individual, majorities.

Benjamin Harrison

In the aftermath of the Civil War and Reconstruction, elections were intensely regional. As a general rule, Republicans had an advantage in the northern and western regions with their 248 electoral votes, while Democrats were generally preferred in the southern region with its 153 electoral votes.[1] At the time, 201 electoral votes were needed for victory. To win an election, then, Democrats needed to pick up at least 48 electoral votes outside the South.

The regional nature of these elections was obviously harmful to the country. Arguably, the Republican advantage during these years had less to do with building national coalitions, and more to do with the fact that Republicans were favored in two regions, while Democrats were favored in only one. Without the Electoral College, however, the country would likely have remained divided along these regional lines for much longer than it did. The incentives inherent in the presidential election process forced candidates to reach out to voters beyond their home base. Democrats could never win without obtaining votes outside the South. Republicans were perhaps less motivated than Democrats to reach out to southern voters; however, their margin of victory when relying upon northern and western voters, alone, was always dangerously narrow.

In 1884, Democrat Grover Cleveland successfully reached out to non-southern regions, and he won the presidency. In the following election, he gained additional support among southern voters, but he lost the votes of many independents in other regions who had stood behind him in the 1884 election. This lost support undermined his re-election bid against Republican Benjamin Harrison. The final election results in 1888 revealed a hefty margin for Harrison in the Electoral College: 233 to 168. Harrison was elected to the presidency, despite the fact that Cleveland had won the popular vote by 0.8 percent.[2]

Cleveland's widest margins of victory were focused in six southern states: Alabama, Georgia, Louisiana, Mississippi, South Carolina, and Texas. In these six states, Cleveland won 72.2 percent of the votes cast for both men with a popular vote tally of 690,404 Cleveland votes to Harrison's 266,158.[3] Harrison's support, by contrast, was less intense but spread across the northern and western portions of the country. His widest margins of victory appeared in multiple regions: Colorado, Kansas, Maine, Minnesota, Nevada, and Vermont gave him 502,261 votes, compared to Cleveland's 317,223 votes. Harrison's vote totals in these six states constituted 61.3 percent of the votes cast for both men.

Overall, Harrison won 20 states across the northern and western regions, while Cleveland's wins were focused in the South. Harrison's win made him the first American President to ascend to the presidency with an undisputed popular vote loss. The victory resulted, in large part, from the manner in which Cleveland alienated voters outside the southern parts of the country during his first term.

Cleveland's initial view of his role as President led to early problems with Congress.[4] Cleveland believed that the legislative and executive powers should be strictly separated. As a result, he began his term by restricting his engagements with Congress. He would make recommendations on issues, but would then simply veto or sign any bills that resulted without making significant efforts to ensure that bills were fashioned in line with his suggestions. His limited involvement caused him to lose influence among members of his party.

The embattled President eventually sought to regain some control by taking a more active stand during the crafting of legislation, but it remained an uphill battle throughout his first term. One Democratic Congressman observed at the time that "[a] President of the United States ought to have great influence with his party, but Mr. Cleveland deliberately threw his away, and he can't now pick it up again."[5] Cleveland's reserve and lost clout among Democrats caused him to miss opportunities to participate in the creation of bills, particularly a tariff bill that would later cause problems for him during his re-election campaign.

Cleveland was further plagued by his inability to curb abuse of the pension system following the Civil War. Congress was generally amenable to requests by Union veterans for pension funds, even when their requests were weak or fraudulent. Cleveland, however, repeatedly vetoed these pension requests, eventually issuing a record number of vetoes during his first term (414).[6] His firm stance earned him the respect of some who were weary of the fraud and waste, but it also increased his unpopularity with Union veterans and others who could not resist the appeal of the "bloody shirt."[7]

Cleveland stumbled again in 1887, committing two political gaffes that caused him to slip even further in the esteem of many northerners and Union veterans. Cleveland had agreed to attend the national encampment of the Grand Army of the Republic (GAR) in St. Louis. He saw the meeting as an opportunity to shake hands with voters and suggested to GAR that his reception there be public, rather than private. Many veterans viewed the request as an inappropriate politicization of their convention, and the *National Tribune* denounced the President's request stating, "Does anyone want the National Encampment running in conjunction with a grand political mass meeting?"[8]

Yet matters continued to worsen. At about the same time as the GAR convention controversy, Cleveland endorsed a proposal to return all Confederate flags captured during the war to their home states. Members of GAR were horrified at the prospect of Confederate flags returned to their southern owners, and they criticized Cleveland harshly for his decision. In the end, Cleveland withdrew his acceptance of the invitation to appear at the GAR encampment, and he stopped the return of Confederate flags to southern states. But the damage was done. The entire series of events contributed to Cleveland's unpopularity among many veterans, particularly those that did not reside in the South.

A last problem that confronted Cleveland during his term eventually led him to propose a tariff reform measure that proved unpopular among the northern states. While Cleveland was in office, the surplus in the government's treasury grew at a rapid clip, to Cleveland's great consternation. At the beginning of his term, the surplus was $17 million. By the end of his term, the surplus had grown to $140 million.[9]

A surplus would doubtless be a welcome asset to many modern Americans, but in the late 1800s, the surplus was a matter of concern. After much investigation, Cleveland determined that tariff reduction was the best method of reducing surpluses. He devoted his entire 1887 annual address to the subject, against the advice of his advisors, who worried that he would alienate the New York vote. His speech was the first annual address to focus exclusively on one subject, and it forced Democrats in the Congress to address the issue.

Unfortunately, the legislation eventually passed by the Democratic House was a watered-down bill that favored the Democratic South over the northern states. True tariff reform was never enacted during Cleveland's term, and many Americans most likely failed to understand the arguments behind his proposal. They thought that he was currying favor with the South, as the Democratic bill appeared to do.

The matter troubled Cleveland, and he attempted a retreat from the issue later in his campaign. He worked to distance himself from discussions of the subject at the Democratic Party Convention, and he appointed anti-tariff reform men to conspicuous positions in his campaign. Yet he remained convinced that he was on the right side of the issue. "My friends," he said, "told me that it would hurt the party; that without it, I was sure to be re-elected . . . . I did not wish to be re-elected without having the people understand just where I stood on the tariff question and then spring the question on them after my re-election."[10] He paused, "Perhaps I made a mistake from the party standpoint; but damn it, it was right. I have at least that satisfaction."[11]

Matters were further complicated for Cleveland when Harrison took advantage of the tariff issue, bringing it up repeatedly even as Cleveland sought an honorable retreat. Harrison's campaign labeled free trade an evil, claiming that it did more to help foreign interests than to help Americans. Those who supported tariffs, then, were pro-American. Those who opposed tariffs were not. "The policy of the Democratic party," Harrison declared in an October 25 speech, "means a vast and sudden increase of importations. Is there a man here so dull as not to know that this means diminished work in our American shops?"[12]

As borne out by history, Cleveland was on the right side of the tariff matter. Unfortunately for him, Harrison grabbed the issue, framing it in a way that caused voters to perceive Cleveland as a President who represented only the South. The proposal for tariff reduction served primarily to antagonize those who were already upset regarding Cleveland's pension vetoes and his proposal to return the Confederate battle standards to southern states. The issue added to veterans' antipathy toward Cleveland, who did not serve in the Civil War and who impoliticly went fishing on Memorial Day, causing many to feel that he did not respect veterans. Cleveland led a lackluster and unenergetic campaign and was never able to regain the tariff issue from the Republicans. He failed to show voters that tariff reform could help the entire nation and that the benefits need not be limited to a handful of southern states.

Harrison's campaign, by contrast, was energetic, well-organized, and monitored the sentiments of voters across the states. Harrison gave more than 80 speeches to nearly 300,000 people in 16 weeks—quite an unusual feat in the late 1800s.[13] During the post-war years, many found it easy to support Harrison, a Civil War veteran who had served with distinction in the Union army. Moreover, those in charge of Harrison's campaign understood and capitalized on the increasingly popular nature of the presidential campaign, and they worked hard to build Harrison's image as an everyday American. The Republican Party even went so far as to solicit a book on Harrison's life from General Lew Wallace. Emblazoned on the book's cover was the apt title: *Life of Ben Harrison by the Author of Ben Hur.*[14] His tactics worked well among a populace that was still enamored of the concept of the "log cabin." His supporters often gloated that, even if Harrison wasn't *born* in a log cabin, at least he was *educated* in a log schoolhouse.[15] Harrison's strategy successfully prevailed over Cleveland, who left to others much of the task of campaigning and spent a large portion of the campaign season in isolation.

Cleveland's proposals may have been good for the country as a whole, but he did not present them in a manner that enabled him to obtain strong cross-country support. Instead, his campaign in 1888 represents the type of campaign that should lose under the system devised by the Founders. If Cleveland had won, then six southern states voting on (what was at least perceived as) a regional matter would essentially have out-voted the northern and western portions of the country combined. A candidate would have won an election, not by tailoring and communicating a message with national appeal, but by amassing landslide victories in a few key states.

The Electoral College in this instance effectively sent a message to future presidential candidates: Do not ignore the interests of the many by catering to the few. Cleveland himself successfully learned this lesson and returned to win election to a second term in 1892.

George W. Bush

The 2000 election made George W. Bush the first President since Benjamin Harrison to win the presidency without also winning the popular vote. Bush lost the popular vote by a fairly close margin: only 540,520 votes nationwide, although more than 100 million votes, total, were cast for the two major party candidates. The close election results should not have been surprising. They followed months of polling that showed the two candidates running neck and neck in a national popular vote tally.

The conventional wisdom in 2000 was that the election results reflected a "closely divided" nation. President Bill Clinton observed soon after Gore's concession speech: "In this election, the American people were closely divided. The outcome was decided by a Supreme Court that was closely divided."[16] He was soon echoed by political commentators, such as Juan Williams who stated, "Never before have we seen the nation so closely divided as this election year. . . . From the vote for president to the Florida Legislature to the courts, decisions are being made by the narrowest of margins in history."[17] Another editorialist similarly observed, "It's eerie how closely divided the nation has become. . . . Five to four court decision. Four to three court decision. Three-hundred thousand margin out of 100 million votes. House and Senate in a virtual tie."[18]

Taken as a whole, the 2000 congressional and presidential elections were, some say, like the perfect storm. They were "the perfect tie."[19] (Assuming, *arguendo*, that the presidential election was essentially a tie, then it could be argued that the Electoral College served as a tiebreaker.) Commentators accurately recognized that *individuals* across state boundaries appeared to be pretty evenly divided; however, *states* were not so evenly divided.

An examination of the vote totals by state or county reflects a nation that leaned heavily toward Bush: Sixty percent of the states favored Bush. He won 2,434 counties nationwide, compared to Gore, who won only 677 counties.[20] The population in the counties won by Bush was 143 million people, compared to the 127 million people who resided in the counties won by Gore.[21] Bush carried the election in 2,427,000 square miles of the country, compared to

580,000 square miles carried by Gore.[22] Bush earned the votes of at least one state in every region of the country. Most of Gore's support was concentrated in several heavily populated regions in the Northeast and on the western seaboard.

Both Bush and Gore won some states by landslides of 15 percent or more, but Bush won 15 of these states, compared to Gore's seven (plus the District of Columbia). Bush's sizeable victories were spread throughout the Midwest and the South. Gore's largest margins of victory were isolated primarily in the Northeast.

State Landslide Victories Won By Bush[23]

State	Margin of Victory	Bush		Gore	
		Popular Vote	Percent	Popular Vote	Percent
Kentucky	15.1%	872,492	56.5%	638,898	41.4%
Indiana	15.6%	1,245,836	56.6%	901,980	41.0%
South Carolina	15.9%	785,937	56.8%	565,561	40.9%
Mississippi	16.9%	572,844	57.6%	404,614	40.7%
Kansas	20.8%	622,332	58.0%	399,276	37.2%
Texas	21.3%	3,799,639	59.3%	2,433,746	38.0%
Oklahoma	21.9%	744,337	60.3%	474,276	38.4%
South Dakota	22.7%	190,700	60.3%	118,804	37.6%
Montana	25.0%	240,178	58.4%	137,126	33.4%
North Dakota	27.6%	174,852	60.7%	95,284	33.1%
Nebraska	28.9%	433,862	62.2%	231,780	33.3%
Alaska	30.9%	167,398	58.6%	79,004	27.7%
Idaho	39.6%	336,937	67.2%	138,637	27.6%
Wyoming	40.1%	147,947	67.8%	60,481	27.7%
Utah	40.5%	515,096	66.8%	203,053	26.3%
TOTALS		**10,850,387**		**6,882,520**	

Gore won fewer state landslide victories, but he gained nearly as many votes in these highly populated states as Bush did in his 15. In his seven states, Gore earned 10,096,548 votes, while Bush earned 10,850,387 in the 15 states that he won by large margins. Exit polls further reflected the extent to which Gore's support was isolated in certain highly populated regions of the country. Polls showed that 71 percent of voters living in cities with populations of 500,000 or more voted for Gore.[24] By contrast, rural voters went 59 percent for Bush and 37 percent for Gore.[25]

State Landslide Victories Won By Gore

State	Margin of Victory	Bush		Gore	
		Popular Vote	Percent	Popular Vote	Percent
New Jersey	15.8%	1,284,173	40.3%	1,788,850	56.1%
Maryland	16.2%	813,797	40.3%	1,140,782	56.5%
Connecticut	17.5%	561,094	38.4%	816,015	55.9%
Hawaii	18.3%	137,845	37.5%	205,286	55.8%
New York	25.0%	2,403,374	35.2%	4,107,697	60.2%
Massachusetts	27.3%	878,502	32.5%	1,616,487	59.8%
Rhode Island	29.1%	130,555	31.9%	249,508	61.0%
D.C.	76.2%	18,073	9.0%	171,923	85.2%
TOTALS		6,227,413		10,096,548	

At the turn of the 20th century, Democrats were strong in the Pacific West and the East, while Republicans had solid support in the South, Mountain West, and Midwest. Political commentators Henry C. Kenski, Brooks Aylor, and Kate Kenski argue that, in 2000, ten states were "core" Democratic states, while 19 "leaned" Democratic.[26] Gore could have won the election if he had obtained the support of all 29 of these states. Unfortunately for his campaign, he lost one of his core states and eight of his "lean Democratic" states. Republicans, by contrast, had 21 Republican and Republican-leaning states, worth about 192 electoral votes. To win the election, Bush would need to win these states and obtain 78 additional electoral votes from Democratic-leaning states. Bush accomplished his task. He won all 21 Republican states, plus he added nine Democratic or Democratic-leaning states to his electoral vote tally. He achieved his goal by creating a cross-regional coalition that supported him on a couple of core issues.

The themes driving the election in 2000 were more nebulous than those driving the 1888 election. The country was doing well economically. This peace and prosperity should have weighed in favor of Vice President Al Gore, the heir-apparent to incumbent President Bill Clinton. Indeed, during the campaign, Gore attempted to capitalize on the economic issue, arguing that a Bush tax cut could endanger the stability of the economy. Exit polls show that 61 percent of those who believed the country to be on the right track voted for Gore.[27] Bush campaign chief strategist Karl Rove later noted that, had Gore been able to take better advantage of the economic issue, he might have won the election.[28] Bush, however, took some wind out of the sails of Gore's economic arguments. He positioned himself as a moderate who would keep prosperity safe. Once he nullified the economic factor (at least to some degree), he was better able to tackle Gore in other areas, in which many perceived that the country was not doing as well.[29]

Perhaps the main issue driving the outcome of the 2000 election concerned "values"—a notoriously hard-to-define concept.[30] Many people felt that the incumbent, Clinton, had performed well in office, but they did not like him personally. His scandal-ridden presidency adversely affected the mood of voters, and Clinton became a political liability for Gore, particularly in many swing states in the South and the Midwest.[31] The Bush campaign capitalized on this discontent surrounding the perceived decline in moral values. Indeed, Bush focused on the morality issue, even as he simultaneously acknowledged one of his opponent's strengths: the country's economic prosperity. Bush's nomination acceptance speech at the Republican Party Convention in Philadelphia opened, "Prosperity can be a tool in our hands—used to build and better our country. Or it can be a drug in our system—dulling our sense of urgency, of empathy, of duty. . . . Our generation has a chance to reclaim some essential values."[32]

Bush's campaign worked to link Gore with the dishonest and unprincipled behavior that voters perceived had intensified during the Clinton administration. Vice presidential candidate Richard Cheney declared, "Mr. Gore will try to separate himself from his leader's shadow. But somehow we will never see one without thinking of the other."[33] Gore further contributed to his own downfall, binding himself to Clinton's failings in the minds of many voters, primarily by his failure to strongly condemn Clinton's actions during the 1998 impeachment proceedings. Diane Wright, a homemaker in Gore's home state of Tennessee, expressed this sentiment. She stated she would likely vote for Bush, "[p]robably because of Clinton. Gore should have been stronger. He could have distanced himself. A lot of people in Tennessee feel that way."[34]

Bush successfully courted voters who were concerned about values, particularly those residing in the conservative South and Midwest. Polls showed that 57 percent of voters believed the country to be on the wrong moral track. Of these people, 62 percent voted for Bush.[35] An additional indicator of the importance placed upon moral issues during the 2000 election is the breakdown of the vote according to religious practice. Of those attending religious services more than weekly, 63 percent voted for Bush. The situation was reversed for those who did not attend religious services: 61 percent voted for Gore.[36] Forty-four percent of voters thought the Clinton scandals were an important issue in the 2000 election.[37] Of those who rated the scandals "very important," 80 percent voted for Bush.[38] Moreover, questions about other moral values, such as stem cell research and abortion, also pulled at the electorate. Many were concerned about judicial nominations, perceiving that liberal, activist judges were leading the nation astray morally. In response, Bush promised to appoint judges who would "strictly interpret the Constitution and not use the bench for writing social policy."[39] Gore instead argued that "[i]t would be likely that [his judges] would uphold *Roe v. Wade*."[40]

In 2000, voters in the majority of states viewed Bush as an honest, sincere man who would strive to do the right thing. They viewed Gore as an experienced candidate, but one who was insincere and too ambitious. These characteristics, whether perceived or real, contributed to his inability to distance himself sufficiently from Clinton's moral failings. Gore made the mistake of thinking that peace and prosperity would carry the day with most of the country. He was right in thinking that it would carry the day with most *individuals*; however, most of these voters resided in the more liberal east and west coasts. Voters in the majority of states, particularly in the more conservative Midwest and South, voted on a different range of issues. To them, honesty, trustworthiness, and other leadership qualities were equally valid issues to consider when casting their votes. Gore was unable to obtain the support of most of these latter individuals.

Bush worked in other ways to broaden his base of support. He deliberately sought to gain the support of many independents by avoiding actions that might be perceived as partisan or solely Republican. Rove noted that Bush gained backing by avoiding the old Republican rhetoric on many issues. Instead, he looked for ways to reach across partisan lines. Rove observed, "When [Bush] talked about welfare, he didn't say, 'Let's get the welfare cheats off the rolls.' He said, 'We're losing some of our best and brightest to dependency on government. How can we help free people to meet their greatest potential in life?'"[41] Moreover, Bush purposely tackled issues that are traditionally considered advantageous for Democrats, such as education, Medicare, and Social Security. He worked to paint a picture of himself as a new kind of Republican, a "compassionate conservative" that could reach across partisan lines. He did not always persuade voters on these issues, but he at least decreased the advantage that Gore had in these areas.[42]

In the end, election results show that Bush succeeded in his efforts to build a cross-regional coalition of voters. Rove noted that Bush made some major (and little discussed) inroads into the Democratic vote. He won a swing of 11.3 million new votes since the 1996 election.[43] New Hispanic voters, alone, grew by 1.5 million.[44] Further, he won a number of traditionally Democratic states, such as West Virginia, that he should not have carried.[45] Gore also increased the number of votes cast for his party since the 1996 election, but these additional votes were from constituencies that consistently vote Democratic anyway. For instance, he gained new votes among labor unions and black voters.[46]

The election of 2000 is a perfect example of why the Electoral College exists. If America operated under a direct election system, Gore would have won despite losing the election in 60 percent of states and more than two-thirds of counties in America. He would have won despite the fact that he had virtually no support in two large regions of the country and the bulk of his support was isolated on the east and west coasts.[47] The rural and less populous states would have been trampled by the will of a few heavily populated regions.

⁂ ⁂ ⁂

The elections of 1888 and 2000 are illustrations of Electoral College success. In each case, the candidate who did a better job of building a national coalition and generating support nationwide was sent to the White House. Harrison and Bush were the appropriate winners for each of these elections. They proved themselves to be better representatives for a diverse, federalist society than Cleveland and Gore, who would have owed their wins, had they occurred, to landslide victories in a few states.

Chapter Seventeen

Roosevelt & Reagan: Landslide Victories

Franklin Delano Roosevelt and Ronald Reagan both came to the presidency during times of economic difficulty, and each conquered the daunting task of uplifting a discouraged country. Both men possessed a unique talent for speaking to people in a manner that restored their hope and made them feel understood. Each President had his detractors; no candidate will ever be supported by *all* voters. However, FDR and Reagan, perhaps better than any other candidate during the 20th Century, attained the goals encouraged by the Electoral College.

The 1936 and 1984 elections proved the ability of these men to achieve support across racial, regional, and ethnic lines. Each President's critics were outnumbered by the great majority of constituents who trusted their President, even if they disagreed with him on the margins. By and large, FDR and Reagan were perceived as *American* Presidents, first and foremost. These two men who obtained such wide cross-country support earned more electoral votes than any other President in U.S. history; they were elected to the White House by electoral landslides.

Franklin Delano Roosevelt

FDR's popularity with the American people cannot be properly appreciated without an understanding of the context in which they first elected him.[1] He assumed the Oval Office during the Great Depression, which began when the New York stock market crashed in 1929. At the time of the crash, Republican President Herbert Hoover was in office and most of the blame for the economic disaster was laid at his feet. During the following presidential campaign between Hoover and FDR, the country was still suffering from the consequences of the economic decline. Thousands of banks had failed, and stock values had dropped to about 20 percent of their previous value.[2] Thirteen million Americans found themselves unemployed by March 1933.[3] Under such circumstances, FDR was elected easily in 1932 on what was essentially an "anti-Hoover" vote.

Almost immediately, FDR proposed sweeping reforms that became known as the New Deal. His package of proposed solutions injected the federal government extensively into many economic and labor matters that had previously remained private. FDR explained his plans to the American public during evening radio talks, called "fireside chats." He also relied upon these chats to give people optimism and a sense of security, despite the nation's economic difficulty.

To many Americans, the New Deal meant relief; they trusted FDR's confident outlook on the future. Others remained worried about FDR's policies, perceiving that government had been inserted too much into private matters; they worried that the end result would be confiscatory taxation and a lack of self-reliance. The J.P. Morgans, for instance, hated FDR, going so far as to forbid the mention of his name in their home.[4] The Morgans and those like them, however, were vastly outnumbered by those who trusted FDR and believed his offer of hope. The gulf between the two groups widened still further between the elections of 1932 and 1936.

Ironically, FDR's New Deal probably prolonged the Depression,[5] due to the greatly increased federal taxes necessary to support the government programs. These new taxes sucked capital out of the private market, making it harder for employers to hire new employees or invest in new businesses. The median unemployment rate was 17 percent throughout the New Deal era.[6] Americans were relying upon a man who was most likely making their economic situation worse. But, for election purposes, it didn't matter. Voters believed in FDR, and they believed his contentions that the New Deal would cure the economy. His appeal to voters in the face of such economic disaster is a huge testament to his ability to make people trust him, even when he may not have deserved it.

FDR was extremely popular by the time the 1936 election rolled around, although the economy was still slow and eight million Americans remained unemployed.[7] Few presidential candidates could have realistically hoped to challenge FDR in his bid for re-election, but Republicans eventually nominated Alfred "Alf" Landon, Governor of Kansas. Landon was the only Republican governor to win reelection during the Democratic landslides of 1934,[8] and he was known for his battles in favor of civil liberties and against the Ku Klux Klan. Of the potential candidates, it seemed that he had the best chance of defeating FDR.[9]

Even Landon, however, was not up to the task. He often seemed to agree with many of FDR's New Deal policies, although he objected that the programs went too far and were "strangling . . . free enterprise."[10] Moreover, Landon was not especially talented at public speaking. His lack of talent may have helped with some voters who viewed his clumsy manner as more sincere than FDR's slick charisma. Nevertheless, Landon's ineptness in public remained mostly a hindrance. Other Republicans labeled him a "pretty poor specimen" or no "world-beater" as the campaign heated up during the summer of 1936.[11] Worse, Landon was a weak campaigner. He stayed at home during much of the campaign and did not participate in the Republican primaries. Instead, most attacks on FDR originated with others in his party.

During the campaign, Republican criticisms focused on allegations that FDR's policies extended the federal government into too many areas of state and private life. Republicans disapproved of FDR's decision to abandon the gold standard and condemned the seemingly permanent federal deficit. Landon won the support of those who were alarmed by ever-increasing federal tax rates, as well as those who felt that FDR's policies undermined such virtues as self-reliance and thriftiness. When all was said and done, though, Landon's supporters were not bound together by any characteristic of Landon or his platform; instead, they were bound together by their dislike of FDR and his programs. Senator Arthur H. Vandenberg stated at the time, "I belong to but one bloc and it has but one slogan—stop Roosevelt."[12] Unfortunately for FDR's detractors, their aversion to the New Deal alone, without some other unifying factor, was not sufficient to stop a President who had much of the country on his side and who was determined to fight.

FDR's campaign turned the election into warfare between the classes. He argued that his New Deal would protect average Americans from Big Business and the wealthy. FDR boasted, "Never before in all our history have these forces been so united against one candidate as they stand today. They are unanimous in their hate for me—and I welcome their hatred."[13] He continued, "[T]he forces of selfishness and of lust for power met their match [during my first term]. I should like to have it said of my second Administration that in it these forces met their master."[14]

Most Americans believed that FDR stood staunchly on their side, opposed to the rich and powerful who would take advantage of them during a time of economic difficulty. Their beliefs were reinforced by FDR's campaign speeches, which often began with FDR's observation: "You look happier today than you did four years ago."[15] As he continued his speech, he would regale the audience with strings of numbers that supposedly indicated how his programs were working and the economy was improving. As FDR campaigned, people often came to hear him speak and would yell their thanks to him as he passed by: "He saved my home," or "He gave me a job."[16] One worker exclaimed in 1936 that FDR was the "only man we ever had in the White House who would understand that my boss is a son-of-a-bitch."[17]

FDR added to his cross-country appeal by putting together his "New Deal Coalition," an alliance of voters from different regional, racial, religious, and ethnic backgrounds.[18] Labor unions, minorities, liberals, and southern Protestants forged a partnership of sorts under this coalition. Catholic voters swung in favor of FDR because he appointed so many Catholics to the bench. During FDR's tenure, one in four judicial appointees was Catholic, as opposed to one in 25 during the previous three administrations.[19] Black voters also began to come to the Democratic side during these years. They appreciated FDR's appointment of blacks to important posts, and they felt that FDR's New Deal programs had offered them relief from economic depression.

On Election Day, the broad-based coalition that FDR put together paid off handsomely. FDR trampled Landon, both in the popular and the electoral votes. He obtained 523 electoral votes to Landon's eight votes and 27,750,866 popular votes to Landon's 16,679,683 votes.[20] FDR won every state in the union except for Maine and Vermont.

FDR's coalition of voters enabled him to obtain the widest margin of victory in the nation's history: 515 electoral votes. Ronald Reagan came closest to beating FDR's record when he defeated Walter Mondale by 512 electoral votes nearly 50 years later.

Ronald Reagan

As with FDR, Reagan's success cannot be fully appreciated without first understanding life in America before his presidency. Reagan initially won the presidency by defeating Jimmy Carter in the election of 1980. Domestically, Carter's administration had been characterized by high inflation, long gas lines, and increasing unemployment. In foreign affairs, voters worried about the proliferation of nuclear arms, the spread of communism, and the possibility of war with the Soviet Union. The nation seemed stuck in despondency. In July 1979, Carter stated on television that the nation was undergoing a "crisis of confidence."[21] Carter had hoped to spur the people to action with his words, but he succeeded only in disheartening them further. His speech became known as the "malaise" speech. Matters degenerated still further late in Carter's term when 66 American hostages[22] were taken and held for more than a year in Iran. The incident left the public even more demoralized. When Reagan arrived on the scene, Americans readily turned to this man who was brimming with optimism about the future.

Reagan obtained early popularity, yet his first term was bumpy. He achieved some early successes, such as convincing Congress to reduce taxes by 25 percent across the board over the course of three years. This proposal, combined with the Tax Reform Act of 1986, would eventually reduce the top tax rate from 70 percent to 28 percent.[23] Reagan found another early victory in the area of defense spending. He obtained massive spending increases in this area, although he failed in his efforts to make parallel cuts in domestic spending.

A last early step taken by Reagan eventually tamed the nation's problem with escalating inflation rates, but not before many people incorrectly concluded that Reagan's policies had failed. Reagan supported efforts by Paul Volcker, then the Federal Reserve chairman, to raise interest rates soon after Reagan entered office. The effort brought inflation down sharply, but it also triggered a short recession.[24]

The recession caused many to believe that Reagan's proposals should be abandoned, and his ideas were labeled "Reaganomics" by many critics. Reagan, however, refused to alter his course. He believed that his actions would alleviate the nation's financial difficulties, but he also knew that such a cure could not happen overnight. He steadfastly waited for recovery to come. In 1983, as Reagan's first round of tax cuts was finally phased in fully, the economy did begin to grow—and it grew rapidly. The economy grew for 15 straight years, creating 20 million new jobs between 1983 and 1989. The gross national product increased by one third during the rest of Reagan's presidency.[25] The so-called "misery index" (inflation plus rate of unemployment) dropped from 20.2 percent during October 1980 to 11.5 percent by 1984. Inflation, alone, decreased to less than five percent, although it had been more than 12 percent during Carter's tenure.[26] Reagan joked, "The best sign that our economic program is working is that they don't call it 'Reaganomics' anymore."[27]

By the time the 1984 election rolled around, Reagan was enormously popular with much of the public. (As with FDR, a smaller contingent of people hated him with an equal intensity.) For a country that had been dejected in the 1970s, Reagan was a refreshing change. He replaced pessimism with optimism. Americans believed in themselves and their country as they had not been able to do for years. In this sense, Reagan was similar to FDR. Each President restored confidence to the American people.

Reagan was inspired by his early hero, FDR, in other ways as well. He echoed FDR's fireside chats, often taking his case straight to the people through television addresses from the Oval Office or in his weekly radio broadcast. Reagan was hopeful about America's future, and his positive outlook spilled over onto voters. In many senses, Reagan campaigned on the idealism of "the future" as much as he campaigned on more tangible issues, such as the economy. His campaign slogan in 1984 was compatible with his sunny personality: "It's morning again in America!" Reagan biographer Lou Cannon has remarked on this Reagan trait: "When Reagan talked this way, in cadences that echoed the optimism of his old hero Franklin Roosevelt, he transcended partisan barriers."[28]

Walter Mondale, the Democratic nominee in 1984, probably never had a chance of defeating Reagan. Sixty percent of voters felt favorably toward Reagan in 1984. This number was higher than that for Mondale or either of the vice presidential candidates.[29] Not only was Reagan personally popular, but the economy was thriving for the first time in years. Most people believed that the economy had improved, and they credited Reagan with the improvement. Their approval of Reagan's economy management weighed more heavily even than their personal financial status when they went to the polls. Those who thought Reagan had helped the economy, even though their personal finances had not changed, voted nine to one for him.[30]

Mondale attempted to combat Reagan's strength in this area in several ways. First, he argued that the economy was not as good as it appeared—but voters didn't believe him.[31] Next, he argued that Reagan was merely rewarding the rich at the expense of the poor. While some voters believed Mondale, the argument did not seem to undermine Reagan's broad support base.[32] Last, Mondale attempted to pin the rising deficit on Reagan, but Americans instead blamed Congress. Approximately 50 percent of voters believed Democratic Congressmen were responsible for the deficit, compared to 30 percent who blamed Reagan.[33] Moreover, Mondale's solution to the deficit—spending cuts and a tax hike—also fell flat with voters, who preferred Reagan's arguments for reduced domestic spending. An ABC/*Washington Post* poll at the time of the election showed an overwhelming dislike for tax increases on the part of the electorate.[34] Mondale had hoped that his tax increase proposal would paint him as an honest man who was willing to be candid regarding the need to raise taxes. Instead, he alienated voters and gave Reagan grounds to compare him to the tax and spenders of the 1970s. Reagan, for his part, largely ignored the deficit during his campaign, instead focusing on the improved economy. His positive focus furthered the contrast between Reagan, the optimist, and Mondale, who increasingly began to look like just another pessimist.

Reagan had a further advantage over Mondale on foreign policy issues. When asked, voters sometimes evidenced disagreement with one or two elements of Reagan's policy, but overall, they liked the image of strength abroad that Reagan fostered. This perception crossed party lines. A plurality of Democrats, 42 percent, believed that a Republican administration would do more to keep the country strong.[35]

Although strong on both domestic and foreign issues, Reagan faced a bigger test with respect to a more personal issue: He would be almost 78-years old at the end of a second term in office, and some commentators argued that he was too old to run for President. Reagan, as always, was ever-ready with humor on the subject, which put people at ease. When accused of dozing during Cabinet meetings, he promptly responded to campaign workers: "Some of you here were up all night . . . . And I can only tell you that, if I could manage it, I would schedule a Cabinet meeting so that we could all go over and take a nap together."[36] At a couple of points during the campaign, it seemed as if the age argument would make some headway. For instance, when Reagan did not perform well in the first presidential debate, the *Wall Street Journal* ran a headline that declared, "Is Oldest U.S. President Now Showing His Age?"[37] Reagan soon put the issue to rest with an improved second debate performance—and a joke. When asked about the age issue, he responded: "I want you to know that also I will not make age an issue of this campaign. I am not going to exploit, for political purposes, my opponent's youth and inexperience."[38] Even Mondale laughed at the line. Reagan's re-election was perhaps guaranteed in that moment.

"Reagan is the most popular figure in the history of the United States," House Speaker Tip O'Neill observed after the election, "No candidate we put up would have been able to beat Reagan this year."[39] His words accurately summarized the wide-ranging appeal that Reagan had successfully nourished. In 1984, Reagan was re-elected by an electoral vote of 525 to 13, and he secured 54,455,075 popular votes to Mondale's 37,577,185. His victory is notable for the diversity of people that it encompassed. Commentators often remark upon Reagan's ability to gain support from the so-called "Reagan Democrats." But his support crossed other lines as well. In 1984, Reagan won a majority of every region, every age group, and every occupation.[40] A majority of both men and women voted for Reagan.[41] Reagan made huge gains among Hispanics, although the Jewish and Black vote still went to Mondale. Reagan won a majority of the blue-collar vote; he was the first Republican to do so since Richard Nixon defeated George McGovern.[42]

George Shultz once stated, "Reagan trusted the American people, and because he did, the American people trusted him."[43] Reagan's concern for Americans was demonstrated in many small ways that added up over the years. For instance, he personally responded to thousands of letters that were written to him by his movie fans and constituents. In 1981, he wrote to a citizen, "You specified that you wanted to hear from me personally, so here I am."[44] This attitude marked his service to the country, and won him support at election time.

Vincent Rakowitz, a retired brewery worker in San Antonio, perhaps best summarized the appeal of Reagan to many voters in 1984: "'He really isn't like a Republican. He's more like an American, which is what we really need.'"[45]

⁂ ⁂ ⁂

The elections of 1936 and 1984 stand as examples of Electoral College success. FDR and Reagan won by decisive electoral victories because they had successfully built inclusive national coalitions that appeared to embrace all Americans, as encouraged by the Electoral College system. Arguably, their success in coalition-building was due, at least in part, to the crises that gripped the nation in the 1930s and 1970s before their presidencies. Perhaps the people were more amenable to working together under one President during a time of disaster, as opposed to a time of prosperity. Yet each President also proved his talent for reaching across lines that normally divide the nation. Each demonstrated the success that can be obtained by any candidate who seeks to build upon the values that are shared by Americans, rather than the issues that divide them. Both FDR and Reagan personified the type of candidate that should win the presidency in a diverse, federalist republic. As a result, each was re-elected to the presidency with an electoral landslide.

Conclusion

The conventional wisdom in the early part of the 21st century—supported by various polls—suggests that the nation remains "closely divided." Several elections in a row have featured a division between "blue" coastal and Northeastern states and "red" southern and Midwestern ones. In many ways, the seemingly permanent division between red and blue resembles a similar division between North and South following the Civil War.

The Electoral College helped to ease tensions between North and South in the late 1800s and early 1900s, and it can work in a comparable manner today. Voters can and should take comfort in its existence. America's election process encourages voters to work together and focus on their similarities. A direct election system would instead highlight differences and drive Americans even further apart.

The Founders worked to create a government in which large and small sovereign states would be able to reside peacefully alongside each other. Their observations of history led them to conclude that pure democracies were inadequate to the task because they allow bare majorities to tyrannize over minority groups. Yet the Founders wanted to retain at least one important feature of these democracies: They wanted the people to have a voice in their government and, thus, in the selection of the nation's Chief Executive. How could this democratic principle be retained while minority groups were simultaneously protected?

The Founders' solution was to create a republican democracy, organized on federalist principles. Where possible, governance would be left close to home so the people could keep their representatives accountable to act wisely. Federal involvement would be relied upon only when necessary. Moreover, the federal Constitution, including its presidential election system, would contain a multitude of safeguards. The majority would retain enough power to rule, but the minority would be given many ways in which to make its voice heard. The freedom of all would thereby be protected.

The Electoral College operates in a different world than the one that existed in 1787. Modern Americans expect the federal government to involve itself in a wider range of activities. They probably possess a more populist mindset than their ancestors did, and they may not recognize the value of republican principles in government. Moreover, modern technological advancements have facilitated communication and commerce in ways that could not have been foreseen by those in the founding generation.

Contrary to the contentions of critics, these changes have not undermined the important benefits of America's unique presidential election system. In many ways, the advantages of the country's election process have instead strengthened over time as the two-party system has solidified and the winner-take-all rule has become the general procedure in presidential elections. The Electoral College, as it operates today, requires presidential candidates to build cross-regional coalitions before they can successfully win the White House. Moreover, the process reinforces the nation's two-party system, which promotes a spirit of moderation and compromise in politics. Last, the Electoral College promotes definitive election outcomes. Even when controversy or fraud becomes a factor, such disputes are isolated to one or a handful of states. The country is given as much stability and certainty as possible in a world full of ambitious politicians.

America conducts democratic presidential elections every four years. However, it conducts these democratic elections at the state level, rather than the national level, for an important reason: Conducting elections by states' electoral votes, rather than individuals' votes, ensures that winning presidential candidates will be the best possible representatives for a nation composed of many diverse states. America's election system ensures that the country will be led by an American President, not a regional one.

Conclusion

The past pages have examined the valuable reasons for keeping the presidential election system instituted by the founding generation, and it has refuted the many criticisms that are often thrown at the Electoral College. This examination reveals that the Founders' faith in the Electoral College is still justified. The Founders would doubtless be proud to see their creation still successfully serving federalist, republican interests more than 200 years after it was first instituted.

The Electoral College has stood the test of time. It will serve the nation well long into the future, just as it has throughout American history.

Appendix A

U.S. Constitution
Article II, Section 1

CLAUSE 1: The executive Power shall be vested in a President of the United States of America. He shall hold his Office during the Term of four Years, and, together with the Vice President, chosen for the same Term, be elected, as follows:

CLAUSE 2: Each State shall appoint, in such Manner as the Legislature thereof may direct, a Number of Electors, equal to the whole Number of Senators and Representatives to which the State may be entitled in the Congress: but no Senator or Representative, or Person holding an Office of Trust or Profit under the United States, shall be appointed an Elector.

CLAUSE 3: The Electors shall meet in their respective States, and vote by Ballot for two Persons, of whom one at least shall not be an Inhabitant of the same State with themselves. And they shall make a List of all the Persons voted for, and of the Number of Votes for each; which List they shall sign and certify, and transmit sealed to the Seat of the Government of the United States, directed to the President of the Senate. The President of the Senate shall, in the Presence of the Senate and House of Representatives, open all the Certificates, and the Votes shall then be counted. The Person having the greatest Number of Votes shall be the President, if such Number be a Majority of the whole Number of Electors appointed; and if there be more than one who have such Majority, and have an equal Number of Votes, then the House of Representatives shall immediately chuse by Ballot one of them for President; and if no Person have a Majority, then from the five highest on the List the said House shall in like Manner chuse the President. But in chusing the President, the Votes shall be taken by States, the Representation from each State having one Vote; A quorum for this purpose shall consist of a Member or Members from two thirds of the States, and a Majority of all the States shall be necessary to a Choice. In every Case, after the Choice of the President, the Person having the greatest Number of Votes of the Electors shall be the Vice President. But if there should remain two or more who have equal Votes, the Senate shall chuse from them by Ballot the Vice President.

CLAUSE 4: The Congress may determine the Time of chusing the Electors, and the Day on which they shall give their Votes; which Day shall be the same throughout the United States.

U.S. Constitution
The 12th Amendment

The Electors shall meet in their respective states and vote by ballot for President and Vice-President, one of whom, at least, shall not be an inhabitant of the same state with themselves; they shall name in their ballots the person voted for as President, and in distinct ballots the person voted for as Vice-President, and they shall make distinct lists of all persons voted for as President, and of all persons voted for as Vice-President, and of the number of votes for each, which lists they shall sign and certify, and transmit sealed to the seat of the government of the United States, directed to the President of the Senate;—the President of the Senate shall, in the presence of the Senate and House of Representatives, open all the certificates and the votes shall then be counted;—The person having the greatest number of votes for President, shall be the President, if such number be a majority of the whole number of Electors appointed; and if no person have such majority, then from the persons having the highest numbers not exceeding three on the list of those voted for as President, the House of Representatives shall choose immediately, by ballot, the President. But in choosing the President, the votes shall be taken by states, the representation from each state having one vote; a quorum for this purpose shall consist of a member or members from two-thirds of the states, and a majority of all the states shall be necessary to a choice. And if the House of Representatives shall not choose a President whenever the right of choice shall devolve upon them, before the fourth day of March next following, then the Vice-President shall act as President, as in case of the death or other constitutional disability of the President. The person having the greatest number of votes as Vice-President, shall be the Vice-President, if such number be a majority of the whole number of Electors appointed, and if no person have a majority, then from the two highest numbers on the list, the Senate shall choose the Vice-President; a quorum for the purpose shall consist of two-thirds of the whole number of Senators, and a majority of the whole number shall be necessary to a choice. But no person constitutionally ineligible to the office of President shall be eligible to that of Vice-President of the United States.

Appendix B

Election Results: 1789-2008[1]

Candidate	Party	Electoral Votes		Popular Vote[2]	
		Actual[3]	Percent[4]	Actual	Percent
1789					
George Washington	F	69			
John Adams	F	34			
Others (10 candidates)	Misc.	35 (total)			
1792					
George Washington	F	132			
John Adams	F	77			
Others (3 candidates)	Misc.	55 (total)			
1796					
John Adams	F	71			
Thomas Jefferson	DR	68			
Others (11 candidates)	Misc.	137 (total)			
1800					
Thomas Jefferson	DR	73			
Aaron Burr	DR	73			
John Adams	F	65			
Others (2 candidates)	Misc.	65 (total)			

AI = American Independent
AM = Anti-Mason
CU = Constitutional Union
D = Democrat
DR = Democratic-Republican
F = Federalist

ID = Independent Democrat
IDR = Ind. Dem.-Republican
L = Libertarian
NR = National-Republican
P = Progressive
PO = Populist

R = Republican
SRD = States' Right Democrat
SD = Southern Democrat
W = Whig
WA = Whig-American

Candidate	Party	Electoral Votes		Popular Vote[2]	
		Actual[3]	Percent[4]	Actual	Percent
1804					
Thomas Jefferson	DR	162	92.0%		
Charles C. Pinckney	F	14	8.0%		
1808[5]					
James Madison	DR	122	69.3%		
Charles C. Pinckney	F	47	26.7%		
George Clinton	IDR	6	3.4%		
1812[6]					
James Madison	DR	128	58.7%		
De Witt Clinton	F/IDR	89	40.8%		
1816[7]					
James Monroe	DR	183	82.8%		
Rufus King	F	34	15.4%		
1820[8]					
James Monroe	DR	231	98.3%		
John Quincy Adams	IDR	1	0.4%		
1824[9]					
John Quincy Adams	DR	84	32.2%	113,122	30.9%
Andrew Jackson	DR	99	37.9%	151,271	41.3%
William H. Crawford	DR	41	15.7%	40,856	11.2%
Henry Clay	DR	37	14.2%	47,531	13.0%
1828					
Andrew Jackson	DR	178	68.2%	642,553	56.0%
John Quincy Adams	NR	83	31.8%	500,897	43.6%
1832[10]					
Andrew Jackson	D	219	76.0%	701,780	54.2%
Henry Clay	NR	49	17.0%	484,205	37.4%
John Floyd	ID	11	3.8%	—	—
William Wirt	AM	7	2.4%	100,715	7.8%
1836					
Martin Van Buren	D	170	57.8%	764,176	50.8%
William H. Harrison	W	73	24.8%	550,816	36.6%
Hugh L. White	W	26	8.8%	146,107	9.7%
Daniel Webster	W	14	4.8%	41,201	2.7%
William P. Mangum	ID	11	3.7%	—	—
1840					
William H. Harrison	W	234	79.6%	1,275,390	52.9%
Martin Van Buren	D	60	20.4%	1,128,854	46.8%

Appendix B

Candidate	Party	Electoral Votes		Popular Vote[2]	
		Actual[3]	Percent[4]	Actual	Percent
1844					
James K. Polk	D	170	61.8%	1,339,494	49.5%
Henry Clay	W	105	38.2%	1,300,004	48.1%
1848					
Zachary Taylor	W	163	56.2%	1,361,393	47.3%
Lewis Cass	D	127	43.8%	1,223,460	42.5%
1852					
Franklin Pierce	D	254	85.8%	1,607,510	50.8%
Winfield Scott	W	42	14.2%	1,386,942	43.9%
1856					
James Buchanan	D	174	58.8%	1,836,072	45.3%
John C. Fremont	R	114	38.5%	1,342,345	33.1%
Millard Fillmore	WA	8	2.7%	873,053	21.5%
1860					
Abraham Lincoln	R	180	59.4%	1,865,908	39.9%
John C. Breckinridge	SD	72	23.8%	848,019	18.1%
John Bell	CU	39	12.9%	590,901	12.6%
Stephen A. Douglas	D	12	4.0%	1,380,202	29.5%
1864[11]					
Abraham Lincoln	R	212	90.6%	2,220,846	55.1%
George B. McClellan	D	21	9.0%	1,809,445	44.9%
1868					
Ulysses S. Grant	R	214	72.8%	3,013,650	52.7%
Horatio Seymour	D	80	27.2%	2,708,744	47.3%
1872[12]					
Ulysses S. Grant	R	286	78.1%	3,598,468	55.6%
Thomas Hendricks	D	42	11.5%	—	—
B. Gratz Brown	D	18	4.9%	—	—
Charles J. Jenkins	D	2	0.5%	—	—
David Davis	D	1	0.3%	—	—
1876					
Rutherford B. Hayes	R	185	50.1%	4,033,497	48.0%
Samuel J. Tilden	D	184	49.9%	4,288,191	51.0%
1880					
James A. Garfield	R	214	58.0%	4,453,611	48.3%
Winfield S. Hancock	D	155	42.0%	4,445,256	48.2%
1884					
Grover Cleveland	D	219	54.6%	4,915,586	48.9%
James G. Blaine	R	182	45.4%	4,852,916	48.2%

Candidate	Party	Electoral Votes		Popular Vote[2]	
		Actual[3]	Percent[4]	Actual	Percent
1888					
Benjamin Harrison	R	233	58.1%	5,449,825	47.8%
Grover Cleveland	D	168	41.9%	5,539,118	48.6%
1892					
Grover Cleveland	D	277	62.4%	5,554,617	46.0%
Benjamin Harrison	R	145	32.7%	5,186,793	43.0%
James B. Weaver	PO	22	5.0%	1,024,280	8.5%
1896					
William McKinley	R	271	60.6%	7,105,144	51.1%
William J. Bryan	D / PO	176	39.4%	6,370,897	45.8%
1900					
William McKinley	R	292	65.3%	7,219,193	51.7%
William J. Bryan	D	155	34.7%	6,357,698	45.5%
1904					
Theodore Roosevelt	R	336	70.6%	7,625,599	56.4%
Alton B. Parker	D	140	29.4%	5,083,501	37.6%
1908					
William H. Taft	R	321	66.5%	7,676,598	51.6%
William J. Bryan	D	162	33.5%	6,406,874	43.0%
1912					
Woodrow Wilson	D	435	81.9%	6,294,326	41.8%
Theodore Roosevelt	P	88	16.6%	4,120,207	27.4%
William H. Taft	R	8	1.5%	3,486,343	23.2%
1916					
Woodrow Wilson	D	277	52.2%	9,126,063	49.2%
Charles E. Hughes	R	254	47.8%	8,547,039	46.1%
1920					
Warren G. Harding	R	404	76.1%	16,151,916	60.3
James M. Cox	D	127	23.9%	9,134,074	34.1
1924					
Calvin Coolidge	R	382	71.9%	15,724,310	54.0%
John W. Davis	D	136	25.6%	8,386,532	28.8%
Robert M. La Follette	P	13	2.4%	4,827,184	16.6%
1928					
Herbert C. Hoover	R	444	83.6%	21,432,823	58.2%
Alfred E. Smith	D	87	16.4%	15,004,336	40.8%
1932					
Franklin D. Roosevelt	D	472	88.9%	22,818,740	57.4%
Herbert C. Hoover	R	59	11.1%	15,760,425	39.6%

Appendix B

Candidate	Party	Electoral Votes		Popular Vote[2]	
		Actual[3]	Percent[4]	Actual	Percent
1936					
Franklin D. Roosevelt	D	523	98.5%	27,750,866	60.8%
Alfred M. Landon	R	8	1.5%	16,679,683	36.5%
1940					
Franklin D. Roosevelt	D	449	84.6%	27,343,218	54.7%
Wendell Willkie	R	82	15.4%	22,334,940	44.8%
1944					
Franklin D. Roosevelt	D	432	81.4%	25,612,610	53.4%
Thomas E. Dewey	R	99	18.6%	22,021,053	45.9%
1948					
Harry S. Truman	D	303	57.1%	24,105,810	49.5%
Thomas E. Dewey	R	189	35.6%	21,970,064	45.1%
J. Strom Thurmond	SRD	39	7.3%	1,169,114	2.4%
1952					
Dwight Eisenhower	R	442	83.2%	33,777,945	54.9%
Adlai Stevenson	D	89	16.8%	27,314,992	44.4%
1956					
Dwight Eisenhower	R	457	86.1%	35,590,472	57.4%
Adlai Stevenson	D	73	13.7%	26,022,752	42.0%
Walter B. Jones	D	1	0.2%	—	—
1960					
John F. Kennedy	D	303	56.4%	34,226,731	49.7%
Richard M. Nixon	R	219	40.8%	34,108,157	49.5%
Harry F. Byrd	D	15	2.8%	—	—
1964					
Lyndon B. Johnson	D	486	90.3%	43,129,566	61.1%
Barry M. Goldwater	R	52	9.7%	27,178,188	38.5%
1968					
Richard M. Nixon	R	301	55.9%	31,785,480	43.4%
Hubert H. Humphrey	D	191	35.5%	31,275,166	42.7%
George C. Wallace	AI	46	8.6%	9,906,473	13.5%
1972					
Richard M. Nixon	R	520	96.7%	47,169,911	60.7%
George S. McGovern	D	17	3.2%	29,170,383	37.5%
John Hospers	L	1	0.2%	3,673	<0.1%
1976					
Jimmy Carter	D	297	55.2%	40,830,763	50.1%
Gerald R. Ford	R	240	44.6%	39,147,793	48.0%
Ronald Reagan	R	1	0.2%	—	—

Candidate	Party	Electoral Votes		Popular Vote[2]	
		Actual[3]	Percent[4]	Actual	Percent
1980					
Ronald Reagan	R	489	90.9%	43,904,153	50.7%
Jimmy Carter	D	49	9.1%	35,483,883	41.0%
1984					
Ronald Reagan	R	525	97.6%	54,455,075	58.8%
Walter F. Mondale	D	13	2.4%	37,577,185	40.6%
1988					
George H.W. Bush	R	426	79.2%	48,886,097	53.4%
Michael S. Dukakis	D	111	20.6%	41,809,074	45.6%
Lloyd Bentsen	D	1	0.2%	—	—
1992					
Bill Clinton	D	370	68.8%	44,909,326	43.0%
George H.W. Bush	R	168	31.2%	39,103,882	37.4%
1996					
Bill Clinton	D	379	70.4%	47,402,357	49.2%
Bob Dole	R	159	29.6%	39,198,755	40.7%
2000					
George W. Bush	R	271	50.4%	50,455,156	47.9%
Albert Gore, Jr	D	266	49.4%	50,992,335	48.4%
2004					
George W. Bush	R	286	53.1%	62,040,610	50.7%
John Kerry	D	251	46.7%	59,028,439	48.3%
John Edwards[13]	D	1	.2%	—	—
2008					
Barack Obama	D	365	67.8%	69,498,516	52.9%
John McCain	R	173	32.2%	59,948,323	45.7%

Notes

Introduction

1. THE FEDERALIST NO. 68, at 410 (Alexander Hamilton) (Clinton Rossiter ed., Signet Classic 2003) (1961).

2. The timeline for the networks' calls can be found in JEFFREY TOOBIN, TOO CLOSE TO CALL: THE THIRTY-SIX-DAY BATTLE TO DECIDE THE 2000 ELECTION 17–25 (2001), among other sources.

3. *See, e.g.*, Matthew Cooper, *College Bound?*, TIME, Nov. 20, 2000, at 42, 42–43 (summarizing the election results as of November 11, 2000).

4. *See* Bush v. Gore, 531 U.S. 98 (2000) (per curiam); Bush v. Palm Beach Cnty. Canvassing Bd., 531 U.S. 70 (2000) (per curiam).

5. All election results cited in this book were obtained from CQ Press's *Presidential Elections. See* CQ PRESS, PRESIDENTIAL ELECTIONS: 1789–2008 (2010).

6. A detailed discussion of the 1876 election can be found in WILLIAM H. REHNQUIST, CENTENNIAL CRISIS: THE DISPUTED ELECTION OF 1876 (2004); *see also* MICHAEL J. GLENNON, WHEN NO MAJORITY RULES: THE ELECTORAL COLLEGE AND PRESIDENTIAL SUCCESSION 16–17 (1992); ROBERT M. HARDAWAY, THE ELECTORAL COLLEGE AND THE CONSTITUTION: THE CASE FOR PRESERVING FEDERALISM 128–37 (1994); PAUL JOHNSON, A HISTORY OF THE AMERICAN PEOPLE 549 (HarperCollins Publishers 1st U.S. ed. 1998) (1997).

The President of the Senate formally declared Hayes the new President when the electoral count was completed at about 4 a.m. on March 2, 1877—two days before Grant's term expired. Because March 4 fell on a Sunday that year, Hayes was sworn in privately at the White House. Formal inauguration ceremonies were held the following day. *See* REHNQUIST, *supra*, at 178–79, 201.

7. The entire slates of electors in South Carolina, Florida, and Louisiana were disputed. One electoral vote was also undecided in Oregon due to a dispute regarding an elector who was deemed ineligible; however, the remainder of the state's vote was decided on Election Day. REHNQUIST, *supra* note 6, at 104–12.

8. *The Edge with Paula Zahn: Florida Supreme Court Takes Center Stage in Election Deadlock* (Fox News television broadcast, Dec. 5, 2000). Gingrich's comments were made before California submitted amended vote totals on December 27, 2000. These amended totals increased Gore's margin over Bush in the popular vote totals, but only slightly. *See* Cooper, *supra* note 3, at 43 (showing Gore with a 1,199,404 lead over Bush in California at November 11, 2000); U.S. Nat'l Archives & Records Admin., *2000 Presidential Election: Popular Vote Totals*, U.S. ELECTORAL C., http://www.archives.gov/federal-register/electoral-college/2000/popular_ vote.html (last visited June 25, 2012) (discussing the amended returns and showing Gore with a 1,293,774 lead over Bush in California).

9. *See, e.g.*, ANN COULTER, SLANDER: LIBERAL LIES ABOUT THE AMERICAN RIGHT 103 (2002); BILL SAMMON, AT ANY COST: HOW AL GORE TRIED TO STEAL THE ELECTION 19–20 (2001). Other political scientists dismiss the idea that turnout was adversely affected.

10. Editorial, *A Fix for the Electoral College*, BOS. GLOBE, Feb. 18, 2008, at A10.

11. Editorial, *Time to Get Rid of the Electoral College*, MIAMI HERALD, Nov. 5, 2008, at A22.

12. Editorial, *Electoral College Dropout: California Should Join the States Seeking Reform of the Presidential Election System*, L.A. TIMES, Aug. 18, 2008, at A14.

13. Editorial, *Flunking the Electoral College*, N.Y. TIMES, Nov. 20, 2008, at A42. *The Times* editorial staff continued: "One of the main reasons the founders created it was slavery." *Id.*

14. Editorial, *One Person, One Vote for President*, N.Y. TIMES, June 22, 2010, at A26.

15. Editorial, *Another Chance to Lead: Electoral College Bill Sets Reform in Motion*, SACRAMENTO BEE, Sept. 6, 2006, at B6.

16. *Id.*

17. *E.g.*, James P. Pfiffner & Jason Hartke, *The Electoral College and the Framers' Distrust of Democracy*, 3 WHITE HOUSE STUDIES 261, 262–63 (2003). These professors explain:

> Lacking space and having to simplify, most textbooks are forced to present a very abbreviated interpretation of the Framers' intent behind the electoral college. While brevity may be the root of misinterpretation, several of these textbooks lead us to believe that the principal explanatory reason for the creation of the electoral college was the Framers' distrust of the people. By mentioning this distrust as a primary reason for the adoption of the electoral college, these textbooks unintentionally foster an incomplete explanation of the origin of the electoral college.

Id. at 262; *see also* Danny M. Adkison & Christopher Elliott, *The Electoral College: A Misunderstood Institution*, 30 PS: POL. SCI. & POL. 77, 77–79 (1997) (discussing errors made in textbooks).

18. Pfiffner & Hartke, *supra* note 17, at 262 (citation omitted).

19. Bruce Bartlett, *Debating the Electoral College*, TOWNHALL.COM (Nov. 20, 2000), http://townhall.com/columnists/brucebartlett/2000/11/20/debating_the_electoral_college.

20. *Id.*; *see also* Byron York, *The Old College Try: How We Pick the Prez*, NAT'L REV., Dec. 4, 2000, at 24, 24.

21. *See* HARDAWAY, *supra* note 6, at 10.

22. A description of the 1968 election can be found at LAWRENCE D. LONGLEY & NEAL R. PEIRCE, THE ELECTORAL COLLEGE PRIMER 2000, at 59–69 (1999).

23. Frank Newport, *Americans Support Proposal to Eliminate Electoral College System*, GALLUP (Jan. 5, 2001), http://www.gallup.com/poll/2140/americans-support-proposal-eliminate-electoral-college-system.aspx.

24. *Time/CNN Poll: America Shows Patience, in Reversal of Fortune*, TIME, Nov. 20, 2000, at 24, 41.

25. CQ PRESS, *supra* note 5, at 170.

26. *Id.* at 260.

27. THE FEDERALIST NO. 68, at 410 (Alexander Hamilton) (Clinton Rossiter ed., Signet Classic 2003) (1961).

28. *See id.* (noting that complaints against the presidential election system have been few and that even the "most plausible" critic concedes that the "election of the President is pretty well guarded").

Notes

29. L. PAIGE WHITAKER & THOMAS H. NEALE, CONG. RESEARCH SERV., RL30804, THE ELECTORAL COLLEGE: AN OVERVIEW AND ANALYSIS OF REFORM PROPOSALS 17 (2004).

30. *Id.* at 18.

31. U.S. CONST. art. V.

32. TARA ROSS, ENLIGHTENED DEMOCRACY: THE CASE FOR THE ELECTORAL COLLEGE 156–58 (2004).

33. *Id.* at 157.

34. *Id.* at 159.

35. JOHN R. KOZA ET AL., EVERY VOTE EQUAL: A STATE-BASED PLAN FOR ELECTING THE PRESIDENT BY NATIONAL POPULAR VOTE (3d ed. 2011).

36. The full text of the compact can be found on NPV's website. *888-Word Interstate Compact*, NAT'L POPULAR VOTE, http://www.nationalpopularvote.com/pages/misc/888wordcompact.php (last visited June 25, 2012).

37. A list of currently participating states can be found on NPV's website. NAT'L POPULAR VOTE, http://www.nationalpopularvote.com (last visited June 25, 2012). A group opposed to the NPV effort also tracks legislative information. SAVE OUR STATES, http://www.saveourstates.com (last visited June 25, 2012).

38. THE FEDERALIST NO. 68, at 410 (Alexander Hamilton) (Clinton Rossiter ed., Signet Classic 2003) (1961).

Chapter One

1. CLARENCE MANION, THE KEY TO PEACE 49 (1951).

2. This author performed a Lexis search in early 2004 and a second search of state websites in 2011. Two references to "democracy" were found in the states' constitutions. *See* CAL. CONST. art. IV, § 1.5; OR. CONST. art. XV, § 10(2)(a). The Constitution of Puerto Rico also references "democracy." *See* P.R. CONST. pmbl.; *id.* art. II, § 19.

3. Professor Judith Best also makes this point. *See* JUDITH A. BEST, THE CHOICE OF THE PEOPLE? DEBATING THE ELECTORAL COLLEGE 34–35 (1996). Actually, there were suggestions to give the colonies representation in the House of Commons. These proposals were initially championed by some colonists, including Benjamin Franklin. *See* GORDON S. WOOD, THE AMERICANIZATION OF BENJAMIN FRANKLIN 78, 115–16 (2004).

4. JAMES MADISON, NOTES OF DEBATES IN THE FEDERAL CONVENTION OF 1787, at 308 (Adrienne Koch ed., W.W. Norton & Co. 1987) (1966).

5. Denny Pilant, *No—The Electoral College Should Not be Abolished*, *in* CONTROVERSIAL ISSUES IN PRESIDENTIAL SELECTION 216, 226 (Gary L. Rose ed., 1991).

6. Thomas Jefferson, *Inauguration Address* (Mar. 4, 1801), *in* THE LIFE AND SELECTED WRITINGS OF THOMAS JEFFERSON 321, 322 (Adrienne Koch & William Peden eds., 1944).

7. U.S. CONST. art. IV, § 4.

8. James A. Gardner, *Madison's Hope: Virtue, Self-Interest, and the Design of Electoral Systems*, 86 IOWA L. REV. 87, 126 (2000).

9. THE FEDERALIST NO. 10, at 76 (James Madison) (Clinton Rossiter ed., Signet Classic 2003) (1961).

10. MADISON, *supra* note 4, at 39.

11. *Id.* at 42.

12. *Id.* at 110.

13. *Id.* at 233.

14. Letter from James Madison to Thomas Jefferson (Oct. 17, 1788), *in* 11 THE

PAPERS OF JAMES MADISON 295, 298 (Robert A. Rutland et al. eds., 1977).

15. 2 THE DEBATES IN THE SEVERAL STATE CONVENTIONS, ON THE ADOPTION OF THE FEDERAL CONSTITUTION, AS RECOMMENDED BY THE GENERAL CONVENTION AT PHILADELPHIA, IN 1787, at 253 (Jonathan Elliot ed., 2d ed. 1836) [hereinafter ELLIOT'S DEBATES].

16. Letter from John Adams to John Taylor (Apr. 15, 1814), *in* 6 THE WORKS OF JOHN ADAMS, SECOND PRESIDENT OF THE UNITED STATES 447, 484 (Charles Francis Adams ed., 2d prtg. 1969).

17. Letter from Benjamin Rush to John Adams (July 21, 1789), *in* 1 LETTERS OF BENJAMIN RUSH 522, 523 (L. H. Butterfield ed., 1951).

18. JOHN WITHERSPOON, *Lecture XII of Civil Society, in* AN ANNOTATED EDITION OF *LECTURES ON MORAL PHILOSOPHY* 140, 144 (Jack Scott ed., 1982).

19. Fisher Ames, Speech in the Convention of Massachusetts, on Biennial Elections (Jan. 1788), *in* 2 WORKS OF FISHER AMES 3, 7 (Seth Ames ed., 1854).

20. PAUL JOHNSON, A HISTORY OF THE AMERICAN PEOPLE 179 (HarperCollins Publishers 1st U.S. ed. 1998) (1997).

21. Patrick Henry, Speech before the Virginia Ratifying Convention (June 5, 1788), *in* THE ANTI-FEDERALIST PAPERS AND THE CONSTITUTIONAL CONVENTION DEBATES 199, 199 (Ralph Ketcham ed., Signet Classic 2003) (1986).

22. *The Address and Reasons of Dissent of the Minority of the Convention of Pennsylvania to their Constituents,* PA. PACKET (Phila.), Dec. 18, 1787, *reprinted in* THE ANTI-FEDERALIST PAPERS AND THE CONSTITUTIONAL CONVENTION DEBATES, *supra* note 21, at 237, 242.

23. 3 ELLIOT'S DEBATES, *supra* note 15, at 22 (emphasis added).

24. *Id.*

25. "Brutus," *To the Citizens of the State of New York,* N.Y. J. (N.Y.C.), Oct 18, 1787, *reprinted in* THE ANTI-FEDERALIST PAPERS AND THE CONSTITUTIONAL CONVENTION DEBATES, *supra* note 21, at 270, 276.

26. *Id.* at 277.

27. Gordon Wood gives a much more detailed account of the conflicting feelings about democratic and republican principles in early America. *See generally* GORDON S. WOOD, THE RADICALISM OF THE AMERICAN REVOLUTION (Vintage Books 1993) (1992). Some of the discussion of democracies v. republics may have been complicated by another discussion: Can "ordinary" men serve as wise elected officials in a republic or will they be too easily swayed by their private business interests? Must educated gentlemen—"men of learning, leisure and easy circumstances . . . if they are endowed with wisdom, virtue & humanity"—serve as elected officials? *Id.* at 254 (citing Charles Nisbet, president of Dickinson College).

28. Walter Berns, *Let's Hear It for the Electoral College, in* AFTER THE PEOPLE VOTE: A GUIDE TO THE ELECTORAL COLLEGE 51, 52–53 (John C. Fortier ed., 3d ed. 2004).

29. THE DECLARATION OF INDEPENDENCE para 2 (U.S. 1776).

30. MADISON, *supra* note 4, at 64.

31. *Id.* at 39.

32. *Id.*

33. *Id.*

34. *Id.*

35. *Id.* at 40.

36. *Id.*

37. THE FEDERALIST NO. 39, at 236 (James Madison) (Clinton Rossiter ed., Signet Classic 2003) (1961).

Notes

38. THE FEDERALIST NO. 49, at 314 (James Madison) (Clinton Rossiter ed., Signet Classic 2003) (1961).

39. 2 ELLIOT'S DEBATES, *supra* note 15, at 434.

40. *Id.*

41. *Id.*

42. WILLIAM G. CARR, THE OLDEST DELEGATE: FRANKLIN IN THE CONSTITUTIONAL CONVENTION 122 (1990) (citation omitted). Many Americans have misquoted this statement in recent years, instead stating that Benjamin Franklin responded: "A democracy, if you can keep it." The misquotes reflect many Americans' declining understanding of their heritage.

43. Indeed, the state legislatures selected each state's Senators until passage of the 17th Amendment provided for direct senatorial elections by the people of each state.

44. *But see* DAVID W. ABBOTT & JAMES P. LEVINE, WRONG WINNER: THE COMING DEBACLE IN THE ELECTORAL COLLEGE 91–93 (1991) (arguing that while Hispanics "have potentially great electoral leverage because of their geographical distribution," they are unable to take advantage of the benefit because of "political differentiations between [sic] Puerto Ricans, Cubans, and Mexican-Americans" and because many Hispanics are not citizens and, thus, cannot vote).

45. *See id.* at 86–87 (listing Jewish voters as an "advantaged group" under the Electoral College system).

46. Editorial, *College Dropouts,* INVESTOR'S BUS. DAILY, Mar. 27, 2006, at A18; *see also Proposals for Electoral College Reform: Hearings on H.J. Res. 28 and H.J. Res. 43 Before the Subcomm. on the Constitution of the House Comm. on the Judiciary,* 105th Cong. 55 (1997) (statement of Curtis Gans, Director, Committee for the Study of the American Electorate), *available at* http://commdocs.house.gov/committees/judiciary/hju57219.000/hju57219_0f.htm.

47. CQ PRESS, PRESIDENTIAL ELECTIONS: 1789–2008, at 156 (2010).

48. Thurmond also received one vote from a fifth state. Preston Parks, a Truman elector in Tennessee, switched his vote to Thurmond. *See id.* at 189, 246.

49. George Edwards criticizes the first edition of *Enlightened Democracy* for providing a "positive example" of Strom Thurmond. GEORGE C. EDWARDS III, WHY THE ELECTORAL COLLEGE IS BAD FOR AMERICA 143 (2d ed. 2011). This paragraph is simply discussing the manner in which the voice of a minority group can be amplified in certain circumstances. This author is not endorsing Thurmond's segregationist views. Moreover, Edwards fails to note that the first edition also impliedly lumps Thurmond in with the "extremist or unhealthy third parties" discussed a few sentences later (in both editions of this book). The Electoral College amplifies minority voices in some instances and diminishes their impact in others. This system cannot perfectly separate the extremists from the reasonable third parties (nor can any system purport to be perfect), but the Electoral College tends to have the overall positive effect of allowing reasonable third parties to impact public policy whereas extremist groups tend to remain on the fringes.

50. *See* discussion *supra* note 49.

51. MADISON, *supra* note 4, at 308.

52. Gray v. Sanders, 372 U.S. 368, 376 n.8 (1963).

53. MADISON, *supra* note 4, at 629; *see also* LUCIUS WILMERDING, JR., THE ELECTORAL COLLEGE 19 (1958).

54. THE FEDERALIST NO. 68, at 410 (Alexander Hamilton) (Clinton Rossiter ed., Signet Classic 2003) (1961).

55. 2 ELLIOT'S DEBATES, *supra* note 15, at 448.

56. S. COMM. ON THE JUDICIARY, DIRECT POPULAR ELECTION OF THE

PRESIDENT, S. REP. NO. 91-1123, at 29 (1970) (minority views of Messrs. Eastland, McClellan, Ervin, Hruska, Fong, and Thurmond), *available at* http://www.ashbrook.org/articles/electoralcollege-directpopular.html.

Chapter Two

1. For information on the events that transpired before the Constitutional Convention commenced, see CATHERINE DRINKER BOWEN, MIRACLE AT PHILADELPHIA: THE STORY OF THE CONSTITUTIONAL CONVENTION MAY TO SEPTEMBER 1787 (2d prtg. 1986); CAROL BERKIN, A BRILLIANT SOLUTION: INVENTING THE AMERICAN CONSTITUTION (1st Harvest ed. 2003); ROBERT M. HARDAWAY, THE ELECTORAL COLLEGE AND THE CONSTITUTION: THE CASE FOR PRESERVING FEDERALISM 69–75 (1994); *see also* Roger A. Bruns, *A More Perfect Union: The Creation of the U.S. Constitution*, U.S. NAT'L ARCHIVES & RECORDS ADMIN., http://www.archives.gov/exhibits/charters/constitution_history.html (last visited June 25, 2012).

2. THE FEDERALIST NO. 40, at 244 (James Madison) (Clinton Rossiter ed., Signet Classic 2003) (1961).

3. The first edition of this book erroneously stated that six states had no delegates in attendance when the Constitutional Convention opened on May 25. The Convention could have begun with six states absent, since a quorum of only seven states was required. In actuality, nine states were represented on May 25; two of these states had only one delegate in attendance. *See* JAMES MADISON, NOTES OF DEBATES IN THE FEDERAL CONVENTION OF 1787, at 23 (Adrienne Koch ed., W.W. Norton & Co. 1987) (1966).

4. BOWEN, *supra* note 1, at 4.

5. JAMES THOMAS FLEXNER, WASHINGTON: THE INDISPENSABLE MAN 207 (Back Bay ed. 1974). It could also be that his nature made him more prone to reflect than speak during debates, as Jefferson once observed of his former colleague's demeanor in the Virginia legislature. BOWEN, *supra* note 1, at 29.

6. JOSEPH J. ELLIS, FOUNDING BROTHERS: THE REVOLUTIONARY GENERATION 120 (15th prtg. 2001).

7. BOWEN, *supra* note 1, at 30.

8. Shlomo Slonim, *Designing the Electoral College*, *in* INVENTING THE AMERICAN PRESIDENCY 33, 33 (Thomas E. Cronin ed., 1989).

9. For detailed discussions of the Convention debates from a variety of viewpoints, see generally *id.* at 33–60; *see also* HARDAWAY, *supra* note 1, at 76–89; William Josephson & Beverly J. Ross, *Repairing the Electoral College*, 22 J. LEGIS. 145, 151–53 (1996); NEAL R. PEIRCE & LAWRENCE D. LONGLEY, THE PEOPLE'S PRESIDENT: THE ELECTORAL COLLEGE IN AMERICAN HISTORY AND THE DIRECT VOTE ALTERNATIVE 10–30 (Yale Univ. Press rev. ed. 1981) (1968).

10. MADISON, *supra* note 3, at 309.

11. *Id.* at 306.

12. *Id.* at 307.

13. *Id.* at 306.

14. *Id.*

15. *Id.* at 326–27.

16. WILLIAM PETERS, A MORE PERFECT UNION 99 (1987).

17. *See* U.S. CONST. art I, § 2, cl. 3; *id.* art. I, § 3, cl. 1; *id.* art II, § 1, cl. 2.

18. *See id.* art II, § 1, cl. 3 (amended 1804).

19. In a similar vein, Derek Muller argues that the ability of states to determine their own elector allocation was an additional important concession—an element of "invisible federalism"—that has had the effect of protecting the stability of American presidential

elections. *See* Derek T. Muller, *Invisible Federalism and the Electoral College*, 44 ARIZ. ST. L.J. (forthcoming 2012).

20. Letter from James Madison to Henry Lee (Jan. 14, 1825), *in* 9 THE WRITINGS OF JAMES MADISON 215, 217 (Gaillard Hunt ed., 1910).

21. LAWRENCE D. LONGLEY & NEAL R. PEIRCE, THE ELECTORAL COLLEGE PRIMER 2000, at 20 (1999).

22. PEIRCE & LONGLEY, PEOPLE'S PRESIDENT, *supra* note 9, at 30 (citation omitted).

23. *Id.*

24. MADISON, *supra* note 3, at 578; *see also* MAX FARRAND, THE FRAMING OF THE CONSTITUTION OF THE UNITED STATES 164 (7th prtg. 1930).

25. U.S. CONST. art. II, § 1, cl. 3; *id.* amend. XII.

26. S. COMM. ON THE JUDICIARY, DIRECT POPULAR ELECTION OF THE PRESIDENT, S. REP. NO. 91-1123, at 37 (1970) (minority views of Messrs. Eastland, McClellan, Ervin, Hruska, Fong, and Thurmond) (quoting Prof. Alexander Bickel), *available at* http://www.ashbrook.org/articles/electoralcollege-directpopular.html.

27. McPherson v. Blacker, 146 U.S. 1, 27, 35 (1892).

28. The states' discretion is the underlying foundation for the selection of presidential electors, but some recent Court decisions reflect a dispute concerning the extent to which the Equal Protection Clause or the First Amendment may curb state discretion once a state legislature has chosen direct popular election as its method of appointing electors. A state legislature does not have to choose direct popular election; however, once it has done so, some federal constitutional rights may be held to attach. *See, e.g.*, Anderson v. Celebrezze, 460 U.S. 780, 794 n.18 (1983); Williams v. Rhodes, 393 U.S. 23, 29 (1968).

29. 531 U.S. 98, 104 (2000) (per curiam).

30. Hall v. Beals, 396 U.S. 45, 52 (1969) (Marshall, J., dissenting) (asserting that the case before the Court was not moot, as held by the majority).

31. Letter from George Washington to James Madison (Nov. 5, 1786), *in* 4 THE PAPERS OF GEORGE WASHINGTON: CONFEDERATION SERIES 331, 332 (W.W. Abbot et al. eds., 1994).

32. 4 THE DEBATES IN THE SEVERAL STATE CONVENTIONS, ON THE ADOPTION OF THE FEDERAL CONSTITUTION, AS RECOMMENDED BY THE GENERAL CONVENTION AT PHILADELPHIA, IN 1787, at 262 (Jonathan Elliot ed., 2d ed. 1836).

33. This number includes resident population overseas or in the military. KRISTIN D. BURNETT, U.S. CENSUS BUREAU, CONGRESSIONAL APPORTIONMENT: 2010 CENSUS BRIEFS 2 tbl.1 (Nov. 2011), *available at* http://www.census.gov/prod/cen2010/briefs/c2010br-08.pdf.

34. Texas Almanac, *Government: State Government*, TEX. STATE HIST. ASS'N, http://www.texasalmanac.com/topics/government/government (last visited June 25, 2012).

35. One interesting twist on this principle could occur in New Hampshire. A group of libertarians is working to recruit 20,000 members to move to New Hampshire. Once there, these libertarians feel that the weight of their voices, together, will be enough to influence local elections, particularly since the population in that state is relatively small. From there, these libertarians hope to grow in influence until they have successfully reduced the size and scope of government, first in their cities and then in their newly adopted state. More information on this project is available at: http://www.freestateproject.org.

36. For instance, a recent U.S. Census Bureau report shows that the most common state-to-state move in 2010 was from California to Texas. The tenth most common move was from California to Nevada. *Mover Rate Reaches Record Low, Census Bureau Reports*, U.S. CENSUS BUREAU (Nov. 15, 2011), http://www.census.gov/newsroom/releases/archives/

mobility_of_the_population/cb11-193.html.

37. *See* NGA CENTER FOR BEST PRACTICES, http://www.nga.org/cms/render/ live/center (last visited June 25, 2012). As mentioned in the first edition of this book, such attempts to learn from other states may sometimes become part of a candidate's campaign platform. During California's 2003 gubernatorial recall election, then-candidate Arnold Schwarzenegger argued that, if elected, he would "[c]reate a working wholesale power market based on the lessons learned from other states . . . . It is time to learn from other successful restructurings enacted by Texas, the New England states, and the Mid-Atlantic states of Pennsylvania, New Jersey and Maryland." TARA ROSS, ENLIGHTENED DEMOCRACY: THE CASE FOR THE ELECTORAL COLLEGE 57 (2004).

38. New State Ice Co. v. Liebmann, 285 U.S. 262, 311 (1932) (Brandeis, J., dissenting).

39. JUDITH A. BEST, THE CHOICE OF THE PEOPLE? DEBATING THE ELECTORAL COLLEGE 37–39 (1996).

40. Obviously, to the extent the judiciary arrogates to itself the power to legislate and oversee the other branches, the less force this argument will have. *See, e.g.*, Lawrence v. Texas, 539 U.S. 558 (2003); Roe v. Wade, 410 U.S. 113 (1973).

41. BEST, *supra* note 39, at 38.

42. HARDAWAY, *supra* note 1, at 77; *see also* BERKIN, *supra* note 1, at 74.

43. The first edition of this book stated that Rhode Island "believed that the rights of the small states would not be respected." ROSS, *supra* note 37, at 59. It would have been better to emphasize the belief of some Rhode Islanders that a more powerful national government would almost certainly result from the Convention; they were generally reluctant to cede power to a centralized government. FRANK GREENE BATES, RHODE ISLAND AND THE FORMATION OF THE UNION 149–60 (N.Y., Macmillan Co. 1898); *see also* Bruns, *supra* note 1. Catherine Bowen adds further color: "It was common knowledge that certain politicians were feathering their nests under the system [in Rhode Island]. A strong central government no doubt would force debts to be paid in specie." BOWEN, *supra* note 1, at 13. Having said that, Rhode Islander's fears were doubtless intensified by the state's small size and a perception that it would be harder to stand up to other states under another system. Rhode Islanders would have remembered that mere years before, in 1782, the Continental Congress had sought an impost on goods imported into the United States. The tax would have hit Rhode Island hard due to its heavy reliance on its maritime industry. Rhode Island opposed and defeated the measure. *See* BATES, *supra*, at 72–83; RON CHERNOW, ALEXANDER HAMILTON 176 (2004); HON. WILLIAM R. STAPLES, LL.D., RHODE ISLAND IN THE CONTINENTAL CONGRESS 380–411 (Reuben Aldridge Guild ed., Providence, Providence Press Co. 1870). Rhode Island had benefited from "one state, one vote" representation in the past and would not easily forget that fact.

44. Following the 2000 election, several small states filed resolutions with the Congress in support of the Electoral College and the protections that it offers to small states. *See, e.g.*, 147 CONG. REC. 14,116–17 (2001); 147 CONG. REC. 7937 (2001); 147 CONG. REC. 6498 (2001).

Chapter Three

1. U.S. CONST. art. II, § 1, cls. 2–4.

2. *Id.* amend. XII.

3. *Id.* art. II, § 1, cl. 2 & 4.

4. George Washington announced his retirement in September 1796, shortly before the presidential election. Farewell Address (Sept. 19, 1796), *reprinted in* 35 THE WRITINGS OF GEORGE WASHINGTON FROM THE ORIGINAL MANUSCRIPT SOURCES 1745-1799,

at 214 (John C. Fitzpatrick ed., 1940). This retirement became effective in March 1797 when John Adams was sworn into office.

5. ROBERT M. HARDAWAY, THE ELECTORAL COLLEGE AND THE CONSTITUTION: THE CASE FOR PRESERVING FEDERALISM 91 (1994) (discussing the Federalist strategy in 1796); see also NEAL R. PEIRCE & LAWRENCE D. LONGLEY, THE PEOPLE'S PRESIDENT: THE ELECTORAL COLLEGE IN AMERICAN HISTORY AND THE DIRECT VOTE ALTERNATIVE 35 (Yale Univ. Press rev. ed. 1981) (1968) (same).

6. Descriptions of the election of 1800 can be found at: DAVID W. ABBOTT & JAMES P. LEVINE, WRONG WINNER: THE COMING DEBACLE IN THE ELECTORAL COLLEGE 13–14 (1991); ROBERT W. BENNETT, TAMING THE ELECTORAL COLLEGE 22–23 (2006); DAVID P. CURRIE, THE CONSTITUTION IN CONGRESS: THE FEDERALIST PERIOD, 1789—1801, at 292–93 (1997); THOMAS FLEMING, DUEL: ALEXANDER HAMILTON, AARON BURR, AND THE FUTURE OF AMERICA 93–97, 101–02 (1999); HARDAWAY, supra note 5, at 91–92; EDWARD J. LARSON, A MAGNIFICENT CATASTROPHE: THE TUMULTUOUS ELECTION OF 1800, AMERICA'S FIRST PRESIDENTIAL CAMPAIGN 241–70 (2007); 4 DUMAS MALONE, JEFFERSON AND HIS TIME: JEFFERSON THE PRESIDENT; FIRST TERM, 1801–1805, at 3–16 (1970); PEIRCE & LONGLEY, supra note 5, at 36–41.

7. Records of the voting can be found at: 10 ANNALS OF CONG. 1022–30 (1801). The voting ensued from February 11 to February 17, 1801. The House did not meet on February 15, which was Sunday. News reports discussing the voting on the floor are also included in a lengthy footnote in the Annals of Congress. See id. at 1028–33 (citing Feb 13, 16 and 18 reports of the National Intelligencer, including individual votes cast by representatives).

8. Letter from Thomas Jefferson to Dr. Benjamin Rush (Jan. 16, 1811), in THE LIFE AND SELECTED WRITINGS OF THOMAS JEFFERSON 607, 610 (Adrienne Koch & William Peden eds., 1944).

9. A description of these events can be found at MALONE, supra note 6, at 487 app. I.

10. FLEMING, supra note 6, at 97 (citation omitted).

11. Donald Lutz et al., The Electoral College in Historical and Philosophical Perspective, in CHOOSING A PRESIDENT: THE ELECTORAL COLLEGE AND BEYOND 31, 37 (Paul D. Schumaker & Burdett A. Loomis eds., 2002) (discussing the negotiations over the 12th Amendment).

12. Amendments to the Constitution, U.S. HOUSE REPRESENTATIVES, http://www.house.gov/house/Constitution/Amend.html (last updated Sept. 20, 2004).

13. U.S. CONST. amend. XII. Additional provisions, such as the timing for the Electoral College vote, can be found in Title 3 of the U.S. Code.

14. See U.S. CONST. art. II, § 1, cl. 3; id. amend. XII.

15. See id. art. II, § 1, cl. 2 & 4; id. amend. XII.

16. Id. art. II, § 1, cl. 2.

17. See id. art. I, § 2, cl. 3; id. art. I, § 3, cl. 1.

18. Id. amend XXIII, § 1. The District of Columbia is entitled to the same number of electors "to which the District would be entitled if it were a State," but it would never have more than three electoral votes unless the least populous state also had more than three electoral votes. The 23rd Amendment provides that D.C. may have "in no event more than the least populous State." Id.

19. These numbers were extrapolated from the results of the 2010 U.S. Census. See 2010 CENSUS, http://2010.census.gov/2010census (last visited June 26, 2012).

20. U.S. CONST. art. II, § 1, cl. 2.

21. Bush v. Gore, 531 U.S. 98, 104 (2000) (per curiam).

22. Id.; see also McPherson v. Blacker, 146 U.S. 1, 34–35 (1892).

23. A discussion of the first several presidential elections can be found at *McPherson*, 146 U.S. at 29–32.

24. *See* L. PAIGE WHITAKER & THOMAS H. NEALE, CONG. RESEARCH SERV., RL30804, THE ELECTORAL COLLEGE: AN OVERVIEW AND ANALYSIS OF REFORM PROPOSALS 1-2 (2004). There have been occasional exceptions to the general rule, as detailed at CQ PRESS, PRESIDENTIAL ELECTIONS: 1789–2008, at 192 (2010).

25. *See, e.g.*, Scott Bauer, *Proposal Would Change Electoral College in Wis.*, ASSOCIATED PRESS (Oct. 12, 2011), *available at* http://seattletimes.nwsource.com/html/politics/2016485205_apuselectoralcollegewisconsin.html; Jeff Brady, *Pa. May Change Electoral College Allocation Rules*, NPR (Sept. 16, 2011), http://www.npr.org/2011/09/16/140543466/pa-may-change-electoral-college-allocation-rules; Valerie Richardson, *Group Seeks to Split Colorado Electors*, WASH. TIMES (June 16, 2004), at A5.

26. ME. REV. STAT. tit. 21-A, § 802 (2009); NEB. REV. STAT. § 32-1038 (2011).

27. *See* CQ PRESS, *supra* note 24, at 189. Nebraska adopted its plan in time for the 1992 presidential election. *See id.* at 192 (discussing Nebraska's adoption of the congressional district system); LAWRENCE D. LONGLEY & NEAL R. PEIRCE, THE ELECTORAL COLLEGE PRIMER 2000, at 106–07 (1999) (same).

28. Maine adopted its District Plan in 1969, putting it into effect for the first time during the 1972 presidential election. *See* CQ PRESS, *supra* note 24, at 192 (discussing Maine's adoption of the congressional district system); LONGLEY & PEIRCE, *supra* note 27, at 106 (same).

29. *See, e.g.*, MICHAEL J. GLENNON, WHEN NO MAJORITY RULES: THE ELECTORAL COLLEGE AND PRESIDENTIAL SUCCESSION 35–44 (1992) (discussing the "constitutional minefield" that must be navigated when determining where the state's power to select electors ends and where congressional power to count electoral votes begins).

30. *See* WILLIAM H. REHNQUIST, CENTENNIAL CRISIS: THE DISPUTED ELECTION OF 1876, at 113–19 (2004).

31. Act of Feb. 3, 1887, ch. 90, 24 Stat. 373 (current version at 3 U.S.C. §§ 1–21 (2006)).

32. Some dispute exists regarding the extent of congressional authority in this area. Both the states and Congress have some power in this area, but where do the boundaries of each power lie? The Constitution gives Congress the power to "determine the Time of chusing the Electors, and the Day on which they shall give their Votes." U.S. CONST. art. II, § 1, cl. 4. It also gives Congress the authority to "count" the electoral votes. U.S. CONST. amend XII. The states are explicitly given their own authority as well, to "appoint, in such Manner as the Legislature thereof may direct, a Number of Electors." U.S. CONST. art. II, § 1, cl. 2. For a deeper discussion of this issue, see Vasan Kesavan, *Is the Electoral Count Act Unconstitutional?*, 80 N.C. L. REV. 1653 (2002); *cf.* Samuel Issacharoff, *Law, Rules, and Presidential Selection*, 120 POL. SCI. Q. 113, 125 (2005) (questioning whether one Congress can bind future Congresses to count electoral votes in any particular fashion). One Electoral College opponent states that laws such as the Electoral Count Act should be upheld as "an attempt to bring order to a process that raises serious danger of uncertain and inconsistent outcomes," despite his own admission that the constitutionality of the law is questionable. BENNETT, *supra* note 6, at 148–50, 206 n.57.

33. 3 U.S.C. § 1 (2006).

34. *See* AFTER THE PEOPLE VOTE: A GUIDE TO THE ELECTORAL COLLEGE 83 app. C (John C. Fortier ed., 3d ed. 2004) (listing the states' procedures for including or excluding the names of electors on their presidential ballots).

35. 3 U.S.C. § 6.

36. For a listing of state laws on the subject, see U.S. Nat'l Archives & Records

Notes

Admin., *What is the Electoral College? State Laws and Requirements*, U.S. ELECTORAL C., http://www.archives.gov/federal-register/electoral-college/laws.html (last visited June 26, 2012); *see also* AFTER THE PEOPLE VOTE, *supra* note 34, at 83 app. C.

37. 3 U.S.C. § 7.

38. *Id.* §§ 9–11.

39. *See id.* §§ 12–13. This deadline falls on December 26 in 2012 and December 28 in 2016.

40. *See id.* § 15.

41. U.S. CONST. amend XII.

42. *Id.*

43. There may be some ambiguity if more than three candidates tie for one or more of the top three spots. *See* William Josephson, *Senate Election of the Vice President and House of Representatives Election of the President*, 11 U. PA. J. CONST. L. 597, 630–31, 633–34 (2009).

44. *See id.* at 613 (discussing the considerations if more than two candidates tie for the top spots).

45. A detailed discussion of these logistical issues is beyond the scope of this book, but these questions are discussed at length in *id.*; *see also* HARDAWAY, *supra* note 5, at 55–61.

46. The Constitution makes provision for what constitutes a quorum of states ("a quorum for this purpose shall consist of a member or members from two-thirds of the states"), but it does not address the subject of quorums within state delegations. U.S. CONST. amend. XII; *see also* Josephson, *supra* note 43, at 630, 636–37.

47. The 1825 House Rules are reprinted in AFTER THE PEOPLE VOTE, *supra* note 34, at 85 app. D (citation omitted).

48. For an argument that multiple interpretations can be given to the phrase "a majority of the votes given," see Josephson, *supra* note 43, at 629. Josephson argues that the phrase could mean "the whole number of votes given *to* such state" as opposed to "a majority of those present and voting." *Id.* This author leans toward the latter interpretation, per the examples in the text.

49. U.S. CONST. amend. XII.

50. *But see* Josephson, *supra* note 43, at 602 n.11 ("When the Twelfth Amendment says 'ballot,' it means the identity of each voter is not revealed, i.e., is secret."). Further discussion of the meaning of the "ballot" requirement can be found at HARDAWAY, *supra* note 5, at 58; Josephson, *supra* note 43, at 632.

51. *See, e.g.,* 10 ANNALS OF CONG. 1032–33 (1801) (quoting the *National Intelligencer*).

52. U.S. CONST. amend. XX, § 1.

53. 3 U.S.C. § 15 (2006).

54. HARDAWAY, *supra* note 5, at 56 (discussing House deliberations in 1992).

55. Seth Tillman has criticized this argument, made in the first edition of *Enlightened Democracy*. He states:

> But any such course is in all likelihood unconstitutional. One House cannot generally bind a successor House. Each House, elected every two years, has equal constitutional powers under the terms of the Constitution, and that temporal equality extends to equal authority to make or unmake House rules governing contingency elections for President.

Seth Tillman, *Betwixt Principle and Practice: Tara Ross's Defense of the Electoral College*, 1 N.Y.U. J.L. & LIBERTY 921, 923 (2005) (book review). Naturally, subsequent Houses would have to readopt these procedures, just as they already readopt their standing rules at the beginning of each Congress (usually adopted en bloc, but with amendments). That fact does not obscure the point that discussing and adopting procedures early, before there is a need for them, will be the best way to create a set of objective, non-partisan rules. Of course the new House would be constitutionally entitled to object to the procedures and to argue for new rules when the time came, but, as a pragmatic matter, they would be more likely to readopt the rules largely as they have already been written. Any other route smacks of partisanship and the type of political gamesmanship that most voters have come to distrust. *Cf.* Josephson, *supra* note 43, at 646ff (discussing steps that can be taken, whether by House Rules or by statute, to address unresolved logistical issues with the House contingent election and encouraging discussion of these steps before an immediate need for them arises).

56. MAX FARRAND, THE FRAMING OF THE CONSTITUTION OF THE UNITED STATES 175 (7th prtg. 1930).

Chapter Four

1. The phrase "one person, one vote" does not appear in the Constitution. It first appeared in a Supreme Court opinion in Gray v. Sanders, 372 U.S. 368, 381 (1963).

2. LAWRENCE D. LONGLEY & NEAL R. PEIRCE, THE ELECTORAL COLLEGE PRIMER 1–14 (1996).

3. *Proposals for Electoral College Reform: Hearings on H.J. Res. 28 and H.J. Res. 43 Before the Subcomm. on the Constitution of the House Comm. on the Judiciary*, 105th Cong. 48 (1997) (statement of Akhil Reed Amar, Professor, Yale University Law School), http://commdocs. house.gov/committees/judiciary/hju57219.000/hju57219_0f.htm.

4. U.S. CONST. amend. X.

5. *Id.* art I, § 8, cl. 3.

6. United States v. Lopez, 514 U.S. 549 (1995).

7. United States v. Morrison, 529 U.S. 598 (2000).

8. On the pretext of lightening the case load of older Justices, FDR proposed adding up to one additional Justice for every member of the Court who was 70 years of age or older. Up to six new Justices could have been appointed under the plan. *See* WILLIAM E. LEUCHTENBURG, FRANKLIN D. ROOSEVELT AND THE NEW DEAL: 1932-1940, at 231–38 (1963) (discussing FDR's battles with the Supreme Court); DIXON WECTER, THE AGE OF THE GREAT DEPRESSION: 1929-1941, at 104–06 (1948); John Wallace, Comment, *Stare Decisis and the Rehnquist Court: The Collision of Activism, Passivism and Politics in* Casey, 42 BUFF. L. REV. 187, 223 (1994) (discussing the court packing plan).

9. 300 U.S. 379 (1937). Justice Roberts's opinion contradicted a stance that he had taken the year before in *Morehead v. New York ex rel. Tipaldo*, 298 U.S. 587 (1936).

10. As the story has traditionally been told, Roberts switched his position specifically because of FDR's court-packing plan. Chief Justice Hughes also became a steadier ally. *See, e.g.,* LEUCHTENBURG, *supra* note 8, at 231–38; WECTER, *supra* note 8, at 104–06. However, recent research into this area suggests that maybe the Court was generally ready to switch its position on New Deal issues, with or without the court-packing plan. *See* BARRY CUSHMAN, RETHINKING THE NEW DEAL COURT: THE STRUCTURE OF A CONSTITUTIONAL REVOLUTION (1998); MARIAN CECILIA MCKENNA, FRANKLIN ROOSEVELT AND THE GREAT CONSTITUTIONAL WAR: THE COURT-PACKING CRISIS OF 1937 (2002); *see also* Alan Brinkley, *AHR Forum: The Debate over the Constitutional Revolution of 1937—Introduction*, 110 AM. HIST. REV. 1046 (2005), *available at* http://www.historycooperative. org/journals/ahr/110.4/brinkley.html. This author takes no position on the matter. For purposes of this book, the important point is that the Court's view of the Commerce Clause radically changed during the Great Depression, apparently to make the New Deal possible. As the Court's rulings have changed, so has public perception of federal power.

11. 301 U.S. 1 (1937).

Notes

12. *Id.* at 30.

13. *Id.*

14. Wickard v. Filburn, 317 U.S. 111, 128 (1942). Mr. Filburn sold a portion of his crop, but used the rest for (1) feeding his poultry and livestock; (2) making flour for home consumption; and (3) seeding a crop for the following year. *Id.* at 114.

15. Patient Protection and Affordable Care Act, Pub. L. No. 111–148, 124 Stat. 119 (2010). Congress passed the law in reliance upon the Commerce Clause, but the Court upheld it on other grounds. Editorial, *The Roberts Rules*, WALL ST. J., June 29, 2012, at A12.

16. Although recent instances of mob violence in various cities may suggest otherwise. *See, e.g.*, Rebecca Camber, *Powerless Police Let Mob Seize Streets*, DAILY MAIL (U.K.), Aug. 9, 2011 at 1; Patrice Hill, *Greek Woes Hit World Markets; Tougher Austerity Plan Spurs Riots; Risk of Default Grows*, WASH. TIMES, June 16, 2011, at A1; *Schell Urges: Stay in Control*, SEATTLE TIMES, Dec. 2, 1999, at A1; *see also* Richard A. Serrano & Tracy Wilkinson, *All 4 in King Beating Acquitted: Violence Follows Verdicts: Guard Called Out*, L.A. TIMES, Apr. 30, 1992, at A1.

17. Ben Wildavsky, *School of Hard Knocks*, U.S. NEWS & WORLD REP., Nov. 20, 2000, at 52, 52.

18. *See* CQ PRESS, PRESIDENTIAL ELECTIONS: 1789–2008, at 125, 215 (2010).

19. The text contains a listing of major candidates only.

20. PAUL JOHNSON, A HISTORY OF THE AMERICAN PEOPLE 331 (HarperCollins Publishers 1st U.S. ed. 1998) (1997) (citation omitted).

21. *Id.* at 332.

22. U.S. CONST. amend. XV.

23. *Id.* amend. XVII.

24. *Id.* amend. XIX.

25. Kevin Phillips, . . . *And Its Musty Old Quirks*, TIME, Nov. 20, 2000, at 67, 67.

Chapter Five

1. RONALD REAGAN, REAGAN, IN HIS OWN HAND 243 (Kiron K. Skinner et al. eds., 2001) (strikeouts in original eliminated and abbreviations expanded).

2. Jeff Greenfield, *The Hidden Beauty of the System*, TIME, Nov. 20, 2000, at 66, 66.

3. *See, e.g.*, Note, *Rethinking the Electoral College Debate: The Framers, Federalism, and One Person, One Vote*, 114 HARV. L. REV. 2526, 2532 n.31 (2001).

4. LAWRENCE D. LONGLEY & NEAL R. PEIRCE, THE ELECTORAL COLLEGE PRIMER 2000, at 136 (1999).

5. JOHN R. KOZA ET AL., EVERY VOTE EQUAL: A STATE-BASED PLAN FOR ELECTING THE PRESIDENT BY NATIONAL POPULAR VOTE 20 (3d ed. 2011).

6. CQ PRESS, PRESIDENTIAL ELECTIONS: 1789–2008, at 171 (2010).

7. *Id.* at 261.

8. *See* U.S. CONST. art. II, § 1, cl. 2.

9. *Id.*

10. Bush v. Gore, 531 U.S. 98, 104 (2000) (per curiam).

11. Although some Nebraskans would like to return to a winner-take-all system. *See, e.g.*, L.B. 21, 102d Leg., 1st Sess. (Nev. 2011).

12. Kathryn Jean Lopez, *Hillary Is Wrong: An Interview with Charles R. Kesler*, NAT'L REV. ONLINE (Nov. 13, 2000) (copy on file with author); *cf.* Norman R. Williams, *Reforming the Electoral College: Federalism, Majoritarianism, and the Perils of Subconstitutional Change*, 100 GEO. L.J. 173, 183–84 (2011) ("[T]he popular provenance of the electors, coupled with the faithful transmittal of electoral preferences by the electors themselves, has fatally undermined any suggestion that the Electoral College is *antidemocratic.* . . . Rather,

the principal charge against the Electoral College is that it is *antimajoritarian*.").

13. Technically, of course, they do not need to win a majority of states in order to win the election. (They need a majority of electoral votes.) Practically speaking, however, they will need to win most states—or close to this majority—in order to obtain an electoral majority. Only two Presidents this century have been elected with less than a majority of states: John F. Kennedy (23 states) and Jimmy Carter (23 states plus D.C.). *See also* discussion *infra* note 4 (Ch. 15) and accompanying text.

14. JAMES MACGREGOR BURNS, THE DEADLOCK OF DEMOCRACY: FOUR-PARTY POLITICS IN AMERICA 251 (1963), *quoted in* JUDITH BEST, THE CASE AGAINST DIRECT ELECTION OF THE PRESIDENT: A DEFENSE OF THE ELECTORAL COLLEGE 66 (1975).

15. *Id.*

16. *Id.*

17. *See, e.g.*, Akhil Reed Amar, *Presidents Without Mandates (With Special Emphasis on Ohio)*, 67 U. CIN. L. REV. 375, 391 (1999) (asserting that the popular vote winner is usually the Electoral College winner, and, thus, it is hard to see why campaign strategies would change).

18. The World Series example is often used as an analogy for the Electoral College. One example can be found at: Michael Herz, *How the Electoral College Imitates the World Series*, 23 CARDOZO L. REV. 1191 (2002).

19. REAGAN, *supra* note 1, at 243 (strikeouts in original eliminated and abbreviations expanded).

20. *E.g.*, Patrice Hill, *W.Va. Miners Favor Bush Over Gore on Fossil Fuels*, WASH. TIMES, Oct. 11, 2000, at A12.

21. ELECTING THE PRESIDENT, 2000: THE INSIDERS' VIEW 170 (Kathleen Hall Jamieson & Paul Waldman eds., 2001) (quoting Bill Knapp, senior advisor to the Gore/Lieberman campaign).

22. *Id.* at 204 (quoting Karl Rove).

23. *See, e.g.*, Adam Nagourney, *Candidates Face Sprawling and Complex Electoral Map*, N.Y. TIMES, May 12, 2004, at A18 (listing West Virginia as a battleground state and noting that the Democratic Party is attempting to regain its support in the state).

24. *See also, e.g.*, Matthew J. Franck, *Junk Arguments Against the Electoral College*, NAT'L REV. ONLINE (Dec. 15, 2008), http://www.nationalreview.com/blogs/print/50572 ("So complaints that candidates only go to one third of the country ring hollow when we reflect that over time there is considerable change in *which* third of the country is most heavily targeted by candidates.").

25. KARL ROVE, COURAGE AND CONSEQUENCE: MY LIFE AS A CONSERVATIVE IN THE FIGHT 164–65 (2010).

26. In this vein, former Federal Election Commission chairman Bradley Smith points out that battleground states
> form a diverse group indeed . . . . [They include] small states and large, east and west, north and south, agricultural and industrial, urban and rural, and states with large minority populations and states with small minority populations. Thus, even on a shrunken battleground, it is likely that pandering too strongly to parochial concerns will be checked by the need to compete in another "battleground" state elsewhere. Worse yet, pandering to extreme might antagonize voters in other states so as to convert safe states into battleground states. Politics is not static.

Bradley A. Smith, *Vanity of Vanities: National Popular Vote and the Electoral College*, 7 ELECTION L.J. 196, 203–04 (2008).

27. If "attention" is purely about campaign visits to each state, then this claim could

Notes

appear erroneous in light of studies such as David Strömberg, *How the Electoral College Influences Campaigns and Policy: The Probability of Being Florida*, 98 AM. ECON. REV. 769, 796 (2008) ("On net, visits per capita are not correlated with size."). However, as noted in the text, "attention" encompasses much more than only advertising dollars spent.

28. *2010 Census Interactive Population Search: California*, U.S. CENSUS BUREAU, http://2010.census.gov/2010census/popmap/ipmtext.php?fl=06 (last visited June 27, 2012).

29. *See Apportionment Data*, U.S. CENSUS BUREAU, http://2010.census.gov/ 2010census/data/apportionment-data-text.php (last visited June 27, 2012).

30. *2010 Census Interactive Population Search: Wyoming*, U.S. CENSUS BUREAU, http://2010.census.gov/2010census/popmap/ipmtext.php?fl=56 (last visited June 27, 2012).

31. *See Apportionment Data, supra* note 29.

32. *See* JUDITH A. BEST, THE CHOICE OF THE PEOPLE? DEBATING THE ELECTORAL COLLEGE 56–58 (1996).

33. *Id.* at 56.

34. *See, e.g.*, ROBERT W. BENNETT, TAMING THE ELECTORAL COLLEGE 162 (2006).

35. *2010 Census Interactive Population Search: Montana*, U.S. CENSUS BUREAU, http://2010.census.gov/2010census/popmap/ipmtext.php?fl=30 (last visited June 27, 2012); *see also Apportionment Data, supra* note 29.

36. LONGLEY & PEIRCE, *supra* note 4, at 153–54.

37. Obviously, to the degree that a large state has a greater chance of being a battleground state, as some game theorists suggest, that would increase the mathematical advantage for those voters even more.

38. GEORGE C. EDWARDS III, WHY THE ELECTORAL COLLEGE IS BAD FOR AMERICA 47 (2d ed. 2011).

39. Electoral College critics find other grounds on which to complain about the inequities created by the system. For instance, significant population shifts in a state may not be accounted for between the decennial reapportionment of electors after each Census. *See, e.g., id.* at 14. This author does not dispute that some inequities exist. But a national implementation of "one person, one vote" was never a goal of the Constitution's presidential election system. Instead, the Constitution aims to create and maintain a political environment that will protect freedom and ensure healthy self-governance.

40. Robert Bennett expresses some confusion about whether Electoral College proponents (and perhaps this author in particular) mean to protect the interests of states, specifically, or if such references are merely "a means to the end of protecting the interests of the individuals within a state." BENNETT, *supra* note 34, at 218 n.71. He dismisses the possibility that states may have interests of their own:

> The notion of state interests may well be useful as a figure of speech, but surely the values of federalism are to be found not in some interests of the states as such, but in the succor they give to individuals through the dispersal of power and through attachments they can provide for the individuals within them.

Id. All of the above interests are protected by our Constitution, which deliberately combines federalist, republican, and democratic principles for this very purpose (as discussed in Chapters One and Two). For those who doubt that states, as entities, have interests that need to be protected, one quick example should help.

Passage of the 17th Amendment in 1913 severely harmed the interests of the states themselves. That amendment altered the careful balance of federalist, republican, and democratic principles in the election procedure for U.S. Senators. Article I, Section 3 of the Constitution had originally provided for the selection of Senators by state legislatures, but the new amendment enabled individual voters to directly elect Senators themselves. The change perhaps seemed harmless at first, but a century later, the ramifications are obvious. The original constitutional provision made Senators accountable to the state legislatures for their votes. The states themselves, as sovereign entities, had a voice in the federal legislative process. They could defend themselves from encroachments upon their power or from unfunded mandates. But the 17th Amendment, as Senator Zell Miller noted in 2004, "was the death of the careful balance between State and Federal Government. . . . Today State governments have to stand in line because they are just another one of the many special interests that try to get Senators to listen to them, and they are at an extreme disadvantage because they have no PAC." ZELL MILLER, ZELL MILLER: A SENATOR SPEAKS OUT ON PATRIOTISM, VALUES, AND CHARACTER 41 (2005).

In short, states have interests, just as individuals do. Moreover, each state legislature would make a different decision about how to prioritize spending, taxes, and the various needs of its residents. The delicate balance in our Constitution was meant to provide maximum protection to each of these interests: the states themselves and their residents, whether individually or as an aggregate of individuals with similar concerns.

Chapter Six

1. Obviously, the two-party system is a factor not only in U.S. presidential elections but also in congressional, state, and local elections. In this vein, Robert Bennett rightly notes other influences that contribute to the strength of America's two-party system. *See* ROBERT W. BENNETT, TAMING THE ELECTORAL COLLEGE 128–29 (2006). While acknowledging the existence of these other factors, the dynamics of presidential elections is the focus of this book. The President is the only elected official who is expected to represent the nation as a whole. His campaign receives a disproportionate amount of attention among voters and media outlets. Any factor that contributes to the strength of the two-party system in presidential politics has extra influence when it comes to reinforcing the strength of the system as a whole.

2. Nader ran in 1996 but obtained less than one percent of the vote. He obtained a larger 2.7 percent of the vote in 2000. Arguably, however, neither Buchanan nor Nader was truly a "major" third-party candidate. Their runs for the presidency likely would have been inconsequential were it not for the close nature of the 2000 election.

3. Analysis after the election showed that, nationwide, Perot votes broke fairly equally between Clinton and Bush. However, the Center for Voting and Democracy reports that the Perot vote did not split equally in each state. To the contrary, Perot's candidacy seems to have worked to Bush's disadvantage in several states that Bush won in 1988 and might otherwise have been expected to win in 1992. *See* Ctr. for Voting & Democracy, *Plurality Wins in the 1992 Presidential Race: Perot's Contribution to Clinton's Victory*, FAIRVOTE, http://archive.fairvote.org/plurality/perot.htm (last updated Dec. 10, 2009).

4. *Cf.* James Risen & Karen Tumulty, *Politicians Rally Around Plan to Balance Budget*, L.A. TIMES, May 17, 1992, at A1 (reporting on the then-building momentum for a balanced budget constitutional amendment, based at least in part on the pressure created as Ross Perot "hammer[s] away at the skyrocketing deficit as a metaphor for Washington's failure to deal with the nation's most serious economic problems," a message that has caused him to surge in the polls).

5. Omnibus Budget Reconciliation Act of 1993, Pub. L. No. 103–66, 107 Stat. 312.

6. *Republican Contract with America*, U.S. HOUSE REPRESENTATIVES, http://www.house.gov/house/Contract/CONTRACT.html (last visited June 27, 2012).

7. At least to the degree that the objective is election. As discussed in the text, third parties may influence politics in other ways, as when Perot supporters made economic issues an important topic of discussion in the 1994 election.

Notes

8. For more information on the 1912 election, see NATHAN MILLER, THEODORE ROOSEVELT: A LIFE 519–31 (1992).

9. The first edition of this book reported slightly different popular vote totals: 6,293,152 for Wilson, 4,119,207 for Roosevelt, and 3,486,333 for Taft. These figures were obtained from the 1997 edition of Congressional Quarterly's *Presidential Elections.* CONG. QUARTERLY, PRESIDENTIAL ELECTIONS, 1789-1996, at 106 (1997). The figures in this edition have been revised to reflect the new numbers reported in the most recent edition of *Presidential Elections. See* CQ PRESS, PRESIDENTIAL ELECTIONS: 1789–2008, at 147 (2010).

10. For more information on the 1836 election, see MAJOR L. WILSON, THE PRESIDENCY OF MARTIN VAN BUREN 14–20 (1984); *see also* PAUL F. BOLLER, JR., PRESIDENTIAL CAMPAIGNS 60–64 (rev. ed. 1996).

11. For more information on the 1840 election, see BOLLER, *supra* note 10, at 65–77.

12. *See, e.g.,* ROBERT M. HARDAWAY, THE ELECTORAL COLLEGE AND THE CONSTITUTION: THE CASE FOR PRESERVING FEDERALISM 20 (1994) ("The Electoral College lesson has been clear throughout American history: accommodate, compromise, merge, persuade, build, and achieve a consensus.").

13. *See, e.g.,* NEAL R. PEIRCE & LAWRENCE D. LONGLEY, THE PEOPLE'S PRESIDENT: THE ELECTORAL COLLEGE IN AMERICAN HISTORY AND THE DIRECT VOTE ALTERNATIVE 211–12 (Yale Univ. Press rev. ed. 1981) (1968). Longley and Peirce instead contend that the two national parties are in decline due to the advances made in mass communication in recent years, among other factors. *Id.*

14. *Id.* at 209.

15. *Id.* at 211.

16. *Id.* at 209.

17. For a discussion of this topic, see Tara L. Branum, *President or King? The Use and Abuse of Executive Orders in Modern-day America,* 28 J. LEGIS. 1 (2002).

18. U.S. CONST. art. II, § 2, cl. 2.

19. *Id.* art. II, § 2, cl. 1; *see also id.* art. II, § 3.

20. *See, e.g.,* Branum, *supra* note 17, at 31 n.144 and accompanying text.

21. 102 CONG. REC. 5150 (1956) (statement of Senator John F. Kennedy).

22. PEIRCE & LONGLEY, *supra* note 13, at 220–22.

23. *Id.*

24. JUDITH A. BEST, THE CHOICE OF THE PEOPLE? DEBATING THE ELECTORAL COLLEGE 55 (1996); *see also* HARDAWAY, *supra* note 12, at 21 ("What the advocates of direct election fail to take into account, however, is that *these consistently large pluralities and majorities are the result of the very Electoral College system they are seeking to destroy.*").

25. Michael J. Glennon, *Nine Ways to Avoid a Train Wreck: How Title 3 Should Be Changed,* 23 CARDOZO L. REV. 1159, 1159 (2002).

26. One commentator rejected the contention that multiple candidacies will grow into a problem, asserting that a 40-percent requirement should do the trick. So lightly did he take the problem of multiple candidacies that he devoted only one small six-sentence paragraph in a 38-page law review article to consideration of the subject. *See* Ky Fullerton, Comment, *Bush, Gore, and the 2000 Presidential Election: Time for the Electoral College to Go?,* 80 OR. L. REV. 717, 744–45 (2001). More thoughtful commentators, even on the pro-NPV side, have acknowledged that the 40 percent requirement may "undermine rather than bolster" the two-party system. BENNETT, *supra* note 1, at 68.

27. Many proposals have been made to modify voting procedures at the ballot box: For example, instant runoffs would allow voters to rank candidates by order of preference and approval voting would allow voters to cast a ballot for any candidate that they find acceptable.

It is beyond the scope of this book to address each of these options, but it is worth noting that some of them could be problematic for many of the same reasons discussed in this subsection. Voting systems that encourage votes for extremist third-party candidates will fracture voters and disrupt America's ability to work together and find a good compromise candidate who can fairly represent the great diversity of voters in this country.

28. This is a number that is always a little bit in flux, but at least one blogger maintains a current list of parties on his website. *See* Ron Gunzburger, *Directory of U.S. Political Parties*, RON GUNZBURGER'S POLITICS1.COM, http://www.politics1.com/parties.htm (last visited June 27, 2012).

29. *See id.* (providing links for the official websites of each political party).

30. BEST, *supra* note 24, at 57.

31. Election results can be found at GROWING PAINS: RUSSIAN DEMOCRACY AND THE ELECTION OF 1993, at 22 tbl 1-3 (Timothy J. Colton & Jerry F. Hough eds., 1998).

32. HARDAWAY, *supra* note 12, at 18–19. Professor Hardaway also argues that Hitler relied upon a similar system to establish a minority power base in Germany that eventually allowed him to rise to power. *Id.* at 18.

33. *See* Norman R. Williams, *Reforming the Electoral College: Federalism, Majoritarianism, and the Perils of Subconstitutional Change*, 100 GEO. L.J. 173, 204 (2011) (discussing the 2002 elections in France). Election totals can be found at Office for Democratic Institutions and Human Rights, *Republic of France Presidential Elections, 21 April and 5 May 2002*, ORG. FOR SECURITY & CO-OPERATION EUROPE (Apr. 21, 2002), http://www.osce.org/odihr/elections/france/16167.

34. *See Who's Running for French President*, ASSOCIATED PRESS, Apr. 20, 2012.

35. Honor Mahony, *France: Hollande Leads, Le Pen Shocks in Third Place*, EUOBSERVER.COM (Apr. 22, 2012), http://euobserver.com/843/115976; Greg Keller, *Hollande Enjoys Upper Hand in French Elections*, ASSOCIATED PRESS, Apr. 23, 2012, http://news.yahoo.com/hollande-enjoys-upper-hand-french-elections-103239471.html.

36. Mahony, *supra* note 35; Keller, *supra* note 35, at 1.

37. Mahony, *supra* note 35; Keller, *supra* note 35, at 1.

38. Sometimes also referred to as "first past the post."

39. The political scientist credited with this theory is Maurice Duverger. *See* MAURICE DUVERGER, POLITICAL PARTIES, THEIR ORGANIZATION AND ACTIVITY IN THE MODERN STATE (Barbara & Robert North, trans., Wiley 1954).

40. *See, e.g.*, William H. Riker, *The Two-Party System and Duverger's Law*, 76 AM. POL. SCI. REV. 753, 760 (1982); *see also* W. M. Dobell, *Updating Duverger's Law*, 19 CANADIAN J. POL. SCI. 585 (1986).

41. *See, e.g.*, Royce Carroll & Matthew Søberg Shugart, Parties, Alliances, and Duverger's Law in India 8–9 (Mar. 20, 2008) (paper presented at the annual meeting of the Western Political Science Association), *available at* http://citation.allacademic.com/meta/p_mla_apa_research_citation/2/3/7/7/9/pages237792/p237792-1.php.

42. *See, e.g.*, Christine Armario, *Meek Says Clinton Never Convinced Him to Quit Race*, CHI. DAILY HERALD, Oct. 29, 2010, at 16; Ralph Z. Hallow, *Libertarian Won't Give Spot to Murkowski: Incumbent Senator Still Weighs Bid to Hold on to Alaska's Seat*, WASH. TIMES, Sept. 13, 2010, at A3 (discussing "frenzied efforts to talk Mrs. Murkowski into dropping out of the race for good"); Editorial, *For Crist's Sake, Drop out; The Turncoat Threatens to Spoil Certain Republican Victory*, WASH TIMES, May 3, 2010, at B2.

43. *See, e.g.*, *Florida Senate—Rubio vs. Meek vs. Crist*, REALCLEARPOLITICS.COM, http://www.realclearpolitics.com/epolls/2010/senate/fl/florida_senate_rubio_vs_meek_vs_crist-1456.html#polls (last visited June 28, 2012) (listing polls).

44. *November 2, 2010 General Election*, FLA. DEP'T ST., DIVISION ELECTIONS,

http://enight.elections.myflorida.com/Index.asp?ElectionDate=11/2/2010&DATAMODE= (last visited June 28, 2012).

45. Bernard Grofman et al., *Introduction: Evidence for Duverger's Law from Four Countries*, in DUVERGER'S LAW OF PLURALITY VOTING: THE LOGIC OF PARTY COMPETITION IN CANADA, INDIA, THE UNITED KINGDOM AND THE UNITED STATES 1, 2 (Bernard Grofman et al. eds., 2009).

46. *Id.*

47. BENNETT, *supra* note 1, at 71.

48. Candidates like George Washington are the rare possible exception. But how often does a George Washington come along?

Chapter Seven

1. NEAL R. PEIRCE & LAWRENCE D. LONGLEY, THE PEOPLE'S PRESIDENT: THE ELECTORAL COLLEGE IN AMERICAN HISTORY AND THE DIRECT VOTE ALTERNATIVE 228 (Yale Univ. Press rev. ed. 1981) (1968).

2. For a discussion of the discrepancy that typically exists between popular vote totals and Electoral College vote totals, see JUDITH A. BEST, THE CHOICE OF THE PEOPLE? DEBATING THE ELECTORAL COLLEGE 9–15 (1996); ROBERT M. HARDAWAY, THE ELECTORAL COLLEGE AND THE CONSTITUTION: THE CASE FOR PRESERVING FEDERALISM 125–28 (1994).

3. The first edition of this book reported slightly different popular vote totals: 5,443,892 for Harrison and 5,534,488 for Cleveland. These figures were obtained from the 1997 edition of Congressional Quarterly's *Presidential Elections*. CONG. QUARTERLY, PRESIDENTIAL ELECTIONS, 1789-1996, at 100 (1997). The figures in this edition have been revised to reflect the new numbers reported in the most recent edition of *Presidential Elections*. See CQ PRESS, PRESIDENTIAL ELECTIONS: 1789–2008, at 141 (2010).

4. The new edition of *Presidential Elections* has revised its vote totals for 1952, just as it did for the 1888 totals. *See* discussion *supra* note 3. The first edition of this book thus reported that Dwight D. Eisenhower won 55.1 percent of the popular vote in 1952. *See* CONG. QUARTERLY, *supra* note 3, at 116. The new edition of *Presidential Elections* states that this number should instead be 54.9 percent. *See* CQ PRESS, *supra* note 3, at 157.

5. *See also* discussion *infra* note 17–18 (Ch. 13) and accompanying text.

6. As Nixon did in 1960. *See* discussion *infra* notes 13–14 and accompanying text.

7. *Cf.* Andrew Gelman, Gary King, & W. John Boscardin, *Estimating the Probability of Events That Have Never Occurred: When is Your Vote Decisive?*, 93 J. AM. STAT. ASS'N. 1 (1998) (estimating the probability that one vote could change the outcome of a presidential election).

8. *See, e.g.*, JUDITH BEST, THE CASE AGAINST DIRECT ELECTION OF THE PRESIDENT: A DEFENSE OF THE ELECTORAL COLLEGE 191–204 (1975) (noting the ability of the Electoral College to isolate incidents of fraud); *see also* HARDAWAY, *supra* note 2, at 25–28 (discussing the 1960 election and the uncertainty that could have resulted from the close count and the alleged fraud).

9. CQ PRESS, *supra* note 3, at 169.

10. Texas then had 24 electoral votes and Illinois had 27. Had those votes been cast for Nixon, rather than Kennedy, the final election tally would have been: Nixon, 270, and Kennedy, 252.

11. Nixon lost Texas by 46,257 votes and Illinois by 8,858 votes. *See id.* at 159.

12. *See* discussion *supra* note 8 and accompanying text.

13. Richard Reeves, Op-ed, *There's Always the Option of Giving In*, N.Y. TIMES, Nov. 10, 2000, at A33.

14. RICHARD NIXON, THE MEMOIRS OF RICHARD NIXON 224 (1978).

15. *See* CQ PRESS, *supra* note 3, at 159.

16. For instance, recounts in New Mexico were briefly discussed, but were not pursued. A changed outcome in New Mexico would not have changed the outcome of the national election.

17. Within certain limits. For instance, the Florida legislature threatened to take direct action to resolve the uncertainty in its state in 2000, but its actions would almost certainly have led to a lawsuit if the court issues had not been resolved instead. *See, e.g.*, ROBERT W. BENNETT, TAMING THE ELECTORAL COLLEGE 134–36 (2006) (discussing the constitutionality of the proposed action in Florida); *see also* Bill Sammon & Steve Miller, *Florida Lawmakers Prepare to Step In*, WASH. TIMES, Dec. 1, 2000, at 1; Bill Sammon, *Florida Lawmakers Call Special Session*, WASH. TIMES, Dec. 7, 2000, at 1.

Chapter Eight

1. *E.g.*, Bruce Bartlett, *Waffling Electors*, TOWNHALL.COM (Dec. 18, 2000), http://townhall.com/columnists/brucebartlett/2000/12/18/waffling_electors; Diane Rado, *Electors Are Thrust Into Prominence*, ST. PETERSBURG TIMES (Florida), Dec. 18, 2000, at 1B.

2. U.S. CONST. art. II, § 1, cl. 3.

3. *Id.* amend. XII.

4. LAWRENCE D. LONGLEY & NEAL R. PEIRCE, THE ELECTORAL COLLEGE PRIMER 2000, at 104 (1999); *see also* JUDITH A. BEST, THE CHOICE OF THE PEOPLE? DEBATING THE ELECTORAL COLLEGE 43–45 (1996); ROBERT W. BENNETT, TAMING THE ELECTORAL COLLEGE 14–17 (2006); GEORGE C. EDWARDS III, WHY THE ELECTORAL COLLEGE IS BAD FOR AMERICA 49–51 (2d ed. 2011); Norman R. Williams, *Reforming the Electoral College: Federalism, Majoritarianism, and the Perils of Subconstitutional Change*, 100 GEO. L.J. 173, 182 (2011).

5. *See, e.g.*, ROBERT M. HARDAWAY, THE ELECTORAL COLLEGE AND THE CONSTITUTION: THE CASE FOR PRESERVING FEDERALISM 85–87 (1994); *see also* Luis Fuentes-Rohwer & Guy-Uriel Charles, *The Electoral College, the Right to Vote, and Our Federalism: A Comment on a Lasting Institution*, 29 FLA. ST. U. L. REV. 879, 896 & n.102 (2001).

6. LONGLEY & PEIRCE, *supra* note 4, at 104.

7. *E.g.*, *id.* at 102; *see also* BEST, *supra* note 4, at 44; L. PAIGE WHITAKER & THOMAS H. NEALE, CONG. RESEARCH SERV., RL30804, THE ELECTORAL COLLEGE: AN OVERVIEW AND ANALYSIS OF REFORM PROPOSALS 1–2 (2004).

8. LONGLEY & PEIRCE, *supra* note 4, at 102.

9. *See* AFTER THE PEOPLE VOTE: A GUIDE TO THE ELECTORAL COLLEGE 83 app. C (John C. Fortier ed., 3d ed. 2004) (listing the method of nomination in each state).

10. *See id.* (delineating which electors are bound and how, by state). A slightly more recent list can be found on the website for the National Conference of State Legislatures. *See The Electoral College*, NAT'L CONF. ST. LEGISLATURES, http://www.ncsl.org/legislatures-elections/elections-campaigns/the-electoral-college.aspx (last updated Apr. 20, 2009).

11. Ray v. Blair, 343 U.S. 214 (1952).

12. *Id.* at 215.

13. *Id.*

14. *Id.* at 230–31.

15. For more information on the difficulties associated with forcing electors to abide by pledges, see BENNETT, *supra* note 4, at 104–15; HARDAWAY, *supra* note 5, at 50.

16. LONGLEY & PEIRCE, *supra* note 4, at 24, 113. According to Longley and Peirce,

the count is as low as nine or as high as 17, depending on whether the disputed votes in 1824 are counted. *Id.* at 113; *see also* JOHN R. KOZA ET AL., EVERY VOTE EQUAL: A STATE-BASED PLAN FOR ELECTING THE PRESIDENT BY NATIONAL POPULAR VOTE 85 (3d ed. 2011).

17. One elector was elected to Congress and thus did not cast his ballot. His replacement defected from the expected vote, voting for Adams instead. One of the other electors voted for William Crawford. The other voted for Andrew Jackson. LONGLEY & PEIRCE, *supra* note 4, at 111–12.

18. Balloting in Minnesota is secret, so the identity of the elector is not known. BENNETT, *supra* note 4, at 224 n.38.

19. *See* WHITAKER & NEALE, *supra* note 7, at 12; *see also* AFTER THE PEOPLE VOTE, *supra* note 9, at 90 app. G (listing faithless electors); CQ PRESS, PRESIDENTIAL ELECTIONS: 1789–2008, at 189 (2010) (same); LONGLEY & PEIRCE, *supra* note 4, at 111–13 (same).

20. *See* discussion *supra* note 18.

21. There is a reasonable argument for excluding Preston Parks from this list. He was nominated to (and pledged to vote for) two different slates of electors: the Democratic slate ('Truman) and the States' Rights slate (Thurmond). Although he'd originally pledged to vote for Truman, he changed his mind and campaigned for Thurmond. His vote for Thurmond could not have been a surprise. *See, e.g.,* EDWARDS, *supra* note 4, at 55; LONGLEY & PEIRCE, *supra* note 4, at 112.

22. *E.g.,* Frank J. Murray, *Bush Electors Ignore Pleas to Defect,* WASH. TIMES, Dec. 15, 2000, at A16. Some even mentioned the possibility before Gore conceded. *See* Edward Walsh, *A Quixotic Effort to Rally the 'Faithless'?: Electors Almost Never Defect,* WASH. POST, Nov. 17, 2000, at A26.

23. NPV agrees: "In summary, faithless electors are a historical curiosity associated with the Electoral College, but they never have had any practical effect on any presidential election." KOZA ET AL., *supra* note 16, at 91.

24. In 2004, one West Virginia Republican elector threatened to exercise his independence. He claimed that he would not vote for George W. Bush, if elected. In the end, he cast his ballot for Bush, as expected. *See* Alexander Keyssar, *The Electoral College Flunks,* N.Y. REV. BOOKS, Mar. 24, 2005, at 16, 16.

25. LONGLEY & PEIRCE, *supra* note 4, at 107.

26. *See* AFTER THE PEOPLE VOTE, *supra* note 9, at 83 app. C; *see also* THOMAS H. NEALE, CONG. RESEARCH SERV., RS20273, THE ELECTORAL COLLEGE: HOW IT WORKS IN CONTEMPORARY PRESIDENTIAL ELECTIONS 3 (2003). Robert Bennett rightly notes that this number is a moving target. BENNETT, *supra* note 4, at 235 n.59. The main point is that voters increasingly view the identity of electors as unimportant.

27. BENNETT, *supra* note 4, at 234 n.58 (citation omitted).

28. U.S. Nat'l Archives & Records Admin., *Frequently Asked Questions: Where Do I Find the Names of the 2008 Presidential Electors?,* U.S. ELECTORAL C., http://www.archives.gov/ federal-register/electoral-college/faq.html#2008names (last visited June 26, 2012).

29. Although, to play devil's advocate for a bit, perhaps it is really about media focus and educating the public about the role of electors. In certain situations (*e.g.,* death of a candidate), electors may need to act as an independent, deliberative body. In those situations, the voting public should know who is acting on its behalf and should cast ballots accordingly. The media can focus on the names and positions of electors just as easily as it can focus on candidates. It could ensure that we know their names, political philosophies and other, relevant details. Mass communication has improved our ability to be informed about electors,

not only candidates.

30. *See, e.g.*, NEAL R. PEIRCE & LAWRENCE D. LONGLEY, THE PEOPLE'S PRESIDENT: THE ELECTORAL COLLEGE IN AMERICAN HISTORY AND THE DIRECT VOTE ALTERNATIVE 160 (Yale Univ. Press rev. ed. 1981) (1968) (opposing the Automatic Plan and relating comments of other opponents).

31. For more information regarding the problems caused by the death of a candidate, see BEST, *supra* note 4, at 46–49; Akhil Reed Amar, *Presidents, Vice Presidents, and Death: Closing the Constitution's Succession Gap*, 48 ARK. L. REV. 215 (1995); John C. Fortier & Norman J. Ornstein, *If Terrorists Attacked Our Presidential Elections*, 3 ELECTION L.J. 597 (2004).

32. If there is no Vice President-elect on January 20, Section 3 of the 20th Amendment arguably can't be applied immediately. *See* William Josephson, *Senate Election of the Vice President and House of Representatives Election of the President*, 11 U. PA. J. CONST. L. 597, 615–17 (2009). A contrary position is taken by the Congressional Research Service, which equates "qualifies" with "elected." *See* THOMAS H. NEALE, CONG. RESEARCH SERV., RS20300, ELECTION OF THE PRESIDENT AND VICE PRESIDENT BY CONGRESS: CONTINGENT ELECTION 5 (2001). A contrary position is also taken by Robert Bennett, who assumes that the congressionally provided line of succession in 3 U.S.C. § 19 (2006) would be used if there were no President-elect and no Vice President-elect. *See* BENNETT, *supra* note 4, at 81.

33. U.S CONST. amend. XX, § 3. In the event that a Vice President-elect was inaugurated as President through operation of the 20th Amendment, the 25th Amendment would then allow him to designate a new Vice President following his inauguration. *See* U.S CONST. amend. XXV, § 2.

34. There is perhaps some disagreement about whether a candidate can be formally declared the President-elect before Congress has counted the votes. Akhil Reed Amar notes that the "legislative history of the 20th Amendment suggests that the electoral college winner is 'President elect' the moment the electoral college votes are cast, and before they are counted in Congress." Amar, *supra* note 31, at 217–18. However, "the text of the Amendment fails to say this explicitly," *id.* at 218, and "[b]oth Article II and the Twelfth Amendment seem to focus on the formal counting of votes in the Congress as the magic, formal moment of vesting in which the winning candidate is elected as 'President.'" *Id.* at 217.

On the other hand, Robert Bennett states that a candidate can be President-elect before the votes are counted by Congress. BENNETT, *supra* note 4, at 119 & 239 n.100. Such a position seems to ignore the fact that Congress at least claims the authority to reject slates of electors and to decide certain election disputes. How can the outcome be known with certainty until Congress has acted? In the case of a candidate who has passed away, Congress could decide not to accept these votes cast for a deceased candidate, as it did in 1873 when Horace Greeley died. The most rational point at which to formally designate a candidate "President-elect" is after Congress has decided which votes to count and accept as valid on January 6.

35. *See* GLYNDON G. VAN DEUSEN, HORACE GREELEY, NINETEENTH-CENTURY CRUSADER 424 (1953) (relating the circumstances of Greeley's death).

36. *See, e.g.*, CQ PRESS, *supra* note 19, at 137, 227; *see also* Amar, *supra* note 31, at 218–19 (discussing the choice confronting the Greeley electors); Fortier & Ornstein, *supra* note 31, at 606 (same); Beverly J. Ross & William Josephson, *The Electoral College and the Popular Vote*, 12 J.L. & POL. 665, 706–07 (1996) (same).

37. *E.g.*, Akhil Reed Amar, *This Is One Terrorist Threat We Can Thwart Now*, WASH. POST, Nov. 11, 2001, at B2; *see generally* Fortier & Ornstein, *supra* note 31.

38. Robert Bennett instead suggests that states pass laws telling their electors how to vote in various circumstances. BENNETT, *supra* note 4, at 119–20.

39. Professor Judith Best has made this suggestion as well. *See* BEST, *supra* note 4, at 48.

40. A separate constitutional provision applies when no candidate receives a majority of the electoral votes and one candidate dies before the contingent election is held. Congress may "by law provide for the case of the death" of such a candidate. U.S. CONST. XX, § 4. For a discussion of automated secondary election procedures that could be designed to work hand in hand with the Automatic Plan, see Chapter Nine.

Chapter Nine

1. Richard C. Baker, *On Becoming President by One Vote*, 48 A.B.A. J. 455, 456 (1962).

2. GEORGE C. EDWARDS III, WHY THE ELECTORAL COLLEGE IS BAD FOR AMERICA 74 (2d ed. 2011).

3. MARTIN DIAMOND, AM. ENTER. INST., TESTIMONY IN SUPPORT OF THE ELECTORAL COLLEGE 7 (1977).

4. U.S. CONST. art. II, § 1, cl. 3.

5. *Id.*

6. Robert Bennett correctly notes an error made at this point in the first edition of *Enlightened Democracy*. ROBERT W. BENNETT, TAMING THE ELECTORAL COLLEGE 199 n.38 (2006). This author noted and apologized for the error in the Study Guide created to accompany *Enlightened Democracy*, shortly after its publication. *See* TARA ROSS, ENLIGHTENED DEMOCRACY: THE CASE FOR THE ELECTORAL COLLEGE, EDUCATORS' STUDY GUIDE C-20 (2005). It is not terribly surprising that Bennett (a law school professor) did not see a study guide created for junior high school students.

The original edition of this book states: "In all cases, the person who placed second in this House election would be Vice President." TARA ROSS, ENLIGHTENED DEMOCRACY: THE CASE FOR THE ELECTORAL COLLEGE 129 (2004). Historically speaking, elections always worked out in this fashion under the Article II provision, but technically, elections could work out slightly differently. Under Article II, the Vice President was to be the candidate who had the greatest number of electoral votes after the President had been elected. On the one occasion that this provision was used, the candidate receiving the highest electoral vote total (once the President was selected) and the candidate receiving the second highest state vote total in the House contingent election were the same person. Technically speaking, they could have been different people. The author again apologizes for the confusion in the Edition One text between the technical rule and historical application of the rule.

7. U.S. CONST. amend. XII; *see also* AFTER THE PEOPLE VOTE: A GUIDE TO THE ELECTORAL COLLEGE 17–19 (John C. Fortier ed., 3d ed. 2004) (describing the contingent election procedures).

8. U.S. CONST. amend. XX, § 3.

9. 3 U.S.C. § 19 (2006); *see also* THOMAS H. NEALE, CONG. RESEARCH SERV., RS20300, ELECTION OF THE PRESIDENT AND VICE PRESIDENT BY CONGRESS: CONTINGENT ELECTION 5 (2001). *But see* discussion *supra* note 32 (Ch. 8).

10. *See, e.g.*, JUDITH A. BEST, THE CHOICE OF THE PEOPLE? DEBATING THE ELECTORAL COLLEGE 13–15 (1996) (relating the primary complaints made about the contingent election procedure).

11. Such a Vice President would doubtless work to frustrate the President's agenda in the Senate—although maybe some would consider that a good thing.

12. *See* discussion *supra* notes 20-21 (Ch. 4) and accompanying text.

13. BENNETT, *supra* note 6, at 76.

14. Professor Bennett's numbers rely upon the 1990 census. *Id.*

15. *See, e.g.*, NEAL R. PEIRCE & LAWRENCE D. LONGLEY, THE PEOPLE'S PRESIDENT: THE ELECTORAL COLLEGE IN AMERICAN HISTORY AND THE DIRECT VOTE ALTERNATIVE 177–79 (Yale Univ. Press rev. ed. 1981) (1968) (discussing reforms that have been proposed to the contingent election procedure); *see also* JUDITH BEST, THE CASE AGAINST DIRECT ELECTION OF THE PRESIDENT: A DEFENSE OF THE ELECTORAL COLLEGE 83–123 (1975) (analyzing various reform proposals for the contingent election procedure); ROBERT M. HARDAWAY, THE ELECTORAL COLLEGE AND THE CONSTITUTION: THE CASE FOR PRESERVING FEDERALISM 153–55 (1994) (same).

16. *Cf.* BEST, THE CASE AGAINST DIRECT ELECTION, *supra* note 15, at 104–05 (noting that runoffs "extend[ ] the electorate's uncertainty" and "would weaken or alter our two-party system"); *see also* HARDAWAY, *supra* note 15, at 154.

17. Professor Best refers to the "second-chance psychology" that can "infect both candidates and voters" when runoffs are introduced into the equation. BEST, THE CASE AGAINST DIRECT ELECTION, *supra* note 15, at 117.

18. *See, e.g., id.* at 85.

19. *See* BEST, THE CHOICE OF THE PEOPLE, *supra* note 10, at 13–15 (arguing that the contingent election procedure is not usually needed and no change is necessary).

20. *See* discussion *supra* notes 45–55 (Ch. 3) and accompanying text.

21. *See* discussion *supra* note 55 (Ch. 3) and accompanying text.

22. DAVID MCCULLOUGH, JOHN ADAMS 475 (2001). Although some might argue that no great harm comes from having Presidents and Vice Presidents of different parties. The President does not have to assign duties to Vice Presidents, although they sometimes do so. As a constitutional matter, the most important task of a Vice President is to be available to serve as President in the event that a President passes away. Moreover, as a historical matter, many Vice Presidents have found themselves in the same situation as Jefferson, even when they were members of the same political party as the President. For instance, Theodore Roosevelt served briefly as Vice President prior to his presidency. He had few responsibilities as Vice President and was reportedly bored and frustrated with his role. *See* NATHAN MILLER, THEODORE ROOSEVELT: A LIFE 346 (1992) (describing Vice President Roosevelt as "[f]rustrated," "feeling unused," and looking for ways to fill his time).

23. *See, e.g.*, HARDAWAY, *supra* note 15, at 153–55, 166–68 (arguing that the contingent election procedure should not be changed).

Chapter Ten

1. Steven Thomma, *Possibility of a President Who Lost Popular Vote Triggers Crisis of Legitimacy*, KNIGHT RIDDER/TRIB. NEWS SERVICE, Nov. 8, 2000.

2. *Id.*

3. Michael Kramer, *Time to Ax Electoral College*, DAILY NEWS (N.Y.), Nov. 9, 2000, at 10.

4. Arthur M. Schlesinger, Jr., *Not the People's Choice: How to Democratize American Democracy*, AM. PROSPECT, Mar. 25, 2002, at 23, 23.

5. *See, e.g.*, Michael Herz, *How the Electoral College Imitates the World Series*, 23 CARDOZO L. REV. 1191 (2002); *see also* Samuel Issacharoff, *Law, Rules, and Presidential Selection*, 120 POL. SCI. Q. 113, 113–14 (2005).

6. *Cf.* Issacharoff, *supra* note 5, at 126 ("[I]t is essential that the rules of presidential selection be, insofar as possible, fixed *ex ante*, and that they have the respect of all relevant actors.").

Notes

7. Joy McAfee, Comment, *2001: Should the College Electors Finally Graduate?: The Electoral College: An American Compromise From Its Inception to Election 2000*, 32 CUMB. L. REV. 643, 661–62 (2001).

8. *Id.* at 662.

9. *See, e.g.*, JUDITH BEST, THE CASE AGAINST DIRECT ELECTION OF THE PRESIDENT: A DEFENSE OF THE ELECTORAL COLLEGE 46 (1975) ("[M]any critics seem to believe that the objection to a minority President need only be stated, not argued."); *see also* ROBERT M. HARDAWAY, THE ELECTORAL COLLEGE AND THE CONSTITUTION: THE CASE FOR PRESERVING FEDERALISM 13 (1994) ("[Such claims] raise the perfectly legitimate question of what is a 'majority.' More precisely, one may ask, a majority of what?").

10. NEAL R. PEIRCE & LAWRENCE D. LONGLEY, THE PEOPLE'S PRESIDENT: THE ELECTORAL COLLEGE IN AMERICAN HISTORY AND THE DIRECT VOTE ALTERNATIVE 236 (Yale Univ. Press rev. ed. 1981) (1968).

11. Paul Starr, *Mr. Bush Gets His Honeymoon*, AM. PROSPECT, Feb. 26, 2001, at 6 (internal citation omitted).

12. Alexander Keyssar, *The Majority's Rules*, L.A. TIMES, May 25, 2003, at R12 (book review). George Edwards offers a different description, calling the relative calm a "surface acceptance of the election results." GEORGE C. EDWARDS III, WHY THE ELECTORAL COLLEGE IS BAD FOR AMERICA 1 (2d ed. 2011). Edwards cites Bush's low approval ratings, especially the wide discrepancy between the ratings of Democrats versus Republicans. *Id.* at 1-2. The discrepancy may have indicated an "extraordinary polarization" between parties, as Edwards states, but it is unfair to blame the situation solely on the 2000 election results. The approval ratings of Bill Clinton and Barack Obama showed even larger discrepancies between the ratings of Democrats v. Republicans. *See, e.g.*, Jeffrey M. Jones, *Obama's Approval Most Polarized for First-Year President*, GALLUP (Jan. 25, 2010), http://www.gallup.com/poll/125345/obama-approval-polarized-first-year-president.aspx.

13. *See also* Bradley A. Smith, *Vanity of Vanities: National Popular Vote and the Electoral College*, 7 ELECTION L.J. 196, 201–02 (2008) (making similar points).

14. *E.g.*, Richard L. Berke, *The 2000 Campaign: The Widening Battle; Bucking History, Tossup States Increase, Forcing Candidates to Rethink Strategies*, N.Y. TIMES, Oct. 27, 2000, at A27.

15. Mary Deibel, *Lawyers Loosed on Campaign Conundrums*, SCRIPPS HOWARD NEWS SERVICE, Nov. 08, 2000; *see also* Jack Kemp, *Case of Civic Virtue vs. Civic Vice*, WASH. TIMES, Nov. 18, 2000, at A12 (discussing a "pre-election memo," prepared by former Solicitor General Walter Dellinger); Paul A. Gigot, *Two Countries, One System*, WALL ST. J., Nov. 9, 2000, at A26 (quoting Dellinger's statements in support of the Electoral College prior to the election).

16. BEST, *supra* note 9, at 47–48.

17. *Id.* at 48.

18. *Id.*

19. Herz, *supra* note 5, at 1196 (quoting Albert R. Hunt, *The Electoral College: Legitimate but Anachronistic*, WALL ST. J., Oct. 26, 2000, at A27).

Chapter Eleven

1. *See generally* WINNER TAKE ALL: REPORT OF THE TWENTIETH CENTURY FUND TASK FORCE ON REFORM OF THE PRESIDENTIAL ELECTION PROCESS (1978) (proposing the Bonus Plan); *see also* NEAL R. PEIRCE & LAWRENCE D. LONGLEY, THE PEOPLE'S PRESIDENT: THE ELECTORAL COLLEGE IN AMERICAN HISTORY AND THE DIRECT VOTE ALTERNATIVE 176-77 (Yale Univ. Press rev. ed. 1981) (1968) (describing the Bonus Plan and how it came to be proposed).

There is nothing intuitive about the number 102, although proponents argue that the two votes represent each state's two Senators (plus two for the District of Columbia). Why not one extra vote per state and the District of Columbia, for an electoral bonus of 51? Or three votes (representing two Senators and one Congressman), for an electoral bonus of 153?

2. *See* JUDITH A. BEST, THE CHOICE OF THE PEOPLE? DEBATING THE ELECTORAL COLLEGE 62 (1996). Currently, 538 electoral votes are awarded, which means that 270 votes are needed to win. The Bonus Plan would bring the total number of votes to 640. A majority of 640 is 321, which means that 219 state electoral votes plus the 102 bonus votes would lead to victory. *Id.*

3. Paul Schumaker, Letter to the Editor, *Not the People's Choice*, AM. PROSPECT, May 6, 2002, at 5.

4. *See* L. PAIGE WHITAKER & THOMAS H. NEALE, CONG. RESEARCH SERV., RL30804, THE ELECTORAL COLLEGE: AN OVERVIEW AND ANALYSIS OF REFORM PROPOSALS 20–22 (2004) (reporting the arguments of District Plan proponents).

5. *See, e.g., id.; see also* DAVID W. ABBOTT & JAMES P. LEVINE, WRONG WINNER: THE COMING DEBACLE IN THE ELECTORAL COLLEGE 126 (1991) (discussing the "crucial shortcoming" of the District Plan: It "does nothing to correct the wrong-winner perversion"); PEIRCE & LONGLEY, *supra* note 1, at 142 (discussing the disparities that would still exist between the popular and electoral vote totals under a District Plan); *cf.* ROBERT W. BENNETT, TAMING THE ELECTORAL COLLEGE 52 (2006) (noting that disparity exists not only because of senate add-on votes but also because of differences in turnout in various states).

6. *See, e.g.*, Ky Fullerton, Comment, *Bush, Gore, and the 2000 Presidential Election: Time for the Electoral College to Go?*, 80 OR. L. REV. 717, 734 (2001) (citing Rhodes Cook, *This Just In: Nixon Beats Kennedy*, WASH. POST, Mar. 25, 2001, at B2). Bush would have won 288 to 250 in the electoral vote. Cook, *supra*, at B2.

7. Proponents sometimes argue that the District Plan would prevent campaigning from focusing on swing states. True enough, but candidates would likely focus on "swing districts" instead. *See* PEIRCE & LONGLEY, *supra* note 1, at 142.

8. *See* BEST, *supra* note 2, at 61–62 (discussing the increased incentives for gerrymandering).

9. *E.g.*, Rachel Saffron, *Electoral College Math*, CAMPAIGNS & ELECTIONS, Apr. 2005, at 11; Sam Hirsch, *Awarding Presidential Electors By Congressional District: Wrong for California, Wrong for the Nation*, 106 MICH. L. REV. FIRST IMPRESSIONS 95 (2008); Harold Meyerson, *A Strategy to Steal the 2012 Election*, STAR-LEDGER (Newark, N.J.), Sept. 22, 2011, at 17. Some have even proposed that states partner up to do it together. Randall Lane, *A Ballot Buddy System*, N.Y. TIMES, Dec. 15, 2008, at A35. However, states may not be able to enter into such a compact, at least not without congressional approval. *See* U.S. CONST. art. I, § 10, cl. 3.

10. Electoral votes can't be divided unless a constitutional amendment is first implemented to automate the casting of these votes. A tenth or hundredth of an elector cannot attend a meeting of the Electoral College in December and cast his one tenth or one hundredth of an electoral vote. Only whole persons can attend the meetings of the Electoral College each presidential election year.

11. WHITAKER & NEALE, *supra* note 4, at 22–24 (relating the logistics proposed for a proportional division of electoral votes).

12. *Id.*

13. *E.g.*, ABBOTT & LEVINE, *supra* note 5, at 121–25; *see also* JOHN R. KOZA ET AL., EVERY VOTE EQUAL: A STATE-BASED PLAN FOR ELECTING THE PRESIDENT BY NATIONAL POPULAR VOTE 112–13 (3d ed. 2011).

Notes

14. *See* BEST, *supra* note 2, at 61–62.
15. *Id.* at 61.

Chapter Twelve

1. *See* Robert W. Bennett, *Popular Election of the President Without a Constitutional Amendment*, 4 GREEN BAG 2d 241 (2001) [hereinafter Bennett, *Popular Election*]; Robert W. Bennett, *State Coordination in Popular Election of the President Without a Constitutional Amendment*, 5 GREEN BAG 2d 141 (2002); *see also* Note, *Rethinking the Electoral College Debate: The Framers, Federalism, and One Person, One Vote*, 114 HARV. L. REV. 2526, 2549 n.112 (2001); Akhil Reed Amar & Vikram David Amar, *How to Achieve Direct National Election of the President Without Amending the Constitution*, FINDLAW'S WRIT (Dec. 28, 2001), http://writ.news.findlaw.com/amar/20011228.html.
2. Bennett, *Popular Election*, *supra* note 1, at 241.
3. *See* U.S. CONST. art. V.
4. Bennett, *Popular Election*, *supra* note 1, at 241.
5. NAT'L POPULAR VOTE, http://www.nationalpopularvote.com (last visited June 28, 2012). The website for a sister group can be found at SUPPORT POPULAR VOTE, http://www.supportpopularvote.com (last visited June 28, 2012).
6. The mechanics of NPV's plan can be found in JOHN R. KOZA ET AL., EVERY VOTE EQUAL: A STATE-BASED PLAN FOR ELECTING THE PRESIDENT BY NATIONAL POPULAR VOTE (3d ed. 2011).
7. U.S. CONST. art. II, § 1, cl. 2.
8. William G. Ross, *Popular Vote Compact: Fraught with Constitutional Perils*, JURIST (Feb. 28, 2012), http://jurist.org/forum/2012/02/william-ross-vote-compact.php.
9. The 11 most populous states, following the 2010 Census, are: California (55 electoral votes), Texas (38), New York (29), Florida (29), Pennsylvania (20), Illinois (20), Ohio (18), Michigan (16), Georgia (16), North Carolina (15), and New Jersey (14).
10. The current status of this legislation can be found at NAT'L POPULAR VOTE, *supra* note 5; SAVE OUR STATES, http://www.saveourstates.com (last visited June 28, 2012).
11. The bill was Senate Bill 2112. *See* An Act Relating to Elections, S. 2112, 2008 Gen. Assemb., Jan. Sess. (R.I. 2008), http://www.rilin.state.ri.us/BillText/BillText08/SenateText08/S2112.pdf. The state legislature explicitly rejected NPV the following year. Senate Bill 161 was approved by the Senate but rejected by the House. *See* An Act Relating to Elections, S. 161, 2011 Gen. Assemb., Jan. Sess. (R.I. 2011), http://www.rilin.state.ri.us/BillText/BillText09/SenateText09/S0161.pdf. Similar bills have since been reintroduced, and NPV continues to lobby for its legislation in the state.

Past Governors of California, Hawaii, and Vermont have vetoed the legislation as well, but the legislation has since passed in each of those states. In Hawaii, the bill passed when the legislature overrode Governor Linda Lingle's veto.

12. *See, e.g.*, Tara Ross & Trent England, *George Soros Supports the Tea Party? What the National Popular Vote Wants You to Believe*, WKLY. STANDARD BLOG (Aug. 16, 2011, 9:31 AM), http://www.weeklystandard.com/blogs/george-soros-supports-tea-party_590271.html.
13. For instance, Laura Brod, a former Minnesota representative, admitted to her status as a paid lobbyist for NPV in a 2011 Vermont legislative hearing.
14. One of the more active groups opposing the National Popular Vote effort is a group called Save Our States. *See* SAVE OUR STATES, *supra* note 10. The Freedom Foundation provided what little funding the project had for its first several years. In the meantime, many of those helping the Save Our States project—or the Electoral College in general—have been volunteers. This author personally travels to testify before state legislative hearings; this travel is entirely self-financed. As of this writing, the group had received two

recent grants, and it hopes to raise more money as awareness of the NPV effort grows.

15. Reportedly, John Koza pledged $12 million to the effort; Tom Golisano pledged up to $30 million. Jonathan Soros pledged $3 million. *See* Debbie Joslin, *NPV—Follow the Money!, in* NATIONAL POPULAR VOTE COMPACT (NPV): REASONS FOR RISK 13, 13 (Oct. 20, 2011), http://www.cordovabreakfastclub.org/wp-content/uploads/2012/01/National-Popular-Vote-Reasons-for-Risk-10-11-DJ.pdf; *see also* Trent England, *NPV Claims Fall Flat*, SAVE OUR STATES (Aug. 4, 2011), http://www.saveourstates.com/2011/npv-claims-fall-flat/.

16. For instance, in Wisconsin, three Republican legislators withdrew their names from the legislation shortly after being convinced to join. *See* Trent England, *NPV Bill Loses Cosponsors: Three Lawmakers Reject NPV After Closer Inspection*, SAVE OUR STATES (Feb. 23, 2010), http://www.saveourstates.com/2010/npv-bill-loses-cosponsors. In South Dakota in 2011, the NPV legislation lost support quickly, and the bill died in committee when one sponsor of the legislation asked that his bill be tabled. *See* An Act to Enact the Agreement Among the States to Elect the President by National Popular Vote, S. 138, 2011 Leg. Assemb., 86th Sess. (S.D. 2011), http://legis.state.sd.us/sessions/2011/Bills/SB138P.pdf. Sponsors have abandoned the NPV legislation in other states as well. *See* England, *supra*; *see also, e.g.*, S.B. 39, 27th Gen. Assemb., 2d. Sess. (Alaska 2011), http://www.legis.state.ak.us/PDF/27/Bills/SB0039A.pdf.

17. *See, e.g.*, Ben Adler, *Would the National Popular Vote Advantage Red-State Republicans?*, AM. PROSPECT (Jan. 9, 2009), http://prospect.org/article/would-national-popular-vote-advantage-red-state-republicans; Saul Anuzis, *National Popular Vote—Why I Support It*, THAT'S SAUL, FOLKS! (Apr. 1, 2010, 11:40 PM), http://www.thatssaulfolks.com/2010/04/01/national-popular-vote-why-i-support-it ("As a conservative and a Republican, there are several other political aspects that I think are important to consider. I believe we are a 'center-right' nation. A national vote system would give our center-right coalition a greater voice in electing the President."); *cf.* Laura Brod, *Don't Rush to Judgment: There Is a Conservative Story to Be Told About the National Popular Vote, in* Ed Morrissey, *Is There a Conservative Case for National Popular Vote?*, HOTAIR (Aug. 15, 2010, 4:30 PM), http://hotair.com/archives/2010/08/15/is-there-a-conservative-case-for-national-popular-vote ("I believe this is a center-right country and that our conservative ideas and ideals will win the day if we take the argument to all people, not just those in battleground states. We leave many conservative votes on the table in red and blue states because candidates are not competing for those votes.").

18. *See also* Tara Ross, *Will Delaware Act Against Its Own Interests?*, SAVE OUR STATES (June 25, 2010), http://www.saveourstates.com/2010/will-delaware-act-against-its-own-interests-2 (discussing Anuzis's lobbying efforts in Delaware).

19. They are less loud about it, probably because they are seeking Republican support and the appearance of bipartisanship; however, at least one liberal publicly labeled pro-Electoral College activists as "haters" who want to stop NPV, since a "national popular vote would disempower the staunchly Republican farm states in the middle of the country." Damon Agnos, *Haters Look to Kill National Popular Vote Bill*, SEATTLE WKLY. BLOG (Mar. 5, 2009, 12:50 PM), http://blogs.seattleweekly.com/dailyweekly/2009/03/haters_look_to_kill_national_p.php; *see also* Trent England, *NPV in the Last Frontier*, SAVE OUR STATES (Mar. 18, 2011), http://www.saveourstates.com/2011/npv-in-the-last-frontier ("They whisper to Republicans that their plan will help Republicans, then whisper to Democrats that NPV will consolidate more power in urban areas.").

20. Texas has been voting Republican in presidential contests since 1980, but its legislative house did not become Republican until relatively late—2002.

Notes

Chapter Thirteen

1. Portions of this chapter are derived from a white paper that this author wrote for the Federalist Society. *See* Tara Ross, *Legal and Logistical Ramifications of the National Popular Vote Plan*, ENGAGE, Sept. 2010, *available at* http://www.fed-soc.org/doclib/20100910_RossEngage11.2.pdf.

2. *See, e.g.*, Bradley A. Smith, *Vanity of Vanities: National Popular Vote and the Electoral College*, 7 ELECTION L.J. 196, 206–08 (2008). NPV's member states could presumably seek agreement on one statutory scheme for conducting recounts, but they could not force non-participating states to adopt such laws.

3. JOHN R. KOZA ET AL., EVERY VOTE EQUAL: A STATE-BASED PLAN FOR ELECTING THE PRESIDENT BY NATIONAL POPULAR VOTE 248 (3d ed. 2011).

4. *Id.*

5. *Id.*

6. 3 U.S.C. § 5 (2006).

7. *See id.*

8. An evaluation of the differences among states' recount criteria is beyond the scope of this book. The important point is that NPV cannot force any state to act upon any particular recount criteria. States will do what they want to do.

9. *See, e.g.*, Smith, *supra* note 2, at 207.

10. NPV advocates often rely heavily on the fact that some states are very lenient in allowing candidates to petition for optional recounts. *See, e.g.*, *U.S. Presidential Election Compact: Hearing on S.B. 39 Before the Sen. Judiciary Comm.*, 27th Leg., 1st Sess. (Alaska 2011) (statement of Laura Brod, former Minnesota State Representative) [hereinafter Statement of Laura Brod]. Without belaboring the point that *petitioning* for a recount is not the same as *obtaining* a recount, NPV's confidence is misplaced. NPV cannot guarantee that any state will continue to allow broad latitude in its optional recounts. Nor can it guarantee that recount laws will not be changed—in both good and bad ways—as politicians react to NPV. The only guarantees are (1) that state recount laws will never be uniform; and (2) political considerations will often weigh heavily with politicians who are in charge of writing state election codes. *See, e.g.*, Smith, *supra* note 2, at 207.

11. Some might doubt that states will compete against each other in this manner. These doubters need look no further than the primary process for nominating presidential candidates. States *already* compete against each other to have the biggest impact possible on the primaries. Why would they not take every opportunity to do the same in the actual presidential election process?

12. KOZA ET AL., *supra* note 3, at 248 (emphasis added).

13. *See id.* ("If, for any reason, the number of presidential electors nominated in a member state in association with the national popular vote winner is less than or greater than that state's number of electoral votes, the presidential candidate on the presidential slate that has been designated as the national popular vote winner shall have the power to nominate the presidential electors for that state . . . .").

14. *Cf.* Derek T. Muller, *Invisible Federalism and the Electoral College*, 44 ARIZ. ST. L.J. (forthcoming 2012) (discussing "State Gamesmanship of the Voting Base").

15. KOZA ET AL., *supra* note 3, at 364.

16. *Id.* at 361.

17. *See also* JUDITH A. BEST, THE CHOICE OF THE PEOPLE? DEBATING THE ELECTORAL COLLEGE 55–58 (1996); ROBERT M. HARDAWAY, THE ELECTORAL COLLEGE AND THE CONSTITUTION: THE CASE FOR PRESERVING FEDERALISM 20–21 (1994).

18. Smith, *supra* note 2, at 207. Norman Williams additionally notes:

The supporters, however, miss the point—it's not the absolute vote spread that matters but the percentage vote margin. Precisely because the number of missed or miscounted ballots rises in proportion to the number of ballots cast, the threshold for triggering mandatory recounts in those states that provide for them is typically specified in percentage terms. Of course, in a nation in which 130 million votes are cast for President (as happened in 2008), a 1% recount threshold would justify a recount where the winning vote margin is 1.3 million votes or less. Moreover, judging by past experience, national elections within that margin are more common than the NPVC supporters misleadingly suggest.

Norman R. Williams, *Reforming the Electoral College: Federalism, Majoritarianism, and the Perils of Subconstitutional Change*, 100 GEO. L.J. 173, 234 (2011) (footnote omitted).

19. Statement of Laura Brod, *supra* note 10. The audio for the committee hearing is available at http://www.legis.state.ak.us/ftr/20110223/sjud/sjud_1333.mp3.

20. *Id.*

21. *Id.*

22. *Id.*

23. Tim Sampson, *Vote of No Confidence*, POLITICS, Aug. 2008, at 12, 14, *available at* http://tsampson.squarespace.com/vote-of-no-confidence/.

24. *Id.*

25. ROBERT W. BENNETT, TAMING THE ELECTORAL COLLEGE 177–78 (2006). This author pressed an NPV supporter to explain some of these problems in 2010:

> Common Cause replied that if such problems arise "it can be addressed." Later, @CommonCauseMA added, "we should have faith that law is correctable."
>
> It will be addressed? The law is correctable? Do NPV or its supporters assume that further statutory corrections will be necessary once its plan is enacted? Apparently. But, in echoes of Pelosi, we have to enact NPV before we know what we will really get at the end of the day. For now, NPV is most interested in getting its foot in the door without raising undue alarm among voters.

Tara Ross, *Anti-Electoral College Advocates: Pass Bill Now, Ask Questions Later*, WKLY. STANDARD BLOG (July 19, 2010, 5:55 PM), http://www.weeklystandard.com/blogs/anti-electoral-college-measure-pass-bill-ask-questions-later.

26. Vikram David Amar, *The National Popular Vote Bill Proposal in California, and Ultimately (Perhaps) in Washington D.C.*, JUSTIA.COM: VERDICT (Aug. 5, 2011), http://verdict.justia.com/2011/08/05/the-national-popular-vote-bill-proposal-in-california-and-ultimately-perhaps-in-washington-d-c.

27. *Id.* (acknowledging questions about where "Congress might derive the power to require such uniformity"); *see also* Vikram David Amar, *Response: The Case for Reforming Presidential Elections by Subconstitutional Means: The Electoral College, the National Popular Vote Compact, and Congressional Power*, 100 GEO. L.J. 237, 252–55 (2011).

28. BENNETT, *supra* note 25, at 234 n.58.

29. If this state wanted to go really crazy, it could revert to an even older form of election—the state legislature could select the electors itself, without reference to a popular election within the state. *See also* Williams, *supra* note 18, at 209–10 (making a similar suggestion). The state may risk being omitted from the election if it takes this route, however. Technically, NPV's compact only requires state election officials to tally votes in those states in which "votes have been cast in a statewide popular election." KOZA ET AL., *supra* note 3, at 248; *see also* Williams, *supra* note 18, at 210 ("The unstated but clear implication is that signatory states are free—indeed, commanded by the NPVC—to ignore nonsignatory states that refuse to conduct a statewide popular election for President.").

30. A discussion of the 1960 election and the confusion in tabulating election results

Notes

can be found at GEORGE C. EDWARDS III, WHY THE ELECTORAL COLLEGE IS BAD FOR AMERICA 67–70 (2d ed. 2011).

31. *See* Alexander S. Belenky, *For National Vote Plan, All States Must Consent*, BUFF. NEWS, Apr. 7, 2009, at A8.

32. Texas could still craft its election in a winner-take-all fashion, despite requiring its citizens to cast ballots for individual election. Alternatively, it could appoint the 38 individuals receiving the highest vote 1`totals, regardless of party affiliation.

33. *See* Williams, *supra* note 18, at 212–14 (discussing several methods by which states could hide their vote totals).

34. Academics such as Bennett laugh off such suggestions, calling it "unlikely" that a vote total would not be available. BENNETT, *supra* note 25, at 176. Why? NPV states may act rashly if they assume that non-participating states will tamely accept the outcome that has been dictated to them by a minority of other states. It is just as likely that at least one state will bristle and react to the fact that it is being backed into a corner.

35. *See* Akhil Reed Amar & Vikram David Amar, *How to Achieve Direct National Election of the President Without Amending the Constitution*, FINDLAW'S WRIT (Dec. 28, 2001), http://writ.news.findlaw.com/amar/20011228.html (contemplating a "National Presidential Vote" system that would tally the votes only of those who registered).

36. KOZA ET AL., *supra* note 3, at 249.

37. *See, e.g.*, David Gringer, *Why the National Popular Vote Plan is the Wrong Way to Abolish the Electoral College*, 108 COLUM. L. REV. 182, 224, 230 (2008).

38. U.S. CONST. art. I, § 10, cl. 1; *see also* Letter from Dr. John R. Koza, Chair, National Popular Vote, to Hon. Joe Paskvan, Alaska State Senate (Feb. 19, 2010), *available at* http://www.nationalpopularvote.com/resources/Withdrawal-V4-2010-2-19-JK-Paskvan. pdf.

39. *See also* Williams, *supra* note 18, at 216 (noting that the federal courts have never applied the Contracts Clause to an unratified interstate agreement).

Chapter Fourteen

1. Portions of this chapter are derived from a white paper that this author wrote for the Federalist Society. *See* Tara Ross, *Legal and Logistical Ramifications of the National Popular Vote Plan*, ENGAGE, Sept. 2010, *available at* http://www.fed-soc.org/doclib/20100910 RossEngage11.2.pdf.

2. Laura Brod, *Don't Rush to Judgment: There Is a Conservative Story to Be Told About the National Popular Vote*, *in* Ed Morrissey, *Is There a Conservative Case for National Popular Vote?*, HOTAIR (Aug. 15, 2010, 4:30 PM), http://hotair.com/archives/2010/08/15/is-there-a-conservative-case-for-national-popular-vote.

3. Richard Bolen, *A Conservative Case for National Popular Vote: Why I Support a State-Based Plan to Reform the Electoral College*, NAT'L POPULAR VOTE (Summer 2010), http://nationalpopularvote.com/pages/blogs/bolen_201008.php.

4. *Id.*

5. Jason Cabel Roe, *Opponents of the National Popular Vote Have It Wrong*, NAT'L POPULAR VOTE (Aug. 6, 2010), http://www.nationalpopularvote.com/pages/blogs/big government_20100806.php.

6. ROBERT W. BENNETT, TAMING THE ELECTORAL COLLEGE 183 (2006).

7. JAMES MADISON, NOTES OF DEBATES IN THE FEDERAL CONVENTION OF 1787, at 309 (Adrienne Koch ed., W.W. Norton & Co. 1987) (1966).

8. *Id.* at 306.

9. *Id.* at 307.

10. Robert Yates, *Notes of the Secret Debates of the Federal Convention of 1787*, THE

AVALON PROJECT: YALE LAW SCH., http://avalon.law.yale.edu/18th_century/yates.asp (last visited June 28, 2012).

11. NPV's proposed contract can be found at JOHN R. KOZA ET AL., EVERY VOTE EQUAL: A STATE-BASED PLAN FOR ELECTING THE PRESIDENT BY NATIONAL POPULAR VOTE 247–49 (3d ed. 2011).

12. *See id.* at 272–73 (explaining why "[n]o single state would be likely to alone enact a law awarding its electoral votes to the nationwide winner").

13. *See, e.g.*, BENNETT, *supra* note 6, at 171 (arguing that congressional approval is not needed but acknowledging "some language in Supreme Court decisions that might suggest that the clause applies").

14. U.S. CONST. art. I, § 10, cls. 1 & 3.

15. Virginia v. Tennessee, 148 U.S. 503, 519 (1893); *see also* Michael S. Greve, *Compacts, Cartels, and Congressional Consent*, 68 MO. L. REV. 285, 300 (2003) (discussing *Virginia v. Tennessee* and its impact on the Court's Compact Clause jurisprudence).

16. A more complete legal analysis of the Court's jurisprudence in this area can be found at Ross, *supra* note 1, at 39-41.

17. Constitutional scholar Michael Greve has written of the "emasculation of the Compact Clause," noting that "one can hardly imagine a state compact that would run afoul of the Compact Clause without first, or at least also, running afoul of other, independent constitutional obstacles." Greve, *supra* note 15, at 288, 308.

18. U.S. Steel Corp. v. Multistate Tax Comm'n, 434 U.S. 452, 473 (1978) ("[T]he test is whether the Compact enhances state power *quoad* the National Government."). Importantly, the Court later discussed the impact of the *U.S. Steel* compact on non-participating states. Writing for the Court, Justice Powell deemed any "[r]isks of unfairness and double taxation" to be "independent of the Compact," at least in this case. *Id.* at 478. He left open the possibility that a compact implicating the "federal structure" could be problematic, but in the case of the Commission, he concluded, "it is not explained how any economic pressure that does exist is an affront to the sovereignty of nonmember States." *Id.* The dissent agreed that impacts upon non-compacting states must be considered. *Id.* at 494 (White, J., dissenting) ("A proper understanding of what would encroach upon federal authority, however, must also incorporate encroachments on the authority and power of non-Compact States.").

19. KOZA ET AL., *supra* note 11, at 227–28. NPV's default position is that the only impact considered is whether state power is increased at the expense of federal power, per the test in *U.S. Steel*, 434 U.S. at 473. However, NPV admits that "there is always the possibility that the U.S. Supreme Court might change the legal standards concerning congressional consent contained in its 1893 and 1978 rulings." *Myths About Congressional Consent*, NAT'L POPULAR VOTE, http://nationalpopularvote.com/pages/answers/m15.php#m15_2 (last visited June 28, 2012). In such a case, it might consider the "possible adverse effects of a compact on non-compacting states in deciding whether congressional consent is required." *Id.*; *see also* KOZA ET AL., *supra* note 11, at 229 (acknowledging that a second test, regarding the impact on non-member states, "might be necessary").

In a podcast debate with this author, John Koza reiterated his claim that effects upon non-participating states need not be considered by the Court. Koza erroneously claimed that only the dissent in *U.S. Steel* mentioned this possibility. *The National Popular Vote Plan— Podcast*, FEDERALIST SOC'Y FOR L. & PUB. POL'Y STUD. (Apr. 20, 2012), http://www.fed-soc.org/publications/detail/the-national-popular-vote-plan-podcast; *see also* discussion *supra* note 18.

20. *Myths About Congressional Consent, supra* note 19 ("The National Popular Vote compact would not 'encroach upon or interfere with the just supremacy of the United States'

Notes

because there is simply no federal power—much less federal supremacy—in the area of awarding of electoral votes in the first place.").

21. *See* discussion *supra* notes 18–19; *see also* Ne. Bancorp, Inc. v. Bd. of Governors of the Fed. Reserve Sys., 472 U.S. 159, 176 (1985) (agreeing with the formulation that a compact cannot "infringe federal supremacy" but also addressing the question of whether the compact in question "enhance[s] the *political* power of the New England States at the expense of other States or [has] an 'impact on our federal structure'" (citing *U.S. Steel*, 434 U.S. at 471)); *U.S. Steel*, 434 U.S. at 494 (White, J., dissenting) ("[T]he purpose of requiring the submission to Congress of a compact (in that case, regarding a boundary) between two States was 'to guard against the derangement of their federal relations *with the other states of the Union*, and the federal government . . . .'" (citing Rhode Island v. Massachusetts, 12 Pet. 657, 726 (1838))) (emphasis added); Derek T. Muller, *The Compact Clause and the National Popular Vote Interstate Compact*, 6 ELECTION L.J. 372, 385 (2007) (arguing that "[e]very Compact Clause case, from *Virginia v. Tennessee* to the modern cases, considers not simply the federal sovereignty interest, but also the interests of non-compacting sister states") (citations omitted).

22. *U.S. Steel*, 434 U.S. at 478.

23. *See, e.g.*, Judith Best, Remarks at MIT Conference: To Keep or Not to Keep the Electoral College: New Approaches to Electoral Reform (Oct. 17, 2008), *available at* http://video.mit.edu/watch/the-electoral-college-experts-debate and audience-dialogue-9432/.

24. The federal government might also argue that NPV affects the balance of power between federal and state governments because the House's role in presidential elections will be effectively removed. Adam Schleifer, *Interstate Agreement for Electoral Reform*, 40 AKRON L. REV. 717, 739–40 (2007). Currently, the House of Representatives selects the President if no candidate obtains a majority of electoral votes. U.S. CONST. amend. XII. NPV eliminates this possibility. *See also* Daniel P. Rathbun, Comment, *Ideological Endowment: The Staying Power of the Electoral College and the Weaknesses of the National Popular Vote Interstate Compact*, 106 MICH. L. REV. FIRST IMPRESSIONS 117, 118 (2008), http://www.michiganlawreview.org/firstimpressions/vol106/rathbun.pdf ("The ability of a few states to determine election outcomes would give 'the states' a unified face and an important advantage in bargaining with the federal government.").

25. *Myths About Congressional Consent*, *supra* note 19.

26. California received preclearance, as it requested. A copy of the letter has been posted on the National Popular Vote website: http://nationalpopularvote.com/resources/CA-Herren-Letter-2012-1-13-DOJ-VRA-Preclearance.pdf. A summary of the requirements of this section of the Voting Rights Act can be found on the Department of Justice website. *See* Civil Rights Division, *Section 5 of the Voting Rights Act*, U.S. DEP'T. JUST., http://www.justice.gov/crt/about/vot/sec_5/about.php (last visited June 29, 2012).

27. As a legal matter, votes will have equal weight if the nation moves to a direct election system. As a practical matter, voters will continue to be unequal, as argued elsewhere in this book.

28. *See generally* JOHN SAMPLES, CATO INSTITUTE, A CRITIQUE OF THE NATIONAL POPULAR VOTE PLAN FOR ELECTING THE PRESIDENT (2008) (discussing which states gain power and which states lose power).

29. KOZA ET AL., *supra* note 11, at 339.

30. *Id.* at 417–19.

31. Bush v. Gore, 531 U.S. 98, 104 (2000) (per curiam).

32. U.S. CONST. art. II, § 1, cl. 2.

33. KOZA ET AL., *supra* note 11, at 272.

34. Thanks to a conversation with Michael Greve, this author has come to the conclusion that she has perhaps been a bit too glib about this matter in the past. She has, for instance, been known to joke that states have "plenary" power and can appoint Mickey Mouse as an elector, if they so choose. They probably could appoint Mickey Mouse—or at least the individual who puts on the mouse suit—but upon considering the ways in which such a principle could be abused, it was perhaps better not to make such loose statements, even in jest.

35. *Cf.* Douglas Laycock, *Equal Citizens of Equal and Territorial States: The Constitutional Foundations of Choice of Law*, 92 COLUM. L. REV. 249, 251 (1992) (arguing that the "fundamental allocation of authority among states is territorial" although the principle "is largely implicit, so obvious that the Founders neglected to state it"). NPV proponent Robert Bennett has also discussed limitations on a state's discretion in choosing its method of elector allocation. BENNETT, *supra* note 6, at 131.

36. NPV responds to this point by noting:

> The Constitutional Convention voted against a number of different methods for selecting the President, including having state legislatures choose the President, having governors make the choice, and a national popular vote.
>
> However, the wording that actually ended up in the Constitution is unqualified and does not prohibit any of the methods that were previously debated.
>
> A majority of the states employed two of the specifically rejected methods in the nation's first presidential election in 1789 (namely, appointment by the legislature and appointment by the governor and his cabinet).

KOZA ET AL., *supra* note 11, at 397. The Constitutional Convention voted against some of these electoral methods, but more importantly, it voted against a national decision on these matters. It explicitly left the decision to the states. *A state* should make a choice for *itself*. NPV contradicts the Convention's outcome by robbing non-participating states of the right to make their own decisions about how Presidents are to be elected; instead, these states are forced into a national popular vote scheme at the behest of a minority of states.

37. It is beyond the scope of this book to offer a detailed legal analysis of some of the claims raised in this subsection. This book seeks only to highlight that there are legitimate grounds for such claims of unfairness and inequality among voters.

38. U.S. CONST. amend XIV, § 1.

39. Bush v. Gore, 531 U.S. 98, 104–05 (2000) (per curiam).

40. *Id.* at 110.

41. *See also* Editorial, *College Dropouts*, INVESTOR'S BUS. DAILY, Mar. 27, 2006, at A18 ("It's odd that those who say the Electoral College disenfranchises voters propose a system that disenfranchises voters.").

42. A thorough evaluation of the differences among states' laws is beyond the scope of this book. The specific differences are not important; what is important is that differences exist. State laws on these matters are often changing anyway.

43. The author is grateful to Paul Windels, an election law lawyer in New York, for pointing out some of these jurisdictional questions. *See* E-mail from Paul Windels III to Tara Ross (Apr. 11, 2012, 14:38 CST) (on file with author).

44. *Myths About the 14th Amendment*, NAT'L POPULAR VOTE, http://www.national popularvote.com/pages/answers/m17.php#m17_4 (last visited June 29, 2012).

45. To say nothing of the jurisdictional issues involved. *See* discussion *supra* note 43.

46. *Bush*, 531 U.S. at 104–05.

47. *See* Norman R. Williams, *Reforming the Electoral College: Federalism, Majoritarianism, and the Perils of Subconstitutional Change*, 100 GEO. L.J. 173, 226–28

Notes

(2011). *But see* Vikram David Amar, *Response: The Case for Reforming Presidential Elections by Subconstitutional Means: The Electoral College, the National Popular Vote Compact, and Congressional Power*, 100 GEO. L.J. 237, 250–51 (2011).

48. *Bush*, 531 U.S. at 104; *see also* KOZA ET AL., *supra* note 11, at 4.

49. McPherson v. Blacker, 146 U.S. 1, 35 (1892) (cited in KOZA ET AL., *supra* note 11, at 4).

50. *In re* Opinion of the Justices, 107 A. 673, 705 (Me. 1919) (cited in KOZA ET AL., *supra* note 11, at 4).

51. KOZA ET AL., *supra* note 11, at 4.

52. U.S. Term Limits, Inc. v. Thornton, 514 U.S. 779, 861 (1995) (Thomas, J., dissenting). The comment was made in dissent, but the other justices did not dispute Thomas on this particular point. *See also* Anderson v. Celebrezze, 460 U.S. 780, 794 n.18 (1983) ("The Constitution expressly delegates authority to the States to regulate the selection of Presidential electors. But, as we have emphasized, 'we must reject the notion that Art. II, § 1, gives the States power to impose burdens on the right to vote, where such burdens are expressly prohibited in other constitutional provisions.'") (citations omitted).

53. U.S. CONST. art. IV, § 4; *see also* Kristin Feeley, Comment, *Guaranteeing a Federally Elected President*, 103 NW. U. L. REV. 1427 (2009).

54. U.S. CONST. art. V.

55. SAMPLES, *supra* note 28, at 13–14.

56. Clinton v. City of New York, 524 U.S. 417 (1998).

57. *U.S. Term Limits*, 514 U.S. at 779.

58. *Id.* at 831.

59. New York v. United States, 505 U.S. 144, 147 (1992); *see also* Rathbun, *supra* note 24, at 118.

60. U.S. CONST. art. II, § 1, cl. 2.

61. *See* discussion *supra* note 11 (Ch. 12) and accompanying text.

62. *See* Bob Mercer, *National Popular Vote Movement Fails in South Dakota*, ABERDEEN NEWS (Oct. 25, 2011, 3:53 PM), http://www.aberdeennews.com/news/aan-national-popular-vote-movement-fails-in-south-dakota-20111025,0,6436939.story; *see also* Valerie Richardson, *Group Seeks to Split Colorado Electors*, WASH. TIMES, June 16, 2004, at A5.

63. Bush v. Gore, 531 U.S. 98, 115 (2000) (Rehnquist, C.J., concurring).

64. *See also* Richard L. Hasen, *When "Legislature" May Mean More than "Legislature": Initiated Electoral College Reform and the Ghost of* Bush v. Gore, 35 HASTINGS CONST. L.Q. 599, 610–16 (2008).

65. For a more thorough discussion of this topic, see Ross, *supra* note 1; *see also* Charles S. Doskow & David A. Sonner, *Vox Populi: Is it Time to Reform the Electoral College?*, FED. LAW., July 2008, at 33, 36–39.

66. KOZA ET AL., *supra* note 11, at 317–20.

67. *Every Vote Equal* also reasonably notes a statement made in the Supreme Court case of *U.S. Term Limits v. Thornton*, 514 U.S. 779 (1995). In the majority opinion, Justice Stevens off-handedly remarked that the Article I legislative duty "parallels the duty under Article II." *See id.* at 805 (cited in KOZA ET AL., *supra* note 11, at 309). However, Stevens was not discussing the definition of legislature. Instead, he was discussing which powers have been delegated to the states and which powers have been reserved by them. *See id.* at 804–05.

68. *See also* Doskow & Sonner, *supra* note 65, at 36 (noting that a state legislature may send legislation to a governor "out of habit" even when it is not necessary).

69. Unless a future effort to obtain legislative approval combined with a gubernatorial signature is successful, of course. *See also* discussion *supra* note 11 (Ch. 12).

70. For instance, does NPV violate Section 2 of the Voting Rights Act? Is preclearance required under Section 5? *See generally* David Gringer, *Why the National Popular Vote Plan is the Wrong Way to Abolish the Electoral College*, 108 COLUM. L. REV. 182 (2008).

Chapter Fifteen

1. Following the 2010 Census, these states are: California (55 electoral votes), Texas (38), New York (29), Florida (29), Pennsylvania (20), Illinois (20), Ohio (18), Michigan (16), Georgia (16), North Carolina (15), and New Jersey (14). *See Apportionment Data*, U.S. CENSUS BUREAU, http://2010.census.gov/2010census/data/apportionment-data.php (last visited June 26, 2012).

2. Indeed, Robert Bennett goes so far as to suggest that the two most populous states— California and Texas—could effectively make such a decision for everyone else. *See, e.g.,* ROBERT W. BENNETT, TAMING THE ELECTORAL COLLEGE 166 (2006).

3. S. COMM. ON THE JUDICIARY, DIRECT POPULAR ELECTION OF THE PRESIDENT, S. REP. NO. 91-1123, at 47-48 (1970) (minority views of Messrs. Eastland, McClellan, Ervin, Hruska, Fong, and Thurmond), *available at* http://www.ashbrook. org/articles/electoralcollege-directpopular.html.

4. CQ PRESS, PRESIDENTIAL ELECTIONS: 1789–2008, at 261 (2010).

5. Holman W. Jenkins Jr., *Democrats in Black and White*, WALL ST. J. POL. DIARY, Dec. 15, 2004 (copy on file with author).

6. *See, e.g.*, DAVID W. ABBOTT & JAMES P. LEVINE, WRONG WINNER: THE COMING DEBACLE IN THE ELECTORAL COLLEGE 51–58 (1991) (discussing the elections of 1948, 1960, and 1968); NEAL R. PEIRCE & LAWRENCE D. LONGLEY, THE PEOPLE'S PRESIDENT: THE ELECTORAL COLLEGE IN AMERICAN HISTORY AND THE DIRECT VOTE ALTERNATIVE 58–84 (Yale Univ. Press rev. ed. 1981) (1968) (analyzing the elections of 1916, 1948, 1960, 1968 and 1976); *see also Proposals for Electoral College Reform: Hearings on H.J. Res. 28 and H.J. Res. 43 Before the Subcomm. on the Constitution of the House Comm. on the Judiciary*, 105th Cong. 26 (1997) (statement of Becky Cain, President, League of Women Voters), http://commdocs.house.gov/committees/judiciary/hju57219.000/hju57219_0f.htm [hereinafter Statement of Becky Cain].

7. *See* PEIRCE & LONGLEY, *supra* note 6, at 59; *see also* Statement of Becky Cain, *supra* note 6, at 26.

8. PEIRCE & LONGLEY, *supra* note 6, at 62; *see also* Statement of Becky Cain, *supra* note 6, at 26; ABBOTT & LEVINE, *supra* note 6, at 52–53 (stating that shifts in California and Ohio would have prevented either Truman or Dewey from gaining an electoral majority, thus throwing the election into the House contingent election); GEORGE C. EDWARDS III, WHY THE ELECTORAL COLLEGE IS BAD FOR AMERICA 72 (2d ed. 2011).

9. PEIRCE & LONGLEY, *supra* note 6, at 84; *see also* Statement of Becky Cain, *supra* note 6, at 26.

10. CQ PRESS, *supra* note 4, at 170; *see also* EDWARDS, *supra* note 8, at 72.

11. *See* JUDITH BEST, THE CASE AGAINST DIRECT ELECTION OF THE PRESIDENT: A DEFENSE OF THE ELECTORAL COLLEGE 72–80 (1975).

12. *Id.* at 79.

13. *Id.* at 72–74.

14. Or perhaps he had good ideas that would have served the country well, but he communicated them in a way that failed to gain the trust of voters in many parts of the country.

15. The 1960 election between Nixon and Kennedy is occasionally cited as an election in which the winner of the popular vote lost the presidency. EDWARDS, *supra* note 8, at 62. In order to reach this conclusion, one has to accept an alternative popular vote count for

Notes

Alabama's election—the outcome in every other state showed a clear popular vote lead for Kennedy. In Alabama, tabulation of the popular vote totals was admittedly confusing because voters cast their ballots for individual electors rather than an entire slate of electors. Adding more confusion to the situation, some of the Democratic electors were committed to Kennedy, while others were not. There is probably no good way to accurately count those votes toward a national total. But it nevertheless seems odd to twist the confusing situation into a claim that Nixon "really" won the national popular vote: He lost the popular vote in all states, excluding Alabama. In the state of Alabama, his top elector received fewer votes than the top elector pledged to Kennedy: 237,981 votes for the Nixon elector and 318,303 votes for the top Kennedy elector. *Id.* at 67. At best, this situation shows the impossibility of compiling a reliable national popular vote total, as NPV hopes to do, when the form of individual state's ballots may vary so drastically.

16. Others have reached the conclusion that the Electoral College cannot properly be blamed if, in fact, popular vote winners did not win the presidency in 1824 and 1876. *E.g.*, BEST, *supra* note 11, at 24–25, 52–54; *see also* ROBERT M. HARDAWAY, THE ELECTORAL COLLEGE AND THE CONSTITUTION: THE CASE FOR PRESERVING FEDERALISM 4 (1994); Denny Pilant, *No—The Electoral College Should Not be Abolished*, *in* CONTROVERSIAL ISSUES IN PRESIDENTIAL SELECTION 216, 219–20 (Gary L. Rose ed., 1991); Grant M. Dixton, *Book Review: The Electoral College Primer*, 34 HARV. J. ON LEGIS. 293, 298 (1997); Arthur Schlesinger, Jr., *It's a Mess, But We've Been Through It Before*, TIME, Nov. 20, 2000, at 64, 65. Others include these elections as ones in which the will of the people was "frustrated." *E.g.*, PEIRCE & LONGLEY, *supra* note 6, at 5; *see also* Akhil Reed Amar, *Presidents Without Mandates (With Special Emphasis on Ohio)*, 67 U. CIN. L. REV. 375, 391 (1999) (referring to Hayes, along with Harrison, as a "clear popular loser"); Abner J. Mikva, *Doubting Our Claims to Democracy*, 39 ARIZ. L. REV. 793, 799 (1997) (discussing the 1876 election). Electoral College opponent George Edwards concedes that the election of 1824 isn't fairly included on the list of instances in which a popular vote loser won the White House. In describing the election, he says that "something approximating a popular vote for president" occurred and recognizes that "we must be cautious about interpreting the vote count as an accurate indicator of public opinion." EDWARDS, *supra* note 8, at 78 (internal reference omitted).

17. A discussion of the 1824 election can be found at PAUL F. BOLLER, JR., PRESIDENTIAL CAMPAIGNS 33–41 (rev. ed. 1996); MICHAEL J. GLENNON, WHEN NO MAJORITY RULES: THE ELECTORAL COLLEGE AND PRESIDENTIAL SUCCESSION 15–16 (1992); HARDAWAY, *supra* note 16, at 123–25.

18. *See* discussion *supra* note 16; *see also* Bradley A. Smith, *Vanity of Vanities: National Popular Vote and the Electoral College*, 7 ELECTION L.J. 196, 212 n.109 (2008) ("One quarter of the states, representing over one quarter of the population, did not vote for president.").

19. Moreover, some states did not include all four candidates on their ballots. BOLLER, *supra* note 17, at 36.

20. A discussion of the 1876 election can be found at WILLIAM H. REHNQUIST, CENTENNIAL CRISIS: THE DISPUTED ELECTION OF 1876 (2004); *see also* BOLLER, *supra* note 17, at 133–41; GLENNON, *supra* note 17, at 16–17; HARDAWAY, *supra* note 16, at 128–37.

21. *See* REHNQUIST, *supra* note 20, at 176–79 (discussing the filibusters); *see also* HARDAWAY, *supra* note 16, at 134–35 (same).

22. PAUL LELAND HAWORTH, THE HAYES-TILDEN DISPUTED PRESIDENTIAL ELECTION OF 1876, at 340–41 (1906), *cited by* BEST, *supra* note 11, at 53; *see also* Smith, *supra* note 18, at 213; Norman R. Williams, *Reforming the Electoral College: Federalism, Majoritarianism, and the Perils of Subconstitutional Change*, 100 GEO. L.J. 173, 201 (2011).

23. Nixon lost Massachusetts and the District of Columbia. He also lost one electoral vote when a faithless elector in Virginia cast a vote for Libertarian candidate John Hospers. Nixon's popular vote total was also a landslide: 47,169,911 to 29,170,383. *See* CQ PRESS, *supra* note 4, at 162, 252.

24. Editorial, *Ronald Reagan, 1911-2004*, LAS VEGAS REV.-J., June 7, 2004, at 6B.

25. *Id.*

26. *The NewsHour with Jim Lehrer* (PBS television broadcast, June 7, 2004).

27. Peggy Noonan, *The Ben Elliott Story: What I Saw at the Funeral*, WALL ST. J., (June 14, 2004), http://online.wsj.com/article/SB122460039897754255.html.

Chapter Sixteen

1. JUDITH BEST, THE CASE AGAINST DIRECT ELECTION OF THE PRESIDENT: A DEFENSE OF THE ELECTORAL COLLEGE 67 (1975).

2. *See* CQ PRESS, PRESIDENTIAL ELECTIONS: 1789–2008, at 141, 231 (2010).

3. The first edition of this book reported slightly different popular vote totals. These figures were derived from the 1997 edition of Congressional Quarterly's *Presidential Elections*. CONG. QUARTERLY, PRESIDENTIAL ELECTIONS, 1789-1996, at 100 (1997). The figures in this edition have been revised to reflect the new numbers reported in the most recent edition of *Presidential Elections*. *See* CQ PRESS, *supra* note 2, at 141.

4. For more information on Cleveland's first term and the 1888 election, see DOROTHY BURNE GOEBEL & JULIUS GOEBEL, JR., GENERALS IN THE WHITE HOUSE 250–54 (1945); HORACE SAMUEL MERRILL, BOURBON LEADER: GROVER CLEVELAND AND THE DEMOCRATIC PARTY 102–34 (1957); RICHARD E. WELCH, JR., THE PRESIDENCIES OF GROVER CLEVELAND 93–99 (1988); *see also* HARRY J. SIEVERS, S.J., BENJAMIN HARRISON: HOOSIER STATESMAN 357–427 (1959); HOMER E. SOCOLOFSKY & ALLAN B. SPETTER, THE PRESIDENCY OF BENJAMIN HARRISON 1–18 (1987).

5. MERRILL, *supra* note 4, at 116.

6. Franklin Delano Roosevelt issued more total vetoes, but they were issued over the course of his more than three terms in office. A list of presidential vetoes can be found at *Summary of Bills Vetoed, 1789-present*, U.S. SENATE, http://www.senate.gov/reference/Legislation/Vetoes/vetoCounts.htm (last visited June 27, 2012).

7. MERRILL, *supra* note 4, at 107.

8. *Id.* at 108.

9. GOEBEL & GOEBEL, *supra* note 4, at 250.

10. MERRILL, *supra* note 4, at 128.

11. *Id.*

12. SOCOLOFSKY & SPETTER, *supra* note 4, at 12 (citation omitted).

13. R. HAL WILLIAMS, YEARS OF DECISION: AMERICAN POLITICS IN THE 1890S, at 3 (1978); *see also* SIEVERS, *supra* note 4, at 371. Harrison did not travel to give his speeches. Voters traveled to see him in Indianapolis, and he gave speeches (often tailored to his audience) from his doorstep.

14. SIEVERS, *supra* note 4, at 369.

15. *Id.* at 357.

16. William J. Clinton, Remarks on the Resolution of the 2000 Presidential Election and an Exchange With Reporters in North Aylesbury, United Kingdom (Dec. 14, 2000), *available at* http://www.presidency.ucsb.edu/ws/index.php?pid=1295#axzz1nhsv9kR2.

17. *Talk of the Nation* (NPR radio broadcast, Dec. 12, 2000).

18. Jack Mabley, *U.S. May Be Divided, But It's Not Unhealthy*, CHI. DAILY HERALD, Dec. 13, 2000, at 16.

19. *E.g.*, JAMES W. CEASER & ANDREW E. BUSCH, THE PERFECT TIE: THE TRUE

Notes

STORY OF THE 2000 PRESIDENTIAL ELECTION (2001) [hereinafter PERFECT TIE].

20. Greg Pierce, *Inside Politics: County By County*, WASH. TIMES, Nov. 15, 2000, at 7.

21. *Id.*

22. *Id.*

23. The first edition of this book reported slightly different popular vote totals for both the Bush and Gore charts. These figures were obtained from the National Archives website. The figures in this edition have been revised to reflect the new numbers reported in the most recent edition of *Presidential Elections. See* CQ PRESS, *supra* note 2, at 169. For each candidate, the percent of votes won also takes into account those votes cast for third-party candidates, although the popular vote tallies of these latter candidates are not listed in the charts.

24. *Breaking Down the Electorate*, TIME, Nov. 20, 2000, at 74, 74 (reporting Voter News Service exit polls). Only 26% of the same population voted for Bush. *Id.*

25. *Id.*

26. Henry C. Kenski et al., *Explaining the Vote in a Divided Country: The Presidential Election of 2000, in* THE 2000 PRESIDENTIAL CAMPAIGN: A COMMUNICATION PERSPECTIVE 225, 232–37 (Robert E. Denton, Jr. ed., 2002).

27. PERFECT TIE, *supra* note 19, at 28 tbl.1.2.

28. *See* ELECTING THE PRESIDENT, 2000: THE INSIDERS' VIEW 212 (Kathleen Hall Jamieson & Paul Waldman eds., 2001) (quoting Karl Rove) [hereinafter ELECTING THE PRESIDENT].

29. PERFECT TIE, *supra* note 19, at 28–29 (discussing Bush' strategy for competing with Gore on economic issues).

30. *Id.* at 29–31 (discussing the importance of values during the campaign); *see also* DAVID FRUM, THE RIGHT MAN: THE SURPRISE PRESIDENCY OF GEORGE W. BUSH 7–9 (2003) (same).

31. *See* Kenski et al., *supra* note 26, at 229–30.

32. George W. Bush, Nomination Acceptance Speech at the Republican National Convention in Philadelphia, Pennsylvania (Aug. 3, 2000), *available at* http://www.pbs.org/newshour/election2000/gopconvention/george_w_bush.html.

33. PERFECT TIE, *supra* note 19, at 30 (quoting Richard Cheney).

34. John F. Harris, *Scrambling on "Friendly" Turf: In Full Roar, Gore Tries To Rally Tennessee Again*, WASH. POST, Oct. 26, 2000, at A1, *quoted in* Kenski et al., *supra* note 26, at 260.

35. PERFECT TIE, *supra* note 19, at 28 tbl.1.2.

36. *Us Versus Us*, ECONOMIST (Nov. 6, 2003), http://www.economist.com/node/2172019.

37. *Id.*

38. *Id.* Twenty-four percent deemed the scandals "very important," while twenty percent rated the scandals "important." *Id.*

39. George W. Bush, The First Gore-Bush Presidential Debate in Boston, Massachusetts, COMM'N ON PRESIDENTIAL DEBATES (Oct. 3, 2000), http://www.debates.org/index.php?page=october-3-2000-transcript.

40. Albert Gore, The First Gore-Bush Presidential Debate in Boston, Massachusetts, COMM'N ON PRESIDENTIAL DEBATES (Oct. 3, 2000), http://www.debates.org/index.php?page=october-3-2000-transcript.

41. ELECTING THE PRESIDENT, *supra* note 28, at 206 (quoting Karl Rove); *see also* Kenski et al., *supra* note 26, at 227–28.

42. *See* PERFECT TIE, *supra* note 19, at 35–36.

43. ELECTING THE PRESIDENT, *supra* note 28, at 203–04 (quoting Karl Rove).

44. *Id.*

45. *Id.*

46. *See* Kenski et al., *supra* note 26, at 229.

47. Edwards disputes this description, arguing that Gore had plenty of support in the states that he lost. GEORGE C. EDWARDS III, WHY THE ELECTORAL COLLEGE IS BAD FOR AMERICA 151 (2d ed. 2011). Edwards is focusing on the support of *individuals*. This chapter is focusing on the support of *states*, as stated at the beginning of this subsection.

Chapter Seventeen

1. More information on FDR's presidency and the 1936 election can be found at: CONRAD BLACK, FRANKLIN DELANO ROOSEVELT: CHAMPION OF FREEDOM 388–92 (2003); PAUL F. BOLLER, JR., PRESIDENTIAL CAMPAIGNS 240–49 (rev. ed. 1996); KENNETH S. DAVIS, FDR, THE NEW DEAL YEARS, 1933-1937: A HISTORY 603–648 (1986); WILLIAM E. LEUCHTENBURG, FRANKLIN D. ROOSEVELT AND THE NEW DEAL: 1932-1940, at 175–96 (1963); DIXON WECTER, THE AGE OF THE GREAT DEPRESSION: 1929-1941, at 101–04 (1948).

2. This number is, of course, a bit of a moving target. Daily trends for the stock market during the 1920s and 1930s can be found at *Dow Jones Industrial Average (1920 - 1940 Daily)*, STOCKCHARTS.COM, http://stockcharts.com/freecharts/historical/djia19201940.html (last visited June 29, 2012).

3. *Franklin D. Roosevelt*, THE WHITE HOUSE, http://www.whitehouse.gov/history/presidents/fr32.html (last visited June 27, 2012).

4. BOLLER, *supra* note 1, at 240.

5. Some dispute this assessment. For analyses supporting the theory that the New Deal prolonged the Great Depression see JIM POWELL, FDR'S FOLLY: HOW ROOSEVELT AND HIS NEW DEAL PROLONGED THE GREAT DEPRESSION (2003); AMITY SHLAES, THE FORGOTTEN MAN: A NEW HISTORY OF THE GREAT DEPRESSION (2007); GENE SMILEY, RETHINKING THE GREAT DEPRESSION (2002).

6. Some have disputed this number, including welfare recipients among those who were "productively employed" during the 1930s. Jim Powell, *Tough Questions for Defenders of the New Deal*, CATO INST. (Nov. 6, 2003), http://www.cato.org/research/articles/powell-031106.html.

7. LEUCHTENBURG, *supra* note 1, at 194; *see also American President: A Reference Resource (Franklin Delano Roosevelt): Campaigns and Elections: The Campaign and Election of 1932*, MILLER CENTER, http://millercenter.org/president/fdroosevelt/essays/biography/3 (last visited June 27, 2012) [hereinafter MILLER CENTER].

8. DAVIS, *supra* note 1, at 623; LEUCHTENBURG, *supra* note 1, at 175. Some might include Governor Frank Merriam of California as a Republican who was re-elected, but technically his first election to the office was in 1936. He was elected Lt. Governor in 1932 and became acting Governor in 1934 due to the death of Governor James Rolph. *The Governor's Gallery: Frank Merriam*, ST. CAL., http://governors.library.ca.gov/28-merriam.html (last visited June 29, 2012).

9. Some Republicans hoped that challenges from dissident elements within the Democratic Party would undermine FDR's candidacy and allow a Republican challenger to squeak through to victory. LEUCHTENBURG, *supra* note 1, at 179. Democratic Senator Huey Long, for instance, had offered an alternative solution to the economic problems gripping the country, and his "Share the Wealth" program had many supporters across the country. Unfortunately for those who did not approve of the New Deal, Long's presidential aspirations were abruptly cut short when he was assassinated in September 1935. *Id.* at 179–80.

Notes

10. BOLLER, *supra* note 1, at 242.

11. LEUCHTENBURG, *supra* note 1, at 175 (citations omitted).

12. WECTER, *supra* note 1, at 102.

13. *Id.* at 103; *see also* BLACK, *supra* note 1, at 389; LEUCHTENBURG, *supra* note 1, at 184.

14. WECTER, *supra* note 1, at 103. Although it should be noted that Roosevelt nevertheless won a surprising number of voters from prosperous Americans. For instance, Boston merchant Edward Filene stated, "Why shouldn't the American people take half my money from me? I took all of it from them." LEUCHTENBURG, *supra* note 1, at 190.

15. LEUCHTENBURG, *supra* note 1, at 193.

16. *Id.*

17. BOLLER, *supra* note 1, at 247 (citation omitted).

18. MILLER CENTER, *supra* note 7; *see also* BLACK, *supra* note 1, at 391 (reporting post-election poll results, which indicated that Roosevelt gained more support among Catholics, Jews, blacks, and southern whites).

19. LEUCHTENBURG, *supra* note 1, at 184; *see also* BLACK, *supra* note 1, at 391.

20. The first edition of this book reported slightly different popular vote totals. These figures were obtained from the 1997 edition of Congressional Quarterly's *Presidential Elections.* CONG. QUARTERLY, PRESIDENTIAL ELECTIONS, 1789-1996, at 112 (1997). The figures in this edition have been revised to reflect the new numbers reported in the most recent edition of *Presidential Elections. See* CQ PRESS, PRESIDENTIAL ELECTIONS: 1789–2008, at 153 (2010).

21. BOLLER, *supra* note 1, at 355 (citation omitted).

22. Sixty-six hostages were originally seized. Fourteen were released during 1979 and 1980, but the remaining 52 hostages remained in captivity until January 20, 1981. *Iran Hostage Crisis*, ENCYCLOPÆDIA BRITANNICA, http://www.britannica.com/EBchecked/topic/272687/Iran-hostage-crisis (last visited June 27, 2012).

23. Dinesh D'Souza, *How Reagan Reelected Clinton*, FORBES (Nov. 3, 1997), http://www.forbes.com/forbes/1997/1103/6010118a.html.

24. *See, e.g.*, James K. Glassman, *Reagan Whipped Inflation*, NAT'L REV. ONLINE (June 16, 2004), http://www.nationalreview.com/articles/211138/reagan-whipped-inflation/james-k-glassman (discussing actions that brought inflation under control during the 1980s).

25. D'Souza, *supra* note 23.

26. Scott Keeter, *Public Opinion in 1984*, *in* THE ELECTION OF 1984, at 91, 93 (Marlene Michels Pomper ed., 1985).

27. D'Souza, *supra* note 23.

28. LOU CANNON, PRESIDENT REAGAN: THE ROLE OF A LIFETIME 435 (PublicAffairs 2d ed. 2000) (1991).

29. Keeter, *supra* note 26, at 93.

30. *Id.* at 99.

31. *See id.* at 95.

32. *See id.* at 97.

33. *Id.* at 95.

34. *Id.* at 96. tbl.4.1.

35. *Id.* at 100.

36. BOLLER, *supra* note 1, at 370 (citation omitted).

37. *Id.* at 371.

38. Ronald Reagan, The Second Presidential Debate in Kansas City, Missouri, COMM'N ON PRESIDENTIAL DEBATES (Oct. 21, 1984), http://www.debates.org/index.php?page=october-21-1984-debate-transcript.

39. BOLLER, *supra* note 1, at 373 (citation omitted).

40. CANNON, *supra* note 28, at 434. Reagan did not win a majority of votes among the unemployed. *Id.*

41. Keeter, *supra* note 26, at 101. An ABC/*Washington Post* poll showed that 54 percent of women supported Reagan, compared to 62 percent of men. By contrast, Mondale received support from 46 percent of women and 38 percent of men. *Id.* at 102 tbl. 4.3.

42. CANNON, *supra* note 28, at 434–35.

43. Peter Roff, *UPI's White House Watch*, UPI.COM (June 11, 2004), http://www.upi.com/Business_News/Security-Industry/2004/06/11/UPIs-White-House-watch/UPI-23891087008848/.

44. REAGAN, A LIFE IN LETTERS xiii (Kiron K. Skinner et al. eds., 2003).

45. CANNON, *supra* note 28, at 435.

Appendices

1. The first edition of this book reported slightly different popular vote totals; those figures were obtained from the 1997 edition of Congressional Quarterly's *Presidential Elections*. CONG. QUARTERLY, PRESIDENTIAL ELECTIONS, 1789-1996 (1997). The figures in this edition have been revised to reflect the new numbers reported in the most recent edition of *Presidential Elections*. CQ PRESS, PRESIDENTIAL ELECTIONS: 1789–2008 (2010).

2. No record of the popular vote was kept until 1824.

3. A list of faithless electors can be found in Chapter Eight.

4. Due to the combined voting procedure for President and Vice President, this figure is not useful until after adoption of the 12th Amendment in 1804.

5. The total number of available elector votes was 176; however, only 175 votes were cast because one Kentucky elector did not vote.

6. The total number of available elector votes was 218; however, only 217 votes were cast because one Ohio elector did not vote.

7. The total number of available elector votes was 221; however, only 217 votes were cast because one Delaware elector and three Maryland electors did not vote.

8. The total number of available elector votes was 235; however, only 232 votes were cast because three electors—from Mississippi, Pennsylvania, and Tennessee—did not vote.

9. The election of 1824 was decided in the House contingent election, since no presidential candidate received a majority of electoral votes. John Q. Adams received the votes of 13 state delegations; Jackson, 7; and Crawford, 4.

10. The total number of available elector votes was 288; however, only 286 votes were cast because two Maryland electors did not vote.

11. The total number of available elector votes was 234; however, only 233 votes were cast because one Nevada elector did not vote. Eleven southern states did not vote because they had seceded from the Union.

12. The total number of available elector votes was 366; however, only 349 votes were cast and counted. The Democratic candidate, Horace Greeley, died between the time of the popular vote and the meeting of the presidential electors. Sixty-three of his electors voted for alternative candidates, but three electors cast their votes for Greeley despite his death. Congress refused to count these last three votes, since they had been cast for a deceased candidate. In addition, Congress refused to accept votes from Arkansas and Louisiana due to disruptive conditions resulting from Reconstruction.

13. An anonymous elector in Minnesota voted for John Edwards instead of John Kerry.

Index

Index

Index